GRAND SLAM

GOLF'S MAJOR CHAMPIONSHIPS

GRAND SLAM

GOLF'S MAJOR CHAMPIONSHIPS

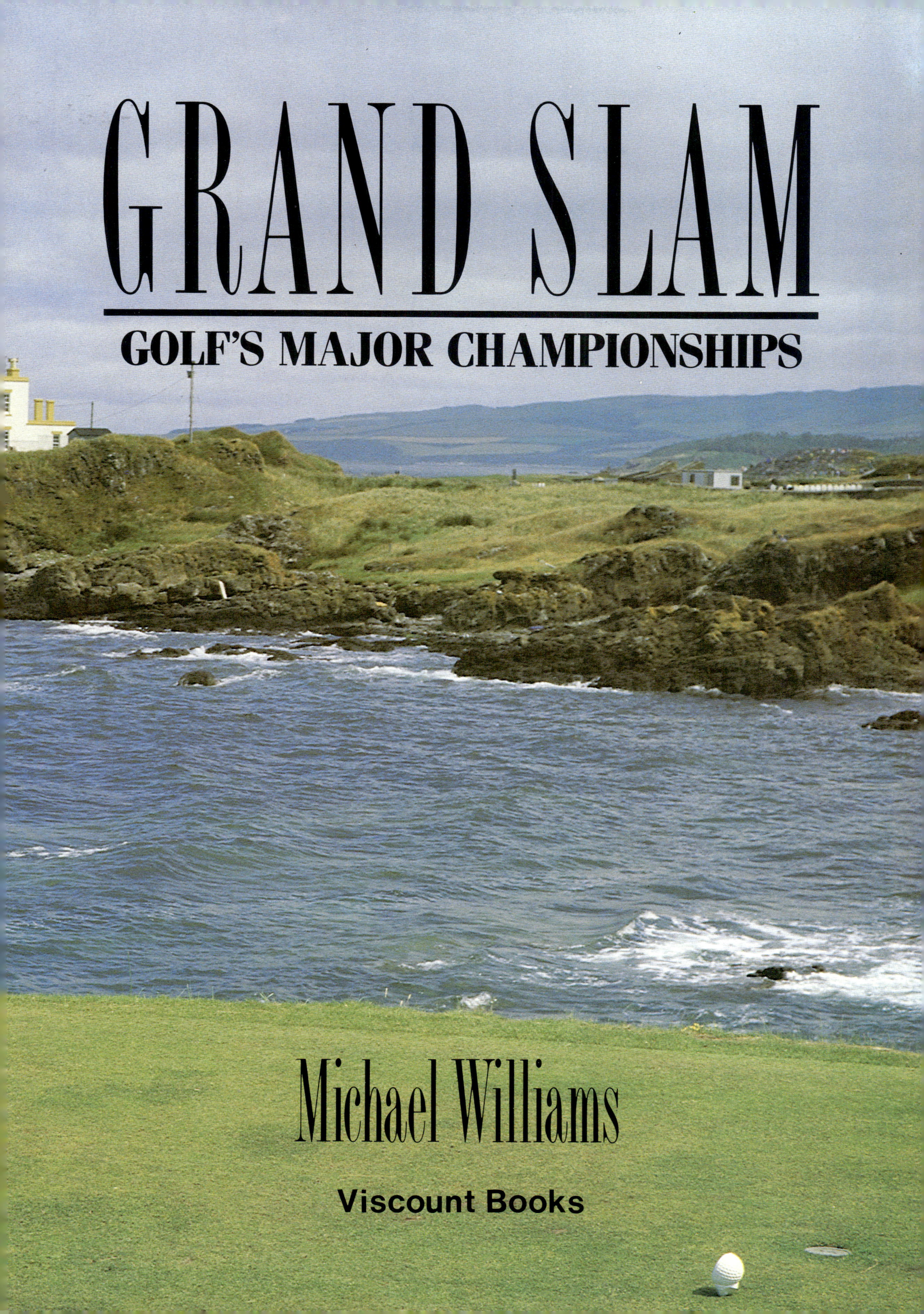

Michael Williams

Viscount Books

Dedication
To Caroline, Sally, Bridget, Roddy

Title page: *On a wild and windy day there are few more intimidating drives than that off the ninth tee at Turnberry. Waves crash on the rocks below while the narrow strip of fairway beyond the rugged coastline is the only haven to the trembling golfer.*

This edition published by Viscount Books 1988
Prepared by
The Hamlyn Publishing Group Limited
a division of The Octopus Publishing Group plc,
Michelin House, 81 Fulham Road,
London SW3 6RB

ISBN 0 600 55934 3

Printed in Spain

CONTENTS

FOREWORD	7
US MASTERS	9
The Augusta National	9
Sarazen's Albatross	12
Guldahl Triumphs	13
Rivalry of Hogan and Snead	14
Coming of Arnold Palmer	16
Player's Indomitable Spirit	20
Roberto's Oversight	23
Nicklaus in Perpetuity	25
Floyd's Five Wood	29
Tom Watson Stands the Heat	31
Sneed's Lingering Death	33
Ballesteros: The Youngest Champion	34
Langer Beats the Twitch	36
Rise of Larry Mize	38
Lyle's Green Jacket	39
US Masters Records	40
US OPEN CHAMPIONSHIP	43
Merion	44
Olympic	46
Inverness	48
Shinnecock Hills	50
Winged Foot	52
Oalkand Hills	54
Oakmont	56
Baltusrol	58
Founding Fathers: Ouimet and McDermott	60
Arise, Sir Walter	63
Men from Overseas	65
An Amateur Called Jones	70
Sarazen, Guldahl and Snead	74
Curtains for Hogan and Palmer	78
Courage of Ken Venturi	81
Ben Hogan: a Golfing Colossus	82
The Golden Years of Nicklaus	84
The Lowest Score of the Lot	87
Watson Has His Moment	89
US Open Records	91
BRITISH OPEN CHAMPIONSHIP	95
Prestwick	96
St. Andrews	98
Muirfield	101
Musselburgh	103
Royal St. George's	105
Hoylake	107
Royal Cinque Ports, Deal	109
Prince's	111
Royal Lytham and St. Anne's	113
Royal Birkdale	115
Royal Troon	117
Carnoustie	119
Portrush	121
Turnberry	123
Vardon Breaks the Deadlock	125
Nicklaus Survives the Old Course	127
Trevino's Good Fortune	130
Hagen, Cotton and Lyle	132
Jones en Route for the Grand Slam	135
Duncan's Recovery	138
Sarazen Returns	139
Jacklin's Hour of Glory	140
Palmer's Honesty	143
Thomson's Success	144
Miller and Watson	145
Weiskopf Conquers Troon	146
Hogan's Progression at Carnoustie	148
Watson's Finest Hour	150
Norman's Talent Fulfilled	152
British Open Records	154
US PGA CHAMPIONSHIP	159
Pebble Beach	160
Pinehurst No. 2	162
Southern Hills	165
Firestone	166
Oak Hill	168
Cherry Hills	170
Hagen the Supreme Match-player	172
Sarazen's Absentmindedness	173
Verb to 'Diegel'	174
Another First for Player	175
Dave Marr: Mind of a Champion	177
Boros Withstands the Pressure	178
Nicklaus's Full House	179
Mahaffey's Dream, Watson's Nightmare	181
Year of the Two Golden Oldies	183
Agony of Greg Norman	185
US PGA Records	187
ACKNOWLEDGMENTS	189
INDEX	190

FOREWORD

I suppose I was about 14 years old when I first became aware of such names as Jack Nicklaus, Arnold Palmer and Gary Player. I had a handicap of about two or three at the time and little dreamed that one day I would be playing alongside them, sometimes even beating them.

We did not get too many golf magazines in West Germany in those days but I do remember that on the wall of the professional's shop at Augsburg, where I was a caddie, there was a swing sequence of Nicklaus, using the driver.

I was only 15 when I turned professional and I did not have the advantage of some of the British and American players, who are able to develop as amateurs. I had to do it the hard way and indeed it was hard.

Some of you will remember the difficulties I had on the greens and that is why I often putt now with the left hand below the right. It gave me a new confidence and played a big part in my winning my first major championship, the Masters in 1985. That was the greatest thrill of my golfing life and I was very proud to see my name going up among so many famous champions.

Being a European my big aim is of course to win the British Open Championship, for more countries are represented in that than in any of the other 'majors' as they have become known. Together with the US Open, Masters and the American PGA, these are the four goals on which we all set our sights each year.

They are therefore the central points in the history of this wonderful game and I am glad that Michael Williams has taken this opportunity to write about the great moments in them, the settings in which the acts were performed and the golfers who filled the leading roles.

Michael has been present at most of them for the past 18 years, which was long before I was ever good enough to play and many of you will be familiar with his graphic but balanced reports in *The Daily Telegraph*, a top British newspaper. The standard of golf writing in Britain is higher than in any other part of the world and I am privileged to be considered a friend of all these reporters even if I may not always agree with exactly what they write!

Golf is a special game and I am sure you will find this a special book.

Bernhard Langer
May 1988.

US MASTERS
The Augusta National

Although tournament golf is now very much an all-the-year-round affair, one season almost overlapping with the next, it nevertheless has its high points. The first of them, which most people see as the launching-pad of a new golfing year, comes with the Masters at Augusta National. For a start, it is played in April and that, in the northern hemisphere, means spring when the grass begins to grow, the first of the flowers come into bloom, and golfers dust off their clubs for another season.

The Masters is the youngest of all the major championships, having come into being as late as 1934. Actually, the club makes no claim to it being a championship; they call it the Masters Tournament since entry is strictly by invitation and the field is restricted to less than 100 players, a dozen or so of them amateurs.

Consequently, the fields are stronger for the US Open, British Open and the American PGA. Yet the invitation to Augusta, when it drops through the letter box some time in January, is among a golfer's most treasured possessions. For the public, too, there has grown up a mystique about the Masters, and the keen golf watcher dreams of one day getting to see it. In most cases it remains a dream for entry is by ticket only and the waiting list is closed.

The first-time visitor to the Masters might be forgiven for wondering what all the fuss is about. The sprawling town of Augusta, deep in Georgia, is not very attractive and the scenery does not improve as one approaches the course along the Washington Road. It is heavily built-up with filling stations and fast food restaurants, and apart from Masters week when banners are stretched across the road indicating the entry gates, the only sign of this world-famous golf course is a small plaque on the main gate which reads 'Augusta National Golf Club'. It is constantly manned by grey-uniformed Pinkertons who turn away any casual visitor.

An 8-foot-high wire fence marks the boundaries of the club and on only one flank, by the fifth hole, is it possible to get a glimpse of a rolling emerald fairway. Enter the main gate, however, and one enters a different world. The approach to the club is down a heavily leafed avenue known as Magnolia Lane, and on either side stretch two immaculate practice grounds which, at the time of the Masters, are like fields of daisies, littered with gleaming white golf-balls, while ever more balls, like tracer bullets, etch themselves against the seemingly permanently deep blue sky. The professionals are at work.

Left: *One of the most popular vantage points at Augusta is by the sixth green, a demanding short hole. From a high tee, the players actually hit their tee shots over the heads of the gallery.*

Right: *The quietly elegant clubhouse of Augusta National, the home of the Masters.*

At the end of Magnolia Lane lies the low green-and-white sprawling wooden clubhouse. Everything at Augusta is green and white, from the canopies outside on the terrace to the towels and the serviettes and the paper cups. The verandah by the small front door is carpeted in green and leads down, via a series of steps, to the locker room, the barber's shop and the professional's shop.

Inside, the thick carpeting tends to make one want to whisper. None of the rooms is large and to the right of the entrance hall a slim spiral staircase leads up to the Holy of Holies, the champions' locker room.

This is separate from the main locker room, which is in another part of the building altogether, and is restricted only to those players who have won the Masters. It lies beyond a shoulder-to-knee swing door and is quite small, so small, in fact, that two players must share the same locker. Outside, on the course side, is another verandah on which Gene Sarazen, always in plus fours, sits and chats as friends pay homage. For it was he, with one shot, who helped to make the Masters.

Beneath is the grass terrace, tables, chairs, umbrellas for shade against the sun and hovering black waiters in mustard-coloured waistcoats. A vast, spreading oak overhangs the lawn. It is golf's greatest and now most traditional meeting place.

Away to the left are the so-called 'cabins', snow white, two of them almost monuments: one was once occupied by President Dwight D. Eisenhower; the other by Bobby Jones. It was here that Jones saw out the last of his days, happy that he had created something that would never perish.

Even before he retired in 1930 Jones had nurtured an ambition to build a golf course, and as soon as he was taken to this former nursery, known as Fruitlands and once owned by a Belgian horticulturist called Baron Berckmann, he knew he had found the ideal landscape. It flowed gently down through pine trees to Rae's Creek and was full of the flowering shrubs that now lend such colour to the Masters as the tournament coincides with their coming into full bloom. Indeed the holes carry the names of many of them: Tea Olive (the first); Flowering Peach (the third); White Dogwood (the 11th); Chinese Fir (the 14th); and Nandina (the 17th). To assist him Jones called upon the distinguished architect, Alister Mackenzie, of Scottish blood, and between them they created a course that is a masterpiece.

Unusually, there is no rough and there are fewer than 50 bunkers. The fairways are of generous width but it is the bordering trees that are the course's first defence. The second is the greens. Some are large, some quite small, but all have wicked contours and are generally as fast as glass. A quite moderate golfer should be able to get round in relative comfort but to score well he must be able to play.

On the fairways there is almost never a bad lie for the course is beautifully maintained, money being no object amongst the small, exclusive membership that comes from all over the United States. Few golf courses in the world are so little played.

Jones's idea in the first place was to stage a tournament for just a few of his friends. Its popularity grew rapidly but it was the chairman of the club, Clifford Roberts, who came to rule it with an iron fist, particularly after the death of Jones in 1971.

Roberts was a man of slow, considered speech and had very set ideas about how the tournament should be run. He allowed no advertising on the course and there was not even a tournament programme, just a single sheet with a map of the course on one side and the starting times on the other. It also carried a message from Jones, written in 1967, which is a model for any tournament:

D.A. Weibring's head begins to come up as he follows the flight of his tee shot to the 16th green at Augusta National.

The 10th hole at Augusta. It is here, on the final afternoon of the Masters, that the fun really begins for it is then, on the homeward stretch, that nerves are as much an ally as skill.

'In golf, customs of etiquette and decorum are just as imortant as rules governing play. It is appropriate for spectators to applaud successful strokes in proportion to difficulty but excessive demonstrations by a player or his partisans are not proper because of the possible effect upon other competitors.

'Most distressing to those who love the game of golf is the applauding or cheering of misplays or misfortunes of a player. Such occurrences have been rare at the Masters but we must eliminate them entirely if our patrons are to continue to merit their reputation as the most knowledgeable and considerate in the world.'

The Masters gave the world the modern system of scoring whereby numbers in red denote by how many strokes a player is under par; numbers in black by how many he is over par. These ever-changing figures on the scoreboards on the last afternoon as players contest the lead are hypnotic to the spectators, many of whom pick their vantage points round the course and never move from them.

The excitement builds to a crescendo on the last afternoon for while the first nine holes have their difficulties, it is over the inward half that the fun begins. The 10th is a magnificent plunging par four between towering pines while the 11th, 12th, and 13th, known as Amen Corner, are all threatened by water.

The flag is invariably tucked on the left of the 11th green, close to a pond dyed blue; the shallow 12th green just beyond Rae's Creek demands a very precisely judged tee shot; while the twisting 13th, with that same creek winding down the left of the fairway and then across the front of the green, demands the bravest of second shots in the bid for a birdie. Curiously, the 13th is shorter than the 10th by 20 yards (18 m) but rated a par five.

There is water, too, to be carried with the second shot to the 15th, the green domed and hard to hold with a wood or long iron. Invariably a birdie four or even an eagle three is required followed by a testing tee shot across more water at the short 16th.

Soon there comes the uphill slog to the 18th with its sharply sloping green beyond the avenue of trees down which an accurate drive must be struck. There the multitude awaits, as too does the green jacket with which every new champion is presented to mark his honorary membership of Augusta National.

Augusta National

Hole	Name	Yards	Par
1	Tea Olive	400	4
2	Pink Dogwood	555	5
3	Flowering Peach	360	4
4	Crabapple	205	3
5	Magnolia	435	4
6	Juniper	180	3
7	Pampas	360	4
8	Yellow Jasmine	535	5
9	Carolina Cherry	435	4
10	Camellia	485	4
11	White Dogwood	455	4
12	Golden Bell	155	3
13	Azalea	465	5
14	Chinese Fir	405	4
15	Firethorn	500	5
16	Red Bud	170	3
17	Nandina	400	4
18	Holly	405	4
		6,905	72

Sarazen's Albatross

The final drama of the Masters is invariably enacted each year at the 15th hole, a par five of 500 yards (457 m), water in front of the green as well as behind. Two grandstands are now erected on either flank and late on the Sunday afternoon they are packed with spectators, eyes straining down the fairway to see whether their man is going to go for the green.

There is a buzz of expectancy as they watch the players summing up the situation, and then a cheer as they see the cover being taken off a wood. A hush descends as the stance is taken, quickly replaced by a buzz of anticipation as the ball climbs, hangs seemingly interminably in the air and then drops. A great groan goes up if the ball falls short and into the water, a thundering cheer if it finds its mark.

In 1935 there was none of this theatre. The Masters was still in only its second year and the wording on the invitation Gene Sarazen received from Augusta National's board of governors was to take part in the 'Annual Invitation Golf Tournament'. Undeterred, the golfing press was already calling it the Masters because of the quality of the field. The quality of the climax that year, as Sarazen holed a full-blooded four wood at the 15th for an albatross two, which in one fell swoop brought him level with Craig Wood – whom he later defeated in a play-off – has been without equal since.

The irony was that only a handful of people saw it; among them, however, was Walter Hagen, with whom Sarazen was playing, and Bobby Jones, who had wandered out to watch. There were no grandstands then, no wildly ecstatic audience on their feet, but just a group of watchers chatting idly by the green. The rest were all up the hill by the 18th and around the clubhouse congratulating Craig Wood on what they thought was outright victory.

Gene Sarazen helped to make the Masters with the albatross two he scored at the 15th hole in 1935. Now he simply gets the Masters under way with a courtesy nine holes on the opening morning.

There have since been many changes to Augusta National to increase its difficulty, but even so the standard of play that year was exceptional. After the first round Grantland Rice wrote: 'A combination of hurricane, typhoon and tornado blew over Augusta National in the first round. But this explosion never came from the elements. It came from the woods and irons of one of the fastest fields that ever wrecked par.'

Henry Picard led with a 67 as five players broke 70 and 10 beat the par of 72. Sarazen had a 68 and Tommy Armour, an eye-witness as his partner, said he had seen its like only from Harry Vardon or Bobby Jones. Shot after shot covered the flag but he missed six putts of between 3 feet and 7 feet (1–2 m). Most players, said Armour, would have been able to kick the ball into the hole.

Sarazen continued to have trouble with his putting in the second round and fell, with a 71, four strokes behind Picard. However, Picard could not keep it up and it was Wood, with a 68, who took over the lead after 54 holes, Sarazen (73) now three behind. Halfway through the final round that margin had been cut to a single stroke but Wood seemed to settle things when he came home in 34 for a 73 and a total of 282, six under par.

News of this came to Sarazen as he was playing the 14th, where he had hooked his drive into an awkward place. Somehow he found a corner of the green and laid a long putt close for his four. He was still three strokes behind. 'It looks as if it is all over,' remarked Hagen as they crossed to the 15th tee. 'Oh, I don't know,' Sarazen is said to have replied. 'They might go in from anywhere.'

Whether this story is apocryphal hardly matters. Sarazen's drive at the 15th came to rest right in the middle of the fairway. However, it was not a good lie and he could not use the three wood he wanted. He had to take his four and close the face – and in it went for the only albatross or double eagle ever recorded here.

It was the same four wood Sarazen had to play for his second to the last as he played the final three holes in par for the tie but though that one shot at the 15th has claimed all the headlines, there were, as he points out, 281 others. Then he had to win the play-off over 36 holes, which he did quite easily by five strokes.

Guldahl Triumphs

This was not the only Masters that fired the public's imagination in the pre-war years. In 1937 and 1938 Ralph Guldahl won successive US Open championships and his victory in the 1939 Masters elevated him to an even loftier pinnacle. His exploits, however, never quite caused the impact they would have done at the hands of others.

He was a big man whose clothes never quite fitted and he would plod along the fairways looking down at his feet. These he would somehow screw into the turf and nothing would budge them as he swung. Only his upper body seemed to move and his face was as inexpressive after a bad shot as it was after a good one. He hit the ball as if wielding an axe.

To get from the ninth green to the 10th tee the players have to pass behind the 18th green and it was as Guldahl was doing so that he heard the announcer informing the crowd that Sam Snead had just finished in 68 for a record 280. Guldahl had been two strokes ahead going into the last round but he was no better than a level par 36 through the turn and knew that he had to come home in 33 to win.

It was a tall order but Guldahl was quickly encouraged when he made a three down the swooping 10th. Two years earlier, in 1937, Guldahl had been in a much more promising position to win the Masters at a similar stage but took a double-bogey five at the 12th and a six at the 13th, and was overtaken by Byron Nelson who played the same two holes in a birdie two and an eagle three.

Now it was Guldahl's turn. He came through the 12th without mishap and then rather skied his drive to the 13th. Undeterred by the prospect of a shot in excess of 200 yards (183 m) to reach the green, he thundered a three wood to 6 feet and then holed the putt for an eagle.

It was as spectacular a thrust as Arnold Palmer was to make many years later on the same hole, and it put Guldahl in the lead. He gained a further insurance with a birdie four at the 15th but still had to take care. A dropped shot at the 17th left him with a four to win. Neither the drive nor the second shot in such circumstances is easy but there was never a doubt about Guldahl's solid four.

Ralph Guldahl was a rugged, muscular golfer but he was good enough to win the US Open twice and the Masters once, in 1939.

Rivalry of Hogan and Snead

It is a fact of golfing life that the exploits of one supreme golfer invariably bring out the best in another. This was certainly true of Ben Hogan and Sam Snead, whose careers ran parallel. Never was their rivalry greater than in the Masters. In the six years between 1949 and 1954 Snead won it three times and Hogan twice.

Hogan had in fact gone close once before. In 1942, shortly before Pearl Harbor, he lost a play-off to Byron Nelson, one of the great players of his time. Unfortunately, that time coincided with the Second World War, when other things mattered more. Exempt from military service, Nelson won 28 tournaments in the space of four years beginning in 1942, 18 of them in 1945, including 11 in succession. Furthermore, he was second seven times and never finished lower than ninth. He had a stroke average of 68.33.

It nevertheless took a great deal out of Nelson and he was often sick with the tension of it all. Indeed, he was so ill during the night before his play-off with Hogan at Augusta that it was suggested he might prefer a postponement. Nelson declined and still played dazzling golf. At one point Hogan completed 11 holes, from the sixth to the 16th, in one under par and still lost ground by five strokes. Nelson had a birdie at the sixth, an eagle three at the eighth and then three successive birdies at the 11th, 12th and 13th. It enabled him, after a poor start, to win by a stroke with a 69 against Hogan's 70.

Byron Nelson was in his prime during the war years. Now he is one of the game's elder statesmen and one of his greatest satisfactions lay in the help he was able to give Tom Watson.

Furthermore, it was reminiscent of the other Masters Nelson won in 1937. Trailing Ralph Guldahl by four strokes going into the last round, he made his decisive move by playing the 12th and 13th holes in five strokes with a birdie two and an eagle three. Guldahl, on the other hand, had a five and a six.

By a coincidence Hogan, Nelson and Snead were all born in 1912, though each developed as golfers at different times. Hogan was the slowest to mature, not winning a major championship until after Nelson had retired into farming. Snead also beat Hogan to it by winning the PGA, British Open and Masters (in that order) first. His first Masters victory in 1949, as high winds whistled through the tall pines, was a majestic triumph. When the wind dropped, Snead blew hot. He had a 67 in each of the last two rounds with some of the finest golf ever seen at Augusta.

Hogan meanwhile was still waiting: and not even competing in the PGA since it was after his accident and he could no longer face 36 holes in a day. For all that Hogan remained, as Gene Sarazen once put it, a 'perpetually hungry' golfer and one very much with the Masters in his sights.

In 1951 the Boston Red Sox were invited to Augusta and their great pitcher, Ted Williams, came out of the locker room saying: 'I just shook a hand that felt like five bands of steel.' It belonged to Hogan, who proceeded to play some of the most clinical, error-free golf as, after three rounds, he stood a stroke behind his arch-rival, Snead, and Skee Riegel.

'Looks like a play-off,' someone said to Hogan before he went out. 'Don't think so,' came the short reply and with two birdies in his first three holes he was away. Hogan was playing the eighth when he heard that Riegel had returned a 71 for 282 and that left him with a 69 to win, Snead having messed things up with an eight at the 11th.

With a birdie at the eighth, Hogan moved to three under par for the round. Level par home, he knew, would be good enough and that is the way he played it, going for absolutely nothing. He deliberately aimed wide of the 11th green because of the water on the left, chipped and single putted. 'If you ever see me on that green,' he once said, 'then I have mis-hit the shot.' Nor did he go for the green at either the 13th or the 15th, though the pitch he played to the former still finished close enough for him to get a birdie. He even preferred to chip from short of the green at the 18th but it was all very carefully planned and with an inward half of 35 for a 68, he won by two.

There is now a tradition at the Masters whereby the defending champion hosts a dinner at the club on the Tuesday evening for all past champions. It was Hogan who started this Masters Club in 1952, honorary membership also being given to Bobby Jones and Clifford Roberts.

Perhaps shaken by the bill, Hogan did not play well that year and was quite embarrassed by a 74,79 finish and Snead romped home in difficult weather. Though now 40, and some thought past his prime, Hogan came to Augusta more determined than ever in 1953, it mattering not one dot that he had not played a tournament for 10 months.

He had slightly changed his putting stance and together with a masterly long-game he totally destroyed the field. It was the complete performance and he broke two records. Lucky perhaps in that every time he went out to play it stopped raining and the sun came out to greet him, Hogan's 205 for 54 holes set one new mark while his 274 for the four rounds was five strokes inside Ralph Guldahl's 1939 record. In sequence Hogan returned 70,69,66,69 and some wondered whether it might ever be beaten. A man not inclined to overstatement, Hogan said: 'They were the best four rounds of tournament golf I have ever played.' He has never changed that opinion.

So that was 2–2 in his 'Masters match' with Snead and in 1954 they tied, though for a long time it was not on them that all eyes were turned but on an engaging amateur with a rustic swing by the name of Billy Joe Patton. He had been invited purely because he had been an alternate on the previous American Walker Cup team.

Nevertheless, Patton led the field after 36 holes and suddenly the public had a 'Jones-like' figure to follow. But the stir he had caused so far was nothing to the mayhem for which he was responsible in the last round, which he began five strokes behind Hogan and two behind Snead.

Hogan heard the noise as he walked down the third fairway but he could not identify quite what it meant. He soon learned; Patton had just holed in one at the sixth. Soon he heard another roar; Patton had birdied the eighth. Then he heard another; Patton had birdied the ninth as well and they were level against par.

The spectators were beside themselves and Patton, like a true Corinthian, was going for everything – it was his undoing. At the 13th, after not the longest of drives, he could

No swing stood the test of time better than that of Sam Snead. He was blessed with the most perfect balance, one of the secrets of golf.

nevertheless not resist going for the green. He found Rae's Creek, thought about playing out of it bare foot, decided against it, forgot to put his shoes back on and pitched in again from the fairway. It cost him a seven.

Hogan knew none of this and made one uncharacteristic error of judgement. Playing the 11th he decided for once that he had to go for the flag and dropped his shot into the water on the left. It probably cost him the tournament for though his 75 for 289 beat Patton by one, it only tied with Snead.

This, then, was the decider; two supreme golfers in the evening of their careers on their favourite battleground. On the first tee, Snead revealed later, 'we wished one another luck. Immediately Ben froze. He went to work to take me apart, concentrating as he always did like there was nothing in this world but his ball and those 18 holes.'

For nine holes there was nothing between them, both out in 35. Snead chipped in at the 10th, Hogan got the stroke back at the 11th, but Snead edged in front again with a four at the 13th. Still there was only a stroke in it as they came to the 16th. Hogan hit the better tee shot but struck a terrible putt, 5 feet (1.5 m) short, and he missed the next.

Perhaps that was the undisputed sign that age was finally catching up on Hogan for, though he took the 18th, Snead won the play-off and the decider with a 70 against a 71. Snead, a Peter Pan figure, continued to grace the Masters for many more years, even into his 70s, but Hogan's appearances grew more infrequent, though not without one final, emotional curtain call. In 1967, then aged 54, he played nine holes in 30 and went round in 66. It was one last look into the past.

Coming of Arnold Palmer

Arnold Palmer was born in Latrobe, bred in Latrobe and lives in Latrobe, a small and pleasant enough town in Pennsylvania. As far as the public is concerned, there is a popular myth that, as a golfer, Palmer was born on the 13th fairway of Augusta National in the 1958 Masters when, in the final round, he wound himself up, lashed a three wood second shot over Rae's Creek and onto the green, holed the putt for an eagle three and went on to win the tournament.

But as regards this eagle three at the 13th, there was in fact general uncertainty at the time as to how significant it had been. For, when playing the previous hole, the 12th, Palmer had embedded his tee shot in the bank

Opposite: *Arnold Palmer was a golfing hero, the crowd sharing his delight as he holes his final putt to win his fourth Masters in 1964.*

A grin of satisfaction from Arnold Palmer as he comes safely out of sand.

at the front of the green. It was virtually unplayable but Palmer was more aware of a special local rule that would give him a free drop than the official on duty by the green.

Consequently, Palmer decided after playing his original ball and holing out in a double bogey five, to drop another ball close to where the first had become embedded. This he holed out in three but such was the confusion that even as he proceeded down the 13th he was still not sure which ball had counted. The spectators, knowing nothing of the local rule brought in after heavy overnight rain, assumed it was a five; so did the television commentators and so therefore did the whole of America.

It was not until the 15th green that Palmer at last had it confirmed that he had indeed taken three at the 12th and he was less surprised than everyone else when the scoreboards were changed to show him two strokes ahead rather than tied for the lead. But that rapidly became an anti-climax when Palmer dropped two strokes in the next three holes for a concluding 73. He in fact won his first Masters sitting in the clubhouse while Doug Ford and Fred Hawkins were missing birdie putts on the 18th green that would have forced a play-off.

In this, television suffered neither its first nor its last confusion. In 1957 Ford had won the Masters by holing a bunker shot on the 18th, 20 minutes before television came on the air, while in 1959 the cameras were so concentrating on Palmer, Stan Leonard, Dick Mayer and Cary Middlecoff at the back of the field that they entirely missed Art Wall make five birdies in the last six holes to win.

It was in 1960 that Palmer really caught the imagination of the public, from East Coast to West and many points beyond. He was by then on his roller coaster, the winner of a dozen tournaments and more, one Masters already behind him and now two major championships that were the making of him.

Palmer led all the way at Augusta that year, a 67 in the first round to set everyone buzzing but then a 73 and a 72 which allowed Dow Finsterwald to get to within a stroke of him. Technically, Finsterwald should have been ahead by a stroke but he called a penalty on himself of which only he was aware. Having missed a putt on one green before holing out the next, he unthinkingly threw the ball back onto the green and tried again the putt he had missed. While practice putting was not allowed on the US Tour, Finsterwald thought it was in the Masters. When he subsequently learned that it was not, and though no one had apparently noticed, he immediately reported the infringement, even in the knowledge that it could lead to disqualification. Officialdom took a slightly more lenient view and imposed on him a two-stroke penalty which turned Finsterwald's second round of 68 into a 70. It

was by those two strokes that he missed tieing with Palmer.

For all that, it was Ken Venturi who very nearly won. When in the final round Palmer failed to birdie either the 13th or 15th, he found that he had been overhauled by Venturi, who had just finished with a 70 for 283. Palmer needed two birdies from the last three holes and after a par three at the 16th, two from two.

At the 17th he was safely on the green with his approach but a good 20 feet (6 m) from the flag. He never looked happy about the putt and twice walked away from it. When at last he took his courage in both hands, there were grave doubts that his ball would ever reach the hole but it fell in with its dying breath. So that was one birdie and Venturi could hardly bare to look at the television monitor in the clubhouse.

It was like a knife into his stomach when next he watched Palmer almost knock the flagstick out of the hole with his six iron second to the 18th. The ball bounced past and then screwed back 5 feet (1.5 m) below the hole. There was never a doubt about a second birdie and victory by a stroke.

Such a finish, soon to be followed by his famous last round of 65 to snatch the US Open at Cherry Hills, gave birth to Arnie's Army. Even the scoreboards at Augusta once carried the message 'Go Arnie Go', though Clifford Roberts soon put a stop to that.

Palmer was a magical figure. Charles Price, in his book *Bobby Jones and the Masters*, wrote: 'Palmer didn't so much walk onto a tee as climb into it, as though it were a prize ring, and then he would look around at the gallery as though he were searching for somebody brave enough to fight him.' He would put more 'body language' into his shots than the rest of the field put together, alternately sinking to his knees in despair or exultantly leaping in the air when he holed a putt. He did not so

A study of concentration as Arnold Palmer anxiously follows a muscular drive.

much hit the ball as bully it and as he did so, his shirt kept coming out and he would have to keep tucking it in again. As Price further described him: 'You could walk an entire round with Palmer without seeing one ball he hit and still know where his shots had gone.'

When Palmer defended the Masters in 1961, it looked for all the world as if he would defeat Gary Player. He came to the last hole needing a par four for victory by a stroke. But he bunkered his second, thinned his recovery, took six and lost by a stroke.

A year later Palmer was back, again closely involved with Player and also Finsterwald, both of whom he beat in a play-off. His habit of winning at Augusta every other year was maintained when in 1964 he did it again with his most comfortable victory of all. Rounds of 69,68,69 and 70 gave him a six-stroke margin over Dave Marr while a total of 276 was only one shot outside the record. Furthermore, Palmer became the first man to win the Masters four times. Already, however, a shadow was beginning to cross his path.

In 1956 Ken Venturi, then still an amateur, might have won the Masters. He led going into the final round but then took 80 and lost by a stroke to Jackie Burke junior.

Player's Indomitable Spirit

Right: *Player's finest hour was when he won his third Masters in 1978 after a final round of 64, the lowest by a champion. Here Tom Watson helps him into his green jacket at the presentation ceremony.*

Opposite top: *'It's looking good', Gary Player seems to be telling himself.*

Below – sequence left to right: *It is all over and Gary Player has come home in 30 for his 64 in the last round of the 1978 Masters. He did not know then that he had won but Severiano Ballesteros clearly thinks that there is not much doubt.*

By the 1960s golf was being dominated by the Big Three: Arnold Palmer, Jack Nicklaus and Gary Player. The odd man out of these three was of course Player, not only because he is quite short but also because he is South African. Size means nothing, however, when you have a heart as big as his.

He drove himself to the absolute limit in his quest to be the best in the world and if he was never quite that, it was nonetheless a damned close-run thing. Between 1958 and 1966 inclusive, a span of nine years, only four golfers had the distinction of donning the green jacket as Masters champion. Palmer did so four times and Nicklaus three. The 'singleton' years belonged to Art Wall in 1959 and Player in 1961. It was the first of Player's three victories over a period of 17 years, even longer than the 15 years that covered his three British Open successes.

To stay at the top as long as that says everything for a remarkable constitution. But Player, like only the few, would beat balls on the practice ground until he was blue in the face. He was also a fanatic about physical fitness and devoted to health foods. He would wear black one day to retain the heat and white another to reflect it. Once, presumably unsure which was the more suitable, he played

in trousers that had one black leg and one white leg!

There was a curious similarity between Player's first British Open victory and his first Masters. He thought he had 'blown' them both but had not. In 1961 he was in only his second full year on the American Tour and Nicklaus was not yet a professional. Mark McCormack, his manager, had convinced Player that it was time to devote himself full-time. Palmer had led all the way through the 1960 Masters and the next year he led for the first two rounds as well.

But Player, a winner already that year of two tournaments, stayed with him, and with a third round of 69 suddenly shot into a four-stroke lead. Victory looked certain when he remained four strokes clear after nine holes of the final round but continuous rain turned into a downpour and play was washed out. He had to start all over again on the Monday.

Out this time in 34, Player continued to look good. But Palmer was one better and when Player took five at the 10th, the heat was on. At the 13th it became too much. He failed to draw his drive as intended and ran out of fairway into the trees on the far side. Instead of playing safe, however, Player still went for the big shot and pulled his two iron into the creek. Having picked out under penalty, he then pitched too strong and took three putts.

For some reason Palmer was playing behind

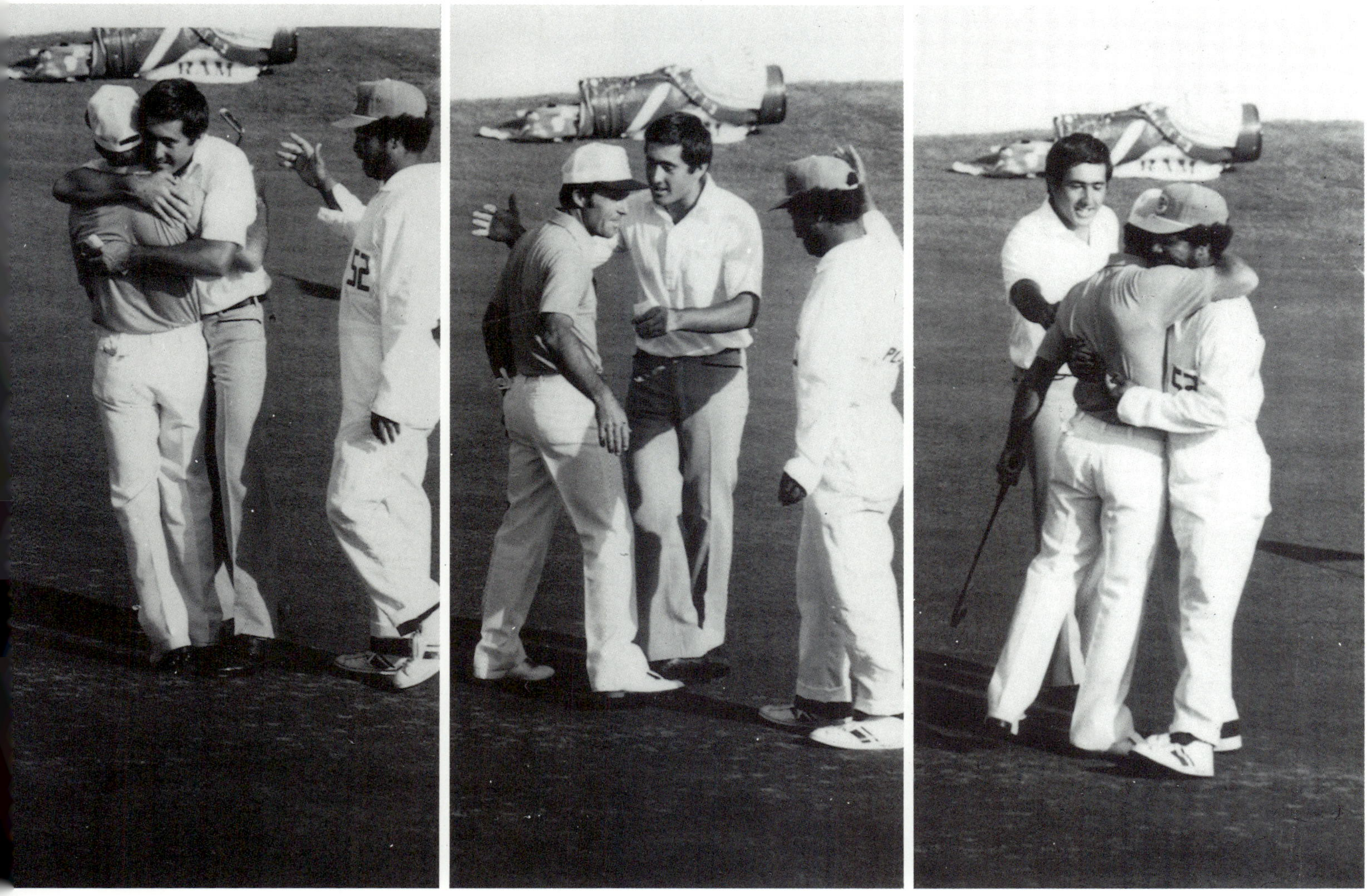

Gary Player's three Masters victories spanned 17 years, from 1961 to 1978.

Player, and when he made a birdie four at the same hole they were level. When Player then took six at the 15th he was behind and in a daze. Somehow he scrambled a four from behind the 17th green and then another four at the last via the right-hand bunker.

All he could then do was wait as he had done in the British Open at Muirfield in 1959 when he thought a six at the last hole had robbed him of the title. But the gods were with him, for Palmer, needing a four to win at the last and a five to tie, also found the right-hand bunker with his second and, to general consternation, took four more to get down.

Player won his second Masters in 1974 in rather more comfort, principally because in the third round he recorded five successive birdies beginning at the 12th. This gave him a 66 and made him one of eight players in contention. His decisive thrust came at the 17th in the last round when he played a stunning pitch right beside the flag for a birdie three. He had two strokes to spare from Dave Stockton and that eternal bridesmaid, Tom Weiskopf.

But there is no doubt as to Player's finest hour at Augusta. That was in 1978, then aged 42. No one ever gave him a thought going into the last round for he was well back, seven strokes indeed behind the leader, Hubert Green, with others in front of him too.

Before he went out someone remarked in jest that all Player needed to stand any sort of chance was eight birdies. 'Don't worry, man,' he replied, 'I want to tell you I can get them.' In fact he made nine, seven in the last 10 holes in a last round of 64 that stands as the lowest by the champion.

There were no expectations for Player even with nine holes to play, for he was still five adrift. Though no one knew it at the time, it was the ninth and 10th holes that got him going; first he hit a seven iron to 12 feet (3.6 m) and then a five iron to 25 feet (7.6 m). Each time his putter did the rest.

Another quite lengthy putt fell for a two at the 12th and he hit the 13th green with a four iron second for his next birdie. At the 15th he had to take wood for his second but made the green and two putted for his four. At the 16th he holed from 15 feet (4.6 m) for a two and such by then was his mood that it is worth recounting again his description of the last hole: 'I hit a drive and six iron to 15 feet,' he said before pausing, 'and nearly missed the putt.'

Player had completed those last nine holes in 30 and never had his putter woven such magic. Five of his seven birdies in those last 10 holes were the result of putts of at least 12 feet (3.6 m).

Green, though he needed a birdie at the 18th to catch Player, would have done so nine times out of ten. But after a magnificent second shot to within a yard of the flag he was disturbed by a television commentator's voice as he was about to putt. He had to start his preparations all over again and missed. When questioned about the incident, Green dismissed it. He had, he said, only himself to blame.

Roberto's Oversight

Golf would not be complete without its tragedies as well as its triumphs. There is nothing, however, that can compare with the misfortune of Roberto de Vicenzo, that most courteous and popular Argentine, who in 1968 tied for the Masters but was never given the chance of competing in the play-off. He was the victim of the harshest rule of all, the clerical error.

What sharpened the agony of it all was that it was also Vicenzo's 45th birthday and no one had ever won the Masters at that age. Furthermore, victory would have brought to a conclusion a most distinguished career that had reached a pinnacle the year before when he won the British Open at Hoylake.

While that last day in Augusta ended awash with tears (not Roberto's it must be quickly added), it had all begun so appropriately and happily. Vicenzo, one of a number of players chasing Gary Player, who was a stroke ahead of the field, holed his approach at the first hole for an eagle two. Immediately the crowd broke into a spontaneous rendering of 'Happy Birthday' and the Argentine remained inspired.

Birdies continued to flow from his fluent, easy swing and with a trio of them at the 12th, 15th and 17th, he came to the last needing a four for a 64. A shade disappointingly, Vicenzo took five at the last but it was a 65 nonetheless for a total of 277. Only Bob Goalby, playing behind, could still beat him and when he took five at the 17th, he was left with a four to tie, which he got.

Down in the depths of the Press room, where the British writers in particular faced the tightest of deadlines because of the six-hour time difference, stories were already being filed announcing a play-off the following day.

However, total consternation and confusion was already reigning around the recorder's tent. A final look at Vicenzo's card, long since signed and handed in, revealed that in the excitement of it all, Roberto had failed to notice that Tommy Aaron, his playing-partner, had put him down for a four at the 17th instead of the three every spectator and television viewer had seen him get. Certainly his total of 65 was correct but the individual scores at each hole added up to 66.

Never had there been so much embarrassment and the rule books were coming out in all

If 1968 at Augusta will always be remembered for the Masters Roberto de Vicenzo lost on a technicality, not enough credit goes to Bob Goalby, who won the title with a last round of 66.

directions to find some loophole so that Vicenzo's score could be corrected. A group of officials hurried up the hill to consult with Bobby Jones, who was then confined to a wheelchair in his cabin by the 10th tee, but he could confirm only that Vicenzo's four at the 17th had to stand because he had signed for it. Therefore it had to be a 66 and Goalby, who had played superbly for a 65 that did not get the limelight it would have done under normal circumstances, was declared the winner.

At least Vicenzo was not disqualified, which he would have been had he signed for a score lower than that which he had actually taken, but the disappointment of finishing second instead of tieing must have been acute. For all that, Vicenzo took it extremely philosophically and without a trace of bitterness. 'What a stupid I am,' he said later when hauled before the Press for a lengthy post-mortem.

This sort of clerical error had of course happened before and it has happened since, though not in the Masters. It highlighted the need for more careful checking of the card by the scorers before a player is allowed to leave the tent. But the ultimate responsibility must always lie with the player himself, and that is as true now as it was then.

Roberto de Vicenzo had less to smile about after his final round in the 1968 Masters. He signed for a four at the 17th when in fact he had had a birdie three and lost by a stroke to Bob Goalby.

Nicklaus in Perpetuity

There has been a curious symmetry about the career of Jack Nicklaus, almost as if it had been pre-ordained. He has won the Masters six times, the PGA five times, the US Open four times, the British Open three times and the American Amateur championship twice. Somehow it reflects the orderliness of the man.

It is doubtful whether anyone has taken such consistent pride in his performance or given of his best when the cause was so obviously hopeless. One of the best illustrations of this came in the 1981 British Open at Royal St. George's, which has never been his favourite course. In the first round he took 83, an unthinkable score for him even in the bad weather that overtook him. Some would have feigned injury overnight or just gone through the motions. Nicklaus did neither. The following morning he was back and completed the 18 holes in 66.

Most remarkable of all has been his durability. By the end of 1987 Nicklaus had played in every major championship since 1962, a quarter of a century and more and a sequence of 104. Furthermore, he was in that time only once a victim of injury, his back giving out on the second morning of the 1983 Masters and forcing him to withdraw.

It took him only one attempt as a professional to win his first US Open and only two each to win his first Masters and PGA. His longest wait was for the British Open for that took him five years.

His planning was meticulous and for years his arrival for the Masters followed the same routine. He would skip the previous week's tournament and go instead to Augusta for two or three days when nobody was around. Once there he would go over his yardages from the previous year, test the speed of the greens and rehearse his game plan. Then, as everyone else began to arrive, he would go away and not come back until late on the Monday, giving him two final days of practice.

Nicklaus was not as popular when he won his first Masters in 1963 as he is now. In his book, *On and Off the Fairway*, a pictorial autobiography, he dubbed himself then a sort of Black Knight and recalls quite vividly how, when he made a bogey, the crowd cheered. Arnold Palmer was their man at that time and they were affronted that anyone, particularly

Jack Nicklaus studies the line of a putt during the 1975 Masters. It was the year of his fifth title.

Age has certainly not wearied Jack Nicklaus. He was 46 when he won his sixth green jacket in 1986.

an overweight, crew-cut ex-collegiate, should threaten him. It was bad enough for Nicklaus to have beaten Palmer in a play-off for the 1962 US Open, but to start winning the Masters as well . . . that was too much.

It was a Masters marred that year by bad weather. Nicklaus had had a 66 in the second round but still trailed Mike Souchak, with whom he was partnered in the third. By the time they reached the 13th, the fairway was awash and Souchak remarked that he did not think they would ever get round, apparently losing interest. Nicklaus half agreed with him but decided to keep plodding on. It was an instinctive reaction and totally justified. When he came to the 18th he found that he was leading.

On the last day the lead kept chopping and changing and with three holes to play it was Sam Snead who was in front. But Nicklaus finished 2,4,4 for a 72 and beat Tony Lema, who was making his first appearance, by a stroke. Snead and Julius Boros tied for third. Nicklaus's winning total of 286 was the third highest in the history of the Masters, but two years later, when he won again, it was with a somewhat better score. On this occasion he broke the record with an aggregate of 271 that has still not been bettered, though it was equalled by Raymond Floyd in 1976.

Nicklaus finished nine strokes ahead of Palmer and Gary Player in 1965 and the quality of his golf that year drew from Bobby Jones the greatest compliment a man can be paid. 'Mr Nicklaus', he said 'plays a game with which I am not familiar.' His rounds were 67,71,64,69 and he tore the field apart. Obviously it was his third round of 64 that wove the magic and for many years it tied the record until the South African, Nick Price, beat it with a 63 in 1986.

Nicklaus played just about as well as he has ever done that afternoon and it could quite easily have been two or three strokes better. His margin of victory still stands as the biggest ever. It is interesting on looking back at the photographs of that time to see Nicklaus wearing a hat, a slight variation to the baseball cap that adorned his head in 1963. In later years Nicklaus invariably played bareheaded, a practice these days followed by all too few.

Only one man has ever successfully defended the Masters and inevitably that was Nicklaus, in 1966. A combination of a very cold spell beforehand, which meant that the course was not in its best condition, and strong winds during the event, led to high scoring. Nicklaus, Tommy Jacobs and Gay Brewer all tied on 288, level par. Scoring had been close throughout; at one time or another 17 players led on their own or tied for the lead, but there wasn't any doubt about the play-off once Nicklaus had holed a long putt for a birdie on the 11th green. He won it with a 70, Jacobs taking 72 and Brewer 78.

Nicklaus considers he has never played quite so badly in a major championship and still won but nor had he ever come quite so close to not playing at all. On the eve of the tournament he learned that a very close friend and his wife, when flying up to watch the Masters from Columbus, had crashed and been killed together with another couple. It was only on the quiet insistence of Nicklaus's wife, Barbara, that he did not scratch.

In 1972 Nicklaus won his fourth Masters to equal Palmer's record and when he added to it the US Open at Pebble Beach, he admitted to the 'possibility but not the probability' of the professional Grand Slam. Lee Trevino put the tin hat on that by chipping in at the 71st hole in the British Open at Muirfield, Nicklaus a stroke behind in second.

At Augusta that year, Nicklaus had led all the way and only a late sequence of bogeys left a glimmer of light to those chasing him. None could take what little opportunity there was and Nicklaus, the only man under par, had three strokes to spare from Tom Weiskopf, Bruce Crampton and Bobby Mitchell.

Three years later came title number five and for sustained excitement, it was very nearly in a class of its own. At the halfway stage Nicklaus, with opening rounds of 68 and 67, was five strokes clear of the field. However, the picture changed swiftly on the Saturday when Johnny Miller made up eight of the 11 strokes by which he was trailing with a 65. It included a brilliant sequence of six consecutive birdies in an outward half of 30. Nor was that all, for Tom Weiskopf, equally inspired, had a 66 to snatch the lead from Nicklaus, who laboured to get a 73.

These three players represented just about the best talent there was in America at that time and their thrust and counter-thrust on the final day was quite spell-binding. Miller continued to play storming 'catch-up' golf and his 66 to follow his third round 65 made up the lowest score for the last 36 holes of a Masters. But it was Weiskopf, with birdies at the 14th and 15th, who wrested the lead at what seemed the crucial moment.

He had, however, to wait on the 16th tee while Nicklaus completed the hole and what he saw sent a shiver down his spine. Nicklaus's tee shot finished some 50 feet from the hole but as soon as he looked at the putt, he had a premonition about it. In it went for a two and Nicklaus leaped feet into the air before running round the green in his excitement. Miller was later asked if he had seen the putt and replied: 'No, but I did find the bear prints in the green', this being a reference to Nicklaus's nickname, the Golden Bear.

At once a shaken Weiskopf caught his mid-iron to the 16th green slightly fat, took four and was behind. Even so both he and Miller came to the last needing birdie threes to tie with Nicklaus and both hit fine second shots to within 10 feet (3 m) or so of the flag. Both missed those putts and Nicklaus, with a concluding 68, had won by a stroke.

As the years passed it seemed that Nicklaus's tally of five Masters titles would stay at that. But his finest hour was yet to come, at the age of 46 in 1986, which made him the oldest winner by nearly four years.

Nicklaus was in a multiple tie for ninth place going into the last round, Greg Norman hold-

The moment when Nicklaus really began to think that victory was his in 1986. He raises his putter aloft after sinking a birdie putt on the 17th green.

ing the lead as he did in all the major championships that year. Nor was there any immediate evidence of a recovery when Nicklaus went through the turn in 35, getting under par only with a three at the ninth. But this birdie opened the floodgates.

He was seven under par for those last 10 holes, coming home in 30 for a 65 just as Gary Player had done eight years earlier with his 64. But Nicklaus's 30 included a bogey four at the 12th, where he was too strong with his tee shot and chipped moderately. This seemed a mortal blow after his birdie threes down the 10th and 11th but he got the stroke back at the 13th and then had a wonderful run of 3,2,3 through the 15th, 16th and 17th: eagle, birdie, birdie. The 12 foot (3.6 m) putt he holed for his eagle was a wonderous moment but, as he said later, 'The more nervous I got, the better I putted. At my age I should have been incapable of even getting the putter back.'

Nicklaus came in to as emotional a reception as there has ever been. But he still had to wait for Norman, who needed a three at the last to win and a par four to tie. Such was the strain of it all, however, that he could not make up his mind over what club to play for his second shot, opted for a soft four iron and cut it wide of the green. Norman took five and lost.

Jack Nicklaus acknowledges the applause at the 1986 prize giving; Bernhard Langer, the 1985 champion, is at his side.

Floyd's Five Wood

Raymond Floyd's golf has somehow never quite received the recognition it deserves. He is a big man, with wide shoulders, built not unlike a quarter-back. But his stride down the fairway is short, almost mincing, while his swing is effective rather than a model for others to follow. He rocks more than rotates. No one could say, however, that he has not been durable. He has been around a long time, winning his first tournament in 1963 and becoming in 1986 the oldest man (43 years and nine months) to win the US Open.

He has (or at least had) the reputation for having something of a short fuse, but there is no denying his record. He is one of only 20 players in the history of the game to have won four major championships and one of only six to have collected the American Triple Crown

In 1976 Raymond Floyd dominated the Masters from first to last. His winning total of 271 equalled the record of Jack Nicklaus.

A look of quiet satisfaction from Raymond Floyd as Jack Nicklaus helps him into his green jacket.

of the US Open, Masters and PGA. Only the British Open, which he has supported faithfully, has eluded him.

A triple millionaire in dollar earnings, Floyd has frequently been written off as over the hill. Yet every time he has come bouncing back. His finest hour was in the 1976 Masters. Only one other man, Jack Nicklaus himself, has so dominated this particular tournament. Yet not even Nicklaus has scored as low as Floyd did through the first 36 and then the first 54 holes. He was 65,66 for the first two rounds for 131 and then he added a 70 in the third for 201, another record. A second 70 on the last day added it all up to 271 and that equalled the tournament best by Nicklaus in 1965. On that occasion Nicklaus won by nine strokes. In 1976 Floyd won by eight.

There was that week a key weapon in Floyd's armoury. Normally the one iron was just about his favourite club but when he began thinking about the Masters a few weeks beforehand, he worked out that in his 11 previous appearances, he had probably used that particular club less than half a dozen times.

As an experiment Floyd had a five wood made up and he used it in the Greensboro tournament that traditionally precedes the Masters. If it worked well there, it worked like a veritable charm at Augusta. There is much more height to the flight of a five wood than there is with a one iron shot, though the overall distance the ball travels is much the same. At Augusta's par fives, which are often the key to victory, Floyd wielded it as to the manner born.

In the first three rounds he was 13 under par for the par fives alone – 12 birdies and one eagle! Only in the last round did his mastery of the long holes marginally lapse, having only one birdie, at the 15th, where he deliberately laid up short of the water and then pitched and single putted.

Still, it was Floyd's supreme confidence at the par fives that was the foundation to his commanding victory: 17 under par in all, 14 of which had come at the long holes. His eight-stroke lead going into the last round was also the biggest in the history of the Masters but he admitted to having only a passing thought for beating the previous best: Nicklaus's 271. He knew he could hardly lose and it was his fervent hope only that he would win in some style, playing decently. He did that all right, repeating the 70 he had had in the third round when only once had he looked in the least bit vulnerable.

At one point then his lead was down to four strokes and when at the 13th he went for the green but found a bunker on the left, he faced a nightmare shot back towards the creek across a slippery green. All sorts of thoughts must have run through his mind but Floyd played a wonderful recovery just a yard beyond the flag and got his birdie.

Tom Watson Stands the Heat

In addition to the six victories of Jack Nicklaus in the Masters, he has also been second on four occasions. On two of them he lost to the same man, Tom Watson. This says much for Watson's character and nerve for there is nothing more forbidding for a golfer than the sound of Nicklaus's feet thundering along behind, knowing full well that with just one slip the great prize will be dashed from his grasp.

In his undergraduate days at Stanford University, Watson 'majored' in psychology and it may have armed him with a deeper knowledge of the pressures likely to be encountered on the big occasion than many realize. Behind a genial, friendly and modest disposition lies a man of steel. It is not surprising that in his time he has also won five British Opens (all at different courses) and one US Open.

His critics have maintained that his driving accuracy is questionable and it is certainly true that the broad fairways of Augusta are hardly claustrophobic. His great strength has always been his short game and no one wins a Masters without a deft touch around the greens and a sure feel on them. His nerve, which was put to the test at Augusta in both 1977 and 1981, came through with flying colours. What was also remarkable was that in 1977 Watson met Nicklaus eyeball-to-eyeball not once but twice. The other occasion was in the British Open at Turnberry and in neither instance did he flinch.

One of the hardest things for Watson in 1977 was that he was playing immediately

'And a vote of thanks to the head greenkeeper', says Tom Watson after he had won the 1981 Masters. Severiano Ballesteros is on his right, Horde Hardin, chairman of Augusta National, on his left.

behind Nicklaus, who is just as slow as he himself is quick and business-like. Consequently Watson had to spend much of the final round standing on the fairway watching Nicklaus putt. It led to an unusual incident that embarrassed both players.

At its peak Tom Watson's short game was in a class of its own.

When Nicklaus holed out for a birdie at the 13th, it seemed to Watson as if his opponent turned towards him and made a gesture as if to

say 'take that'. Afterwards, when it was all over, Watson made a rather acid comment about it and Nicklaus was genuinely horrified, assuring his young rival that all he was doing was waving in acknowledgement to the cheers of the crowd. At once Watson realized how mistaken he had been and promptly apologized for even having suspected a bit of gamesmanship was afoot.

Watson (70,69,70) had gone into the last round a stroke ahead of Rik Massengale, who then went out in 32 which got him nowhere since Watson was the same. Massengale faded but Nicklaus grew stronger. Slowly Nicklaus closed the three-stroke difference between them at the beginning of the day and with Watson on the 17th and Nicklaus on the 18th, they were level.

It was then that Watson sank a long curling putt for a birdie and the roars that greeted it came rolling up the 18th fairway just as Nicklaus was about to hit. It changed his whole thinking. His intention had been to go for the middle of the green and settle for a tie – unless of course he could get lucky and hole the putt. That Watson birdie, however, meant that Nicklaus had to go for a matching one. He hit the ball fat into a bunker, took five and lost by two strokes. Even so, he was round in 66, Watson in 67. Final rounds by the first and second players do not come much better.

In 1981 there was another show-down between them, though it was not stage-managed as it might have been and did not have quite the drama of four years earlier. Nicklaus had led after 36 holes with 70 and 65 – four strokes ahead of Watson – but took 75 on the third day, largely because he was in the water at both the 12th and 13th. Consequently, Watson's 70 jumped him ahead, Greg Norman lying third. Both Watson and Nicklaus rubbed their hands in delight at the prospect of playing one another head-to-head and were as astonished as they were dismayed on learning that they had been split up, Nicklaus to play in the penultimate pairing with John Mahaffey and Watson with Norman.

Augusta's officials do think in quaint ways at times and defended the first and third players partnering one another as normal practice. Whether it made any difference or not no one will ever know but Nicklaus was very lack-lustre, taking 38 to the turn. He pulled himself together on the homeward run but Watson remained in charge, surviving just two slight crises. At the 13th he was in the creek but instead of the customary six, he got up and down in two to save par. Then at the 17th he saved par as well from the front bunker, to which he seemed this year to have a fatal attraction; he was in it three times in the four rounds. Watson had fully expected to have to score in the 60s to win. Instead he had a 71 but with a total of 280 beat Nicklaus and Johnny Miller by two.

Sneed's Lingering Death

Some golfers are fortunate in their time to snatch victory from the jaws of defeat. Many more have suffered defeat when victory seemed assured. High among these victims of misfortune is Ed Sneed in the 1979 Masters, the first to be decided by sudden death.

For three rounds Sneed had played some of the finest golf of his life, under 70 each time as he returned 68,67,69. He led the field by five strokes and with three holes to play in the final round still had three shots to spare.

By then Fuzzy Zoeller, who had begun the day six strokes behind, had just finished in 70. He had hit a massive second shot to the 15th for one birdie, made another at the 17th and then single putted to save par at the last. Zoeller, making his first appearance in the Masters, then retired to the clubhouse for a customary beer and a seat in front of the television set to watch Sneed complete what seemed his inevitable victory.

In another part of the clubhouse Jack Nicklaus, Arnold Palmer and Gary Player were also watching the game on television. They, better than anyone, knew what Sneed was going through and foresaw the difficulties. They were not altogether surprised therefore when he took three putts at the 16th, or even when the 17th cost him three more. Now it was par to win. Tom Watson, Sneed's partner, needed a birdie to tie. Sneed just missed the 18th green on the right, chipped quite well but his putt for the title hung on the lip. He looked at it for a long time in disbelief but his ball stayed above ground. Watson got his four and it was a three-way play-off, Sneed labelled now with a record he could have done without. No man had ever before taken with him a five-stroke lead into the last round and failed to hold it. Such was the price of his concluding 76.

Watson had the best chance at the 10th hole, the first in the 'sudden-death', but missed the putt. Sneed was bunkered by the green at the 11th and made his last heroic gesture, very nearly holing his recovery. Zoeller, after a mammoth drive that left him with only an eight iron to the green, was closer, putting. He holed out for the birdie and threw his putter to the sky.

Left: *Fuzzy Zoeller, the first winner of the Masters after a sudden-death play-off, in 1978.*

Below: *Together with Horton Smith in the Masters' inaugural year of 1934 and Gene Sarazen in 1935, Fuzzy Zoeller also won the Masters at his first attempt.*

Ballesteros: The Youngest Champion

In 1980 Severiano Ballesteros became the youngest winner of the Masters, aged just 23. Here he plays his approach to Augusta's seventh green.

By 1980 the Masters was into its 44th year and a clear pattern had been set. It took an experienced hand to win. Only ten of its champions had not passed their 30th birthday. The course took years to get to know and some spent many years just dreaming about it. One, Bert Yancey, even built models of it which he would study in his every idle moment.

But patterns and tradition are meaningless when genius is at work. Severiano Ballesteros was and still is a golfing genius, as he had indicated he would become when, at the age of 19 and hardly able to utter a single word of English, he had led through the first three rounds of the British Open at Royal Birkdale, yielding ultimately only to the experience and brilliance of Johnny Miller.

That was in 1976. Now, four years on, the first day of the Masters coinciding with the Spaniard's 23rd birthday, Ballesteros gave an exhibition of golfing excellence that was years ahead of his time. It was his fourth appearance in the Masters and for three and a half rounds there was, if the expression will be excused, a God-like air about him. His first three rounds were 66,69,68 and he was seven strokes clear of the field. The final round saw him out in 33 to go 10 ahead. He was then 16 under par for the tournament and needed only two more birdies, sitting ducks for him, to break the record.

The record stayed intact. Ballesteros, human at last, took 39 to come home but it was a matter of little consequence. He still won by four strokes from Gibby Gilbert and the Australian, Jack Newton, thereby becoming only the second winner from outside America. Gary Player had been the first. Ballesteros's British Open victory the year before at Royal Lytham had not been widely appreciated by Americans; he had been too wild, too much of an escape artist for it to have been other than a fluke. At Augusta Ballesteros proved absolutely how wrong they had been.

The official history of the US Masters records: 'Ballesteros *was* the tournament in 1980, as he roamed the 7,040 yards of the Augusta National Golf Course with a brilliant display of boldness, recovery, charisma and class. His instinct with a golf club has gained for him at a tender golfing age the respect and admiration of competitors and those who follow the game.'

There was no caution about the Spaniard's game. He went 110 per cent into everything, even his putts which he would thump into the back of the hole almost as if he intended to dent it. Certainly there were still some wild moments. Playing the 17th in the third round, he landed his ball in the middle of the seventh green. He got a free drop of course and still made a birdie.

His English had improved out of all recognition and he was revealing a nice touch of humour. When questioned about his seven-stroke lead going into the final round, he said it felt as if he were playing off a handicap of seven with everyone else scratch. He did not, in other words, give a thought to losing. Youth seldom does.

For all that Ballesteros did wobble. From a seemingly unassailable lead of 10 strokes with nine holes to play, it dwindled to two. The Spaniard took three putts at the 10th; he was in the water at the 12th and took five; he was in

Left: *Ballesteros watches a lofted pitch home in on the flagstick.*

the water again at the 13th and took six. 'So stupid,' he told himself as he came off that green. 'I was very angry. What are you doing? I asked myself. Now you must try very hard or you will lose the tournament.'

It was over the next two holes that he won it, distancing himself again from the mounting challenge of Gilbert. At the 14th his drive was not good, finding the rough. Newton, his partner, did not think Ballesteros could possibly get the ball anywhere within putting range. Ballesteros made a birdie. At the 15th he ripped a four iron second onto the green, watched Newton's slightly longer putt roll for ever, 'went to school' on it and caressed his ball to within inches of the hole to make another birdie. He was safe at last.

When Ballesteros won again in 1983, the manner of it was totally different. Friday's play was washed out by a thunderstorm of remarkable intensity and Saturday's uncompleted because of more rain. When finally the sun did come out Ballesteros found himself after three rounds a stroke behind Raymond Floyd and Craig Stadler, a stroke ahead of Tom Watson and Jodie Mudd. It was an intriguing situation and Ballesteros, with a marginally shorter swing that gave him, he felt, greater control, made the sort of start that is given only to the greatest.

He opened birdie, eagle, par, birdie and killed the tournament stone dead. Watson, his partner, could not believe it. 'I thought,' he said later, 'that if I could shoot 34 on the front side, I'd be fine. I shot 34 and was four shots out.' Even so, Watson might have got back into the picture. He did not because he took three putts on each of the ninth, 10th and 11th greens.

Ballesteros was cruising by the time he came to the last hole, through the green in two, though it hardly mattered. Then he duffed his chip, which was hardly the stroke of a champion. His next was. He chipped again and holed it. He won by four strokes from Ben Crenshaw and Tom Kite having played the last round in 69.

Below: *When Ballesteros won his second Masters in 1983, he fluffed his chip on the 72nd hole. But he made no mistake with the next, holing it for a four-stroke victory from Ben Crenshaw.*

Langer beats the twitch

If it is true to say that a man who can putt is a match for anyone, it must equally be true to say that a player who cannot putt is a match for no one. Normally putting becomes a problem only as the years advance, when the nerves take over. It is called 'the twitch', an involuntary jerk of the hand (nearly always the right) and consequently also of the clubhead when striking the short putts. It can happen, it is said, even to a violinist, certainly to a darts player. There is no known cure and, as the saying goes, 'once you've got 'em, you've got 'em'.

Bernhard Langer, the finest golfer by a mile yet to have emerged from West Germany, got 'em early. He was still on the foothills of his career when he became so afflicted that other players could not bear to watch his quite pathetic attempts to hole putts that ought not to have given him a second thought. From 2 feet (0.6 m) he was quite likely to send the ball skidding 5 feet (1.5 m) past.

Langer's victory in the 1985 Masters was therefore a triumph of mental discipline, even more so than the product of the countless hours he put in with an equally countless succession of putters. Basically, he beat the twitch by putting cross-handed, placing the left hand below the right, which is the instinctive manner a small child grips a club.

Yet if the Masters that year was the story of one man's rise from the ashes of despair, so too was it the story of another man who started in despair, climbed out of it until he had a clear view of the promised land ahead and then, as suddenly, had his dreams dashed again. Like Langer, Curtis Strange had never won a major championship. Furthermore, it never even crossed his mind that he might win this one when he played the first round in 80 strokes.

Overnight Strange booked his flight home to Virginia. He never made it. What followed very nearly provided the greatest recovery the Masters has known. Strange had a 65 in the second round (as indeed did Sandy Lyle who had had a 78 in the first). He had made the cut after all. By then Strange was back to one over par in total. His progress continued. In the third round he had a 68 and astonishingly was only a stroke behind Raymond Floyd, the leader at four under par.

Langer had not been in the running until the 13th hole of the third round. He had begun 72,74 and was not making up any ground. He did not hit a good drive at the 13th but it was, he decided, worth having a go at the green with his three wood. Langer's heart sank as soon as he hit it for his ball was never going to make the carry over Rae's Creek. But he had a stroke of luck. His ball bounced the burn and he holed the putt for an eagle three. At that moment Langer's whole life began to change.

He had two birdies in the next two holes, made 68 and became a contender.

Just as this year was a Masters that Langer won (he played the last 24 holes in eight under par, finishing with another 68), it was also a Masters that Strange lost. The American, who could be mistaken for a company executive for his neat appearance and grey flecked hair, had the title in his grasp after nine holes of the final round, out in 32 and now four strokes clear of the field.

He was still three ahead with six to play and in such circumstances it would, in hindsight, have been prudent had he 'laid up' at the 13th. But he had hit a good drive and only had 208 yards (190 m) to the green. He put his ball in the creek, tried to play out of it, failed and took six. It was a set-back more than a disaster; the disaster came at the 15th.

Strange's drive was, as the pros might say, 'dead solid perfect', a good 300 yards (274 m) and right in the middle of the fairway. He had, he estimated, only a four iron to the green and he looked up expectantly as soon as he struck it. He watched his ball climb to the apex of its flight and then fall. It landed on the bank that fronts the green and trickled back into the water. Stunned, he took a second six and the lead was Langer's, the West German having previously made four at the same hole.

When Langer then made three at the 17th, Ballesteros, himself a contender and indeed joint runner-up with Strange and Floyd, walked across the green and put his arm round Langer's shoulder. He said: 'It's all yours. Well done. You've played some great shots.'

Above all, however, Langer had holed some great birdie putts: 14 feet (4.3 m) at the third, 18 feet (5.5 m) at the fifth, 13 feet (3.9 m) at the 12th, 4 feet (1.2 m) at the 13th, 4 feet (1.2 m) at the 15th, 14 feet (4.3 m) at the 17th. However, he had proved a twitcher can still win.

Opposite: *Only four non-Americans have won the Masters: Gary Player, Seve Ballesteros, Bernhard Langer and Sandy Lyle. It was not all plain sailing for Langer in 1985 as here he recovers from a bunker.*

Left: *All muscle and concentration, Bernhard Langer watches a shot en route to his first victory in a major championship.*

Rise of Larry Mize

Right: *Larry Mize can hardly believe his good fortune. He has just holed a chip to beat Greg Norman at the second extra hole in a sudden death play-off in 1987. Severiano Ballesteros had been eliminated at the previous hole.*

Below right: *In 1986 Greg Norman had a chance to tie Jack Nicklaus but took five at the last. A year later he got into a play-off and lost again. The Australians's dashing style nevertheless makes him one of the most appealing sights in the game.*

Below: *Larry Mize, the first Augusta-born golfer to win the Masters, extricates himself from a bunker.*

There has been only one other sudden-death play-off in the Masters and that was in 1987 when Larry Mize, born and bred in Augusta, had the sort of finish that is the stuff of fairytales. No previous local lad had come home to beat the world in his own back yard, even if that yard was Augusta National, hardly a playground for him in his youth!

Most eyes had nevertheless been on Ben Crenshaw, tied with Roger Maltbie going into the last round, Bernhard Langer and Greg Norman, both a stroke behind, and Seve Ballesteros, another shot back. It was Norman, Ballesteros and Mize who became the central figures, Mize finishing first and brilliantly so with a birdie at the 18th where he needed only a nine iron for his second.

Then came Ballesteros and Norman, Ballesteros saving par out of a bunker, Norman convinced he had holed a winning putt until at the last split-second it veered left. Nevertheless, it was in many ways now the perfect climax, Norman and Ballesteros, the two best players in the world, together for the play-off. No one paid too much notice to Mize.

Golf rarely follows the script, however, and when Ballesteros took five at the first extra hole, he was out of it, tearfully so; it is acceptable to cry in victory, not in defeat. Norman did not cry, but he must have felt like it. Against all the odds Mize holed a chip from off the green at the 11th. No one will ever know how brilliant or just lucky was the stroke but it was sensational.

Lyle's Green Jacket

If Europe's historic Ryder Cup victory at Muirfield Village in the autumn of 1987 (their first in America) seemed a hard if not impossible act to follow, Sandy Lyle, a member of that winning team, managed it in the spring of 1988 when he became the first Briton to win the Masters.

That he arrived at Augusta as leader of the American money list, having already won two tournaments, the Phoenix and Greensboro Opens, was not altogether in his favour for nearly 40 years had passed since Sam Snead had taken the Greensboro and Masters titles 'back to back'. But Lyle has never had a superstitious nature, taking each week as it comes and seeing no reason at all why form should suddenly run out. So it proved in a quite momentous four days as Lyle, after a quiet opening round of 71 in a difficult wind, followed it with a 67 and then a 72 for a two-stroke lead.

People cast their minds back to 1973 when Peter Oosterhuis had threatened a first British victory with a three-stroke lead going into the final round. It was an advantage quickly lost and for a terrible half hour or so it looked as if Lyle might have the cup dashed from his lips as well.

Having gone out in 34, thanks in some measure to a most unlikely two at the fourth where he chipped in after hitting his tee shot clean through the back of the green, Lyle stood three strokes clear of American Mark Calcavecchia.

There is an air of immense calmness about Lyle at all times and as he stood repeatedly waiting for those ahead of him to clear the green, there seemed almost no way that he could now lose his grip. But the Masters has long had a tradition of becoming a tournament within a tournament over the last nine holes and this was no exception. In a trice Lyle had taken three putts at the 11th; then put his tee shot into Rae's Creek short of the 12th green to drop two more shots and promptly wasted a golden opportunity of a retrieving birdie at the 13th when he hit not much more than a long pitch into a bunker behind the green.

These were seemingly mortal blows as the lead was taken up by Calcavecchia and when Lyle next failed to make a birdie at the long 15th, taking three to get down from the edge of the green, his cause seemed irretrievable. But, against all the odds, Lyle holed a wickedly fast putt on the 16th green for a two and then, needing a four to tie Calcavecchia at the last, went one better with a birdie. There has never been one like it in the whole history of the Masters.

Bunkered from the tee despite using a 'safe' one iron, Lyle was left with a 150 yard (137 m) shot from the sand uphill to the distant green. Fortunately his ball was lying clean on a slight upslope. Even so it was a staggering shot in the circumstances, right behind the flag and then screwing back off the ridge to within 8 feet (2.5m). It was a straight putt and Lyle, nerves no doubt screaming, got it dead right.

Sandy Lyle looks up expectantly as another long iron rips towards a distant green in the 1988 Masters.

US Masters

Players from US unless otherwise stated
An asterisk (*) denotes an amateur
Prize money unchanged unless shown

1934 ($5,000)
284 Horton Smith 70,72,70,72 ($1,500)
285 Craig Wood 71,74,69,71
286 Billy Burke 72,71,70,73
Paul Runyan 74,71,70,71

1935
282 Gene Sarazen 68,71,73,70
Craig Wood 69,72,68,73
284 Olin Dutra 70,70,70,74
Sarazen won play-off 144, Wood 149

1936
285 Horton Smith 74,71,68,72
286 Harry Cooper 70,69,71,76
287 Gene Sarazen 78,67,72,70

1937
283 Byron Nelson 66,72,75,70
285 Ralph Guldahl 69,72,68,76
286 Ed Dudley 70,71,71,74

1938
285 Henry Picard 71,72,72,70
287 Ralph Guldahl 73,70,73,71
Harry Cooper 68,77,71,71

1939
279 Ralph Guldahl 72,68,70,69
280 Sam Snead 70,70,72,68
282 Billy Burke 69,72,71,70
Lawson Little, Jnr. 72,72,68,70

1940
280 Jimmy Demaret 67,72,70,71
284 Lloyd Mangrum 64,75,71,74
285 Byron Nelson 69,72,74,70

1941
280 Craig Wood 66,71,71,72
283 Byron Nelson 71,69,73,70
285 Sam Byrd 73,70,68,74

1942
280 Byron Nelson 68,67,72,73
Ben Hogan 73,70,67,70
283 Paul Runyan 67,73,72,71
Nelson won play-off 69, Hogan 70

1943–1945 No competition

1946 ($10,000)
282 Herman Keiser 69,68,71,74 ($2,500)
283 Ben Hogan 74,70,69,70
287 Bob Hamilton 75,69,71,72

1947
281 Jimmy Demaret 69,71,70,71
283 Byron Nelson 69,72,72,70
Frank Stranahan 73,72,70,68

1948
279 Claude Harman 70,70,69,70
284 Cary Middlecoff 74,71,69,70
287 Chick Harbert 71,70,70,76

1949
282 Sam Snead 73,75,67,67
285 Johnny Bulla 74,73,69,69
Lloyd Mangrum 69,74,72,70

1950 ($12,000)
283 Jimmy Demaret 70,72,72,69 ($2,800)
285 Jim Ferrier 70,67,73,75
287 Sam Snead 71,74,70,72

1951 ($18,450)
280 Ben Hogan 70,72,70,68 ($3,000)
282 Skee Riegel 73,68,70,71
286 Lloyd Mangrum 69,74,70,73
Lew Worsham Jnr. 71,71,72,72

1952 ($24,600)
286 Sam Snead 70,67,77,72 ($4,000)
290 Jack Burke Jnr. 76,67,78,69
291 Al Besselink 70,76,71,74
Tommy Bolt 71,71,75,74
Jim Ferrier 72,70,77,72

1953 ($26,800)
274 Ben Hogan 70,69,66,69
279 Porky Oliver Jnr. 69,73,67,70
282 Lloyd Mangrum 74,68,71,69

1954 ($33,500)
289 Sam Snead 74,73,70,72 ($5,000)
Ben Hogan 72,73,69,75
290 Billy Joe Patton* 70,74,75,71
Snead won play-off 70, Hogan 71

1955 ($34,250)
279 Cary Middlecoff 72,65,72,70
286 Ben Hogan 73,68,72,73
287 Sam Snead 72,71,74,70

1956 ($42,000)
289 Jack Burke Jnr. 72,71,75,71 ($6,000)
290 Ken Venturi* 66,69,75,80
291 Cary Middlecoff 67,72,75,77

1957 ($53,300)
283 Doug Ford 72,73,72,66 ($8,750)
286 Sam Snead 72,68,74,72
287 Jimmy Demaret 72,70,75,70

1958 ($60,050)
284 Arnold Palmer 70,73,68,73 ($11,250)
285 Doug Ford 74,71,70,70
Fred Hawkins 71,75,68,71

1959 ($76,100)
284 Art Wall Jnr. 73,74,71,66 ($15,000)
285 Cary Middlecoff 74,71,68,72
286 Arnold Palmer 71,70,71,74

1960 ($87,050)
282 Arnold Palmer 67,73,72,70 ($17,000)
283 Ken Venturi 73,69,71,70
284 Dow Finsterwald 71,70,72,71

1961 ($99,500)
280 Gary Player (S. Africa) 69,68,69,74 ($20,000)
281 Arnold Palmer 68,69,73,71
Charlie Coe* 72,71,69,69

1962 ($109,100)
280 Arnold Palmer 70,66,69,75
Gary Player (S. Africa) 67,71,71,71
Dow Finsterwald 74,68,65,73
Palmer won play-off 68, Player 71, Finsterwald 77

1963 ($112,500)
286 Jack Nicklaus 74,66,74,72
287 Tony Lema 74,69,74,70
288 Julius Boros 76,69,71,72
Sam Snead 70,73,74,71

1964 ($129,800)
276 Arnold Palmer 69,68,69,70
282 Dave Marr 70,73,69,70
Jack Nicklaus 71,73,71,67

1965 ($137,675)
271 Jack Nicklaus 67,71,64,69
280 Arnold Palmer 70,68,72,70
Gary Player (S. Africa) 65,73,69,73

1966 ($152,880)
288 Jack Nicklaus 68,76,72,72
Tommy Jacobs 75,71,70,72
Gay Brewer 74,72,72,70
Nicklaus won play-off 70, Jacobs 72, Brewer 78

1967 ($163,350)
280 Gay Brewer 73,68,72,67
281 Bobby Nichols 72,69,70,70
284 Bert Yancey 67,73,71,73

1968 ($172,475)
277 Bob Goalby 70,70,71,66
278 Roberto de Vicenzo (Argentina) 69,73,70,66
279 Bert Yancey 71,71,72,65

1969 ($186,975)
281 George Archer 67,73,69,72
282 Tom Weiskopf 71,71,69,71
George Knudson (Canada) 70,73, 69,70
Billy Casper 66,71,71,74

1970 ($194,301)
279 Billy Casper 72,68,68,71 ($25,000)

US Masters

Gene Littler 69,70,70,70
280 Gary Player (S. Africa) 74,68,68,70
Casper won play-off 69, Littler 74

1971 ($197,976)
279 Charles Coody 66,73,70,70
281 Johnny Miller 72,73,68,68
Jack Nicklaus 70,71,68,72

1972 ($204,649)
286 Jack Nicklaus 68,71,73,74
289 Tom Weiskopf 74,71,70,74
Bruce Crampton 72,75,69,73
Bobby Mitchell 73,72,71,73

1973 ($224,825)
283 Tommy Aaron 68,73,74,68 ($30,000)
284 Jesse C. Snead 70,71,73,70
285 Peter Oosterhuis (GB) 73,70,68,74
Jack Nicklaus 69,77,73,66
Jim Jamieson 73,71,70,71

1974 ($229,549)
278 Gary Player (S. Africa) 71,71,66,70 ($35,000)
280 Dave Stockton 71,66,70,73
Tom Weiskopf 71,69,70,70

1975 ($242,750)
276 Jack Nicklaus 68,67,73,68 ($40,000)
277 Johnny Miller 75,71,65,66
Tom Weiskopf 69,72,66,70

1976 ($254,852)
271 Ray Floyd 65,66,70,70
279 Ben Crenshaw 70,70,72,67
282 Jack Nicklaus 67,69,73,73
Larry Ziegler 67,71,72,72

1977 ($280,477)
276 Tom Watson 70,69,70,67
278 Jack Nicklaus 72,70,70,66
280 Tom Kite 70,73,70,67
Rik Massengale 70,73,67,70

1978 ($283,877)
277 Gary Player (S. Africa) 72,72,69,64 ($45,000)
278 Rod Funseth 73,66,70,69
Hubert Green 72,69,65,72
Tom Watson 73,68,68,69

1979 ($299,625)
280 Fuzzy Zoeller 70,71,69,70 ($50,000)
Tom Watson 68,71,70,71
Ed Sneed 68,67,69,76
Zoeller won play-off at 2nd extra hole

1980 ($359,849)
275 Severiano Ballesteros (Spain) 66,69, 68,72 ($55,000)
279 Gibby Gilbert 70,74,68,67
Jack Newton 68,74,69,68

1981 ($362,587)
280 Tom Watson 71,68,70,71 ($60,000)
282 Jack Nicklaus 70,65,75,72
Johnny Miller 69,72,73,68

1982 ($368,652)
284 Craig Stadler 75,69,67,73 ($64,000)
Dan Pohl 75,75,67,67
285 Severiano Ballesteros (Spain) 73,73, 68,69
Jerry Pate 74,73,67,71
Stadler won play-off at 1st extra hole

1983 ($519,699)
280 Severiano Ballesteros (Spain) 68, 70,73,69 ($90,000)
284 Ben Crenshaw 76,70,70,68
Tom Kite 70,72,73,69

1984 ($611,400)
277 Ben Crenshaw 67,72,70,68 ($108,000)
279 Tom Watson 74,67,69,69
280 Gil Morgan 73,71,69,67
David Edwards 71,70,72,67

1985 ($700,793)
282 Bernhard Langer (W. Germany) 72,74,68,68 ($126,000)
284 Curtis Strange 80,65,68,71
Severiano Ballesteros (Spain) 72, 71,71,70
Raymond Floyd 70,73,69,72

1986 ($805,000)
279 Jack Nicklaus 74,71,69,65 ($144,000)
280 Greg Norman (Australia) 70,72,68, 70
Tom Kite 70,74,68,68

1987 ($903,100)
285 Larry Mize 70,72,72,71 ($162,000)
Greg Norman (Australia) 73,74, 66,72
Severiano Ballesteros (Spain) 73, 71,70,71
Mize won play-off at 2nd extra hole,
Ballesteros eliminated at 1st

1988 ($1,000,000)
281 Sandy Lyle (GB) 71,67,72,71 ($813,800)
282 Mark Calcavecchia 71,69,72,70
283 Craig Stadler 76,69,70,68

Sandy Lyle's last stroke and the one that won him the 1988 Masters. His birdie three on the final hole, after a magnificent recovery from a fairway bunker, beat Mark Calcavecchia by a shot and crowned Lyle as the first British golfer to win one of golf's most coveted prizes.

Unlike the British Open, the control of which was not taken over by the Royal and Ancient until 1919, the American Open championship has always been played under the auspices of the United States Golf Association. These two bodies, working in close harmony, now represent the government of the game.

The first US Open was played at Newport, Rhode Island, in 1895 and for a number of years it was dominated by British professionals who had emigrated to the States with the idea of making their fortunes, which some of them did. It was not until 1911 that a home-bred American, Johnny McDermott, finally broke the stranglehold.

More popularly, the turning of the tide is regarded as having come in 1913 when an amateur, Francis Ouimet, beat Harry Vardon and Ted Ray in a play-off. Since then only four overseas players have won the US Open, Ray in 1920, Gary Player in 1965, Tony Jacklin in 1970 and David Graham in 1981.

The championship has always spread itself, north, south, east and west across America. A total of 47 different courses have been used with Oakmont and Baltusrol top of the list with six apiece. It was at Baltusrol in 1980 that Jack Nicklaus set the lowest winning aggregate with a total of 272.

Nicklaus is also one of only four players to have taken the title four times. The others are Willie Anderson at the beginning of the century, Bobby Jones and Ben Hogan. The oldest winner was Raymond Floyd at Shinnecock Hills in 1986 at the age of 43 years and nine months against the 43 years and four months of Ray and the 43 years and three months of Julius Boros. McDermott was the youngest champion, only 19 when he broke the British domination.

The biggest span between first and last victories has been the 18 years of Nicklaus, whose first win was in 1962 and his last in 1980. Five amateurs have been crowned champion; Johnny Goodman was the last in 1933 but none was able to repeat his victory, other than Jones, who won four times.

As with the British Open, prize money has multiplied enormously. It began at $335 in 1895, topped $1,000 in 1919 and $10,000 in 1947. It passed $50,000 in 1960, $100,000 in 1965 and $500,000 in 1983. In 1987 it stood at $825,000 with Scott Simpson, the winner, receiving $150,000.

US OPEN CHAMPIONSHIP

Left: *A cloud of sand follows an explosion shot by Scott Simpson as he heads for a US Open victory at the Olympic Club, San Francisco, in 1987.*

Right: *The smile of the champion as Scott Simpson holds aloft the US Open trophy after beating Tom Watson by a stroke at Olympic.*

Merion

Though unusually short at 6,544 yards (5,984 m), Merion is a classic US Open course and a true favourite with the USGA. It has staged the premier championship four times and been host to many other national championships, including the 1930 Amateur when Bobby Jones set the seal on his celebrated Grand Slam.

Merion's confined area – no more than 110 acres (45 hectares), about half the size of some championship venues – together with Ardmore Avenue which cuts clean through the middle of the course, are not its most endearing qualities. For all the difficulty of spectator movement however, Merion has survived.

No clubhouse is so close to the first tee, a mere step or two from the door while there are several more unusual features. The bunkers, once dubbed 'the white faces of Merion' for the glaring quality of the sand, are dotted with great clumps of spiky grass. Nor are there any flags at Merion. Instead, the flagsticks are topped by oval wicker baskets. Thereby, so it is said, the player is given no clue as to the direction of the wind!

In 1960 Jack Nicklaus, playing for the United States at Merion in the world amateur team championship for the Eisenhower Trophy, scored a remarkable 269 for the 72 holes, 11 under par. It heralded the beginning of one of the greatest careers golf has known, though at the height of it, Nicklaus was confounded by a course that had not changed one iota. In the 1971 US Open neither he nor Lee Trevino, with whom he tied, could do better than match the par of 280. Trevino then won the play-off with a 68 against a 71 and in so doing began a memorable spell during which he took both the Canadian Open and then the British Open at Royal Birkdale.

Much of Merion's defence lies in the speed of its greens for though two of the first four holes measure between them 1,135 yards (1,037 m) (535 yards/489 m at the second and 600 yards/548 m at the fourth), six of the par fours are of less than 400 yards (366 m). The 13th is also a real little teaser at 129 yards (118 m).

From then on, however, the finish asks any number of fascinating questions with two doglegs, one left and the other right, at the 14th and 15th, a second shot over a quarry at the 16th, then a long par three, and finally one of the great last holes.

Such are the demands of the 18th drive from deep in the woods that Paul Runyan once used

The 13th hole at Merion is a real little teaser, only 129 yards in length but severely bunkered and with a sloping green that is like glass.

Lee Trevino removes his cap and punches the air as another putt finds its mark.

his wedge to advance his ball to the forward tee and then hit a wood to the fairway which rises to a crest and then dips into a valley before rising again to a distant green. The one iron second shot Ben Hogan rifled to the green to secure a tie in the 1950 US Open is still held as one of the master strokes of all time.

Just as memorable was the flawless last round of 67 David Graham had in winning the 1981 US Open. He did not miss a fairway or green by more than inches at any time and completed those last five punishing holes in two birdies and three pars.

Curiously, Merion was designed by an architectural amateur in Hugh Wilson, who was a member of the club when it was affiliated to the Merion Cricket Club. He was sent to Britain to take a post graduate course on linksland with the specific task of then coming home and building a championship golf course.

There is no more celebrated hole than the 11th, a classic short par four to a dropping fairway and then a pitch beyond a babbling brook. It was on this very green that Bobby Jones beat Eugene Homans by eight and seven to complete his Grand Slam and here, too, that Bobby Cruickshank, having had the good luck to see his pitch bounce onto the green off a half-submerged rock, threw his club into the air only to have the smile wiped from his face when it descended onto his head.

Merion

Hole	Yards	Par	Hole	Yards	Par
1	355	4	10	312	4
2	535	5	11	370	4
3	183	3	12	405	4
4	600	5	13	129	3
5	426	4	14	414	4
6	420	4	15	378	4
7	350	4	16	430	4
8	360	4	17	224	3
9	195	3	18	458	4

Yards 6,544 Par 70

Merion's impressive club house, from which one steps almost immediately onto the first tee.

Olympic

It is testimony to the strength of the Lakeside course at the Olympic Club in San Francisco that only one of the 18 holes has a fairway bunker. It comes into play on the sixth. The course is difficult enough without any more.

Set in the side of a hill along a series of almost steps down to a lake that lies beyond the boundaries of the course, it is one of two 18-hole lay-outs. The other is the Ocean course, looking out towards the Pacific and quite different, not only in character but also even in climate.

Quite often the rolling fog which can 'cut in half' the Golden Gate Bridge, perhaps the most famous landmark of this intriguing city, prevents play on the Ocean while the Lakeside remains clear.

Not, however, clear of trouble. The main feature of Lakeside is its many dog-legs, some quite sharp but mostly a gentle bend through great avenues of eucalyptus, cypress and cedar. Unusually, too, for an American course, there are no water hazards. But the greens are small and well bunkered while a generally damp climate encourages the rough to be heavy and clinging.

There have been three Opens at Olympic and two of them caused golfing sensations. In 1955 Ben Hogan was actually congratulated on television on what would have been a record fifth victory. However, the little-known Jack Fleck was still out on the course and he tied the great man and then beat him in the play-off.

Eleven years later the world was equally ready to acclaim a second US Open victory for Arnold Palmer. But an extraordinary collapse over the last nine holes led to another play-off which Billy Casper won. How were the mighty fallen!

In 1987 there was another unexpected winner when Scott Simpson, finding an inspired

Below: *Billy Casper used to eat buffalo steaks to keep his weight in check. But he was still a great golfer, US Open champion in 1959 and 1966.*

Right: *The 18th at Olympic is one of the shortest finishing holes in championship golf; no more than a drive (perhaps with a long iron) and pitch but a marvellous natural vantage point for spectators. It was here that Ben Hogan took six and lost a play-off against Jack Fleck in 1955.*

putting touch over the closing holes, held off the challenge of Tom Watson, who was within a whisker of forcing yet a third play-off with the most gallant of long putts from the fringe of the 18th green.

Somehow Olympic is a course on which things simply 'happen'. In tune with the Opens, there was the US Amateur championship of 1981 in the wake of the Walker Cup match at Cypress Point just down the Californian coast. The Amateur does not normally attract a great deal of attention in the United States these days but the progress of Nathaniel Crosby this year more and more captured the imagination of the public. The son of Bing, he became a youthful hero to crowds which swelled by the day as he battled his way to the title, enjoying every minute of it with a series of ever more dazzling strokes. Sadly, for young Nat had much to offer, it was a swing that never quite stood up to the professional arena he was later to enter.

Nowhere is there a more natural amphitheatre for the climax of a championship than at the 18th at Olympic. A towering hillside climbs all around the tiny, fiercely sloping green, offering a natural vantage point to the masses. And looking down on it from an even greater height is the rather inelegant clubhouse, all red brick and deep windows. Inside, there is not so much a locker room as a series of locker rooms, private sanctuaries with doors of their own.

At a mere 340 yards (310 m) or so the 18th is unusually short for a finishing hole and makes up for what has gone before. It is by its nature a course that plays longer than the 6,714 yards (6,139 m) used for the 1987 Open. However, in this instance the 17th, normally a par five, became a par four, thereby reducing the overall par from 71 to the USGA's ideal of 70. With its sharply sloping fairway and narrow entrance to the green, it played more like a four-and-a-half.

Above: *There is only one fairway bunker at Olympic but no lack of them at the short holes. This is the third.*

Olympic

Hole	Yards	Par	Hole	Yards	Par
1	533	5	10	422	4
2	394	4	11	430	4
3	223	3	12	390	4
4	438	4	13	186	3
5	457	4	14	417	4
6	437	4	15	149	3
7	288	4	16	609	5
8	137	3	17	428	4
9	433	4	18	343	4

Yards 6,714 Par 70

Inverness

It is hard to believe in these days of multi-million dollar golfers, managers to look after their business affairs and even, in some cases, their own aircraft to transport them from one venue to the next, that once the professional was held very much as a second-class citizen and barred even from entering the clubhouse.

When, in 1920, Inverness was accorded its first US Open, the club decided that such discrimination was too old-fashioned and opened its doors wide in welcome. So touched were the professionals that Walter Hagen arranged a collection among them and then presented to the club a grandfather clock which, to this day, stands in the main entrance lobby. It carries the inscription:

God measures men by what they are
Not what in wealth possess.
This vibrant message chimes afar
The voice of Inverness.

Though Dick Wilson updated the course in the mid-fifties, the original design by Donald Ross provided its basic character and it remains one of the celebrated venues for the US Open, which has now been held here four times.

There is ample room from the tee but the greens tend to be small and well bunkered on a rolling terrain through avenues of evergreens and hardwoods. Two holes, the seventh and 18th, are especially notable.

The seventh is a classically strong par four played from a high tee to a broad fairway but the problem lies in which line to take. The easier approach from the fairway on a hole that swings left to a pulpit green is from the right side. However, that means a big carry over a snake-like burn. The safer drive down the left leaves the more difficult approach while the slightly domed green can be treacherously fast.

In the 1986 PGA championship both Bob Tway and Greg Norman were safely on the green in two, neither more than 15 feet (4.6 m) away but putting down the slope. Both seemed hardly to breathe on their putts but still putted clean off the green and had to chip back amid blushes.

Inverness's 18th is one of the shortest finishing holes in championship golf, though not quite as short as the last at Olympic. The slightly raised green is surrounded by a nest of bunkers and clinging rough and it provided some high drama in the 1986 PGA for when Tway bunkered his approach from the rough, it seemed that the title was destined to go to Norman even though a four-stroke lead had slowly ebbed away. Instead, Tway holed out from the sand for a birdie three and in a flash Norman's dream was shattered. He had led going into the last round just as he had led going into the final round of the Masters, US Open and British Open. But it was only this last title he had secured.

That first US Open at Inverness in 1920 was notable for it being the last to be won by a

It was at Inverness in 1920 that professionals were first admitted to the clubhouse. The players, led by Walter Hagen, promptly presented the club with a chiming clock in recognition.

Left: *A hushed crowd watches a bunker shot at the 18th hole at Inverness in the 1986 PGA.*

Below: *'It's in' and Bob Tway leaps in the air in excitement after holing the bunker shot that won him the 1986 PGA.*

British golfer, Ted Ray, until Tony Jacklin succeeded him 50 years later. Ray's was an unlikely victory, for Harry Vardon appeared to have the championship in his grasp with a lead of five strokes and only seven holes to play. But a gale sprang up and Vardon, who was then 50, weakened and was beaten by a stroke. In the field for the first time was an 18-year-old amateur, Bobby Jones. He tied eighth.

By 1931, when next the Open went to Inverness, Jones had retired and there resulted the longest championship on record. With a birdie three at the last, George Von Elm tied Billy Burke and they went into a 36-hole play-off. Again they tied and again Von Elm made a three at the 18th. So that meant another 36 holes, which was the way things were done in those days, making the total confrontation of 144 holes. Finally it was Burke who prevailed, by just one stroke.

Inverness

Hole	Yards	Par	Hole	Yards	Par
1	398	4	10	363	4
2	385	4	11	378	4
3	185	3	12	167	3
4	466	4	13	523	5
5	401	4	14	448	4
6	220	3	15	458	4
7	452	4	16	405	4
8	528	5	17	431	4
9	420	4	18	354	4

Yards 6,928 Par 71

Shinnecock Hills

Opposite top: *The 18th green at Shinnecock Hills with its natural vantage point for spectators.*

Opposite bottom: *Professionals do not hole every putt, not even Raymond Floyd on his way to winning the 1986 US Open.*

Though the game is the same, the golf courses on which the US Open is staged can seldom be compared with those which stage the British Open. There is some similarity between Pebble Beach, along that gorgeously rugged Californian coastline, and Turnberry in Scotland but, broadly speaking, there is not the same 'naturalness' about much of the American golfing terrain. The hand of man is more evident than the hand of nature.

A glorious exception is Shinnecock Hills on Long Island. From the crest of the hill on which the low, white, ranch-style clubhouse sits, one can look out and take in a scene that at once reminds the British visitor of Sunningdale, Woodhall Spa or Blairgowrie. Shinnecock Hills is much closer to the sea than any of these, but it is not a links despite the proximity of the Atlantic.

The crested fairways nevertheless give an impression of the swell of the ocean while the rough is severe enough for Jack Nicklaus to have lost a ball in it when driving off the 10th tee in the 1986 US Open. He couldn't remember ever having done that before in a major championship, other than in a water hazard.

That the championship went back to Shinnecock Hills in 1986 reflected a flash of inspiration by the United States Golf Association. The only previous Open held there had been as long ago as 1896 when the championship was still being played over 36 holes. Though within a two-hour train journey of New York, the rather narrow roads and sparse hotel accommodation was considered unsuitable for a modern Open. In fact it ran as smoothly as any in recent years, coping not only with the usual large crowds but also, on the first day, weather that seemed to have been imported from Scotland at its bleakest.

Shinnecock was one of the five founding clubs of the USGA; it has claims to being the first 'formalized' club and the first to have 18 holes. It was a Scottish professional, Willie Dunn, who was responsible for the original lay-out. He was brought across the Atlantic from Biarritz where he had had a chance meeting with William K. Vanderbilt, a prominent sportsman and son of the founder of the Vanderbilt dynasty. Together they toured the area of Southampton and presently came across the sandhills of Shinnecock that reminded Dunn so much of home. An adjacent railroad made it ideal for New Yorkers anxious to try their hand at this new game of golf.

Most of the building of the original course was done by hand and the bunkers are said to be made up of old Indian burial grounds. Rumour has it that a bunker shot was quite

Below: *No American course bears a closer resemblance to those in Britain than Shinnecock Hills, site of two US Opens as far apart as 1896 and 1986. This is the first hole.*

likely to bring to light an old bone or two!

Stanford White, the most fashionable architect of the day, was commissioned to design the clubhouse, which is substantially unchanged a century later and much smaller than the brash palaces that dominate many of the American country clubs. To the 12 original holes, another six were soon added but the Shinnecock Hills of today owes most to a prominent golf course architect, Dick Wilson, who was called in to supervise changes in the early 1930s.

He made full use of the outstanding features and took account of the prevailing wind off the Atlantic by designing the longer holes so that they played downwind and the shorter holes into it.

When the wind blew during the first round of the 1986 US Open, no one succeeded in breaking the par of 70 and at its finish Raymond Floyd was the only man in red figures. He scored 279 for the 72 holes and became the championship's oldest winner.

Shinnecock Hills

Hole	Yards	Par	Hole	Yards	Par
1	394	4	10	409	4
2	226	3	11	158	3
3	453	4	12	472	4
4	408	4	13	377	4
5	535	5	14	444	4
6	471	4	15	397	4
7	188	3	16	544	5
8	367	4	17	172	3
9	447	4	18	450	4

Yards 6,912 Par 70

Winged Foot

It is unlikely that any golfer left with five pars to win a US Open would choose to get them at Winged Foot. They measure a total of 2,179 yards (1,992 m), which is an average of 435 yards (398 m) and the shortest is 417 yards (381 m). All are par fours. Finishing stretches do not come much harder than that.

Winged Foot has the recognizable hand of A.W. Tillinghast, who also designed Baltusrol, San Francisco, Quaker Ridge, Ridgewood, Five Farms and Fresh Meadow and, as an examination of even the modern game, lives by its results. There have been four US Opens played amid the rolling, heavily wooded acres of the West course at Winged Foot on the periphery of New York, and only two players have scored lower than 280, which is now the four-round par.

That was in 1984 when Fuzzy Zoeller and Greg Norman tied on 276, Zoeller winning the play-off in an unexpected canter. Yet in 1974 Hale Irwin won with a seven-over-par total of 287, which gives some idea of the difficulty of the course. In 1959 Billy Casper had scored five strokes better than that, though it is worth pointing out that in doing so he used his putter only 114 times, an average of 28.5 putts per round. To draw a comparison with the winning score in 1929, when Bobby Jones beat Al Espinosa in another play-off, is less valid because of the equipment then in use. Suffice to say that they tied on 294.

There are two courses at Winged Foot, the other being the East. Some members maintain that it is just as good as the West. However, it is the latter that has taken the spotlight and its feature is very much the par fours. Ten of them, including of course the last five, are all in excess of 400 yards (366 m) and that is something for men rather than boys. The short holes, on the other hand, are nicely varied while there are also two teasing drive-and-pitch holes.

Adding to the difficulty are the large, and also deep, bunkers. These may not be prolific but they are certainly strategic. 'I always adhere to my theory', said Tillinghast once, 'that a controlled shot to a closely guarded green is the surest test of any man's golf.'

It is certainly no coincidence that Winged Foot has produced many fine golfers and once they were even able to boast both the US Open and Amateur champions. Dick Chapman won

One of the enormous bunkers that characterize Winged Foot. Here Tom Kite, so often so near and so often so far from a major championship title, comes out of the sand at the seventh hole.

the American Amateur championship in 1940 and a year later Craig Wood, the head professional, added to it the Open title.

There are two distinct loops at Winged Foot, the ninth and 18th holes both returning to the gabled clubhouse, and it is first and foremost a driver's course. Nearly 8,000 trees were felled in the original building of the West course but enough remain to provide continual avenues down which the ball must be hit long and straight. The elevation of many of the greens also means that the second shots must carry all the way rather than bounce forward onto the green.

The club takes its name from an early association with the New York Athletic Club in Manhattan, a number of whose members decided to form a suburban golf club. In due course the affiliation was severed but the 'winged foot' emblem has remained.

Perhaps an illustration of the demands of the course can be given by a temporary English member. So lost in concentration had he been in a particularly well played round that later, when changing in the locker room, he asked his neighbour how he had got on. 'I lost,' came the reply. 'Bad luck, who to?' he was then asked. 'You,' said the victim.

Above: *The ninth green at Winged Foot and beyond it the elegantly gabled clubhouse.*

Winged Foot

Hole	Yards	Par	Hole	Yards	Par
1	446	4	10	180	3
2	411	4	11	333	4
3	216	3	12	535	5
4	460	4	13	212	3
5	515	5	14	418	4
6	324	4	15	417	4
7	161	3	16	452	4
8	442	4	17	444	4
9	456	4	18	448	4

Yards 6,870 Par 70

Below: *Fuzzy Zoeller has the unusual distinction of having won two major championships, both of them after play-offs. He was successful in the 1979 Masters and then in the 1984 US Open at Winged Foot.*

Oakland Hills

Whenever one thinks of Oakland Hills, in a sprawling suburb of Detroit, the name of Ben Hogan springs to mind. It was here in 1951 that the 'Wee Ice Mon', as the Scots were later to dub him after his Open championship victory at Carnoustie, won one of his most celebrated US Opens.

It was celebrated because of the then severity of a golf course that had strong men trembling with apprehension. Afterwards, in his speech of thanks following a final round of 67 – one of only two all week that broke 70 – Hogan spoke his now famous line: 'I'm glad that I brought this course, this monster, to its knees.'

Hogan's total was 287 and only Clayton Heafner also managed to break 290. The 'monster' image therefore lives on, though subsequent events have indicated that it is now more imagined than real. When next the US Open was held at Oakland Hills in 1961, Gene Littler scored 281 while 10 other players either bettered or matched Hogan's aggregate 10 years earlier.

Furthermore, when Andy North won his second US Open at Oakland Hills in 1985 – an unusual record since he can claim only one other tournament victory in his whole career – he did so with a score of 279 as this time 19 players either matched or bettered Hogan's previous score of 287.

Not all of this can be put down to improved equipment and greater ability across the board. In 1951 the USGA were anxious to create a monster and they called in Robert Trent Jones to supervise the necessary changes to a course designed by Donald Ross who, when he first set eyes on the expanse of rolling woodland, remarked: 'The Lord intended this for a golf course.'

Jones's changes included the addition of 66 bunkers and a re-shaping of the fairways so that they bore some resemblance to the shape of an hour glass.

In other words there were two distinct target areas on each of the par four and par five holes: one for the drive and the other for the shot to the green. But bordering these target areas were also some challenging bunkers and any stroke that did not find the target was almost certain to be severely punished.

Hogan was not the only man to be confounded in the early rounds (he began with a

The finishing hole at Oakland Hills, one of the best of the US Open courses.

76), but he warmed to his task and in the last round, often driving with a brassie or spoon, he produced what he has always held to have been the greatest round he ever played.

By 1961, however, both the course – and more, perhaps, the USGA – had mellowed. The rough was no longer as thick as it had been 10 years earlier and many of the bunkers had been removed. It remains one of the supreme tests of championship golf in America but to continue to call it a monster would be an overstatement.

For all that, the rough is still a factor, as T.C. Chen, of Taiwan, would verify. In the 1985 Open there was a very real possibility that the Orient might celebrate its first victory in a major championship. Chen was four strokes clear of the field playing the fifth hole in the final round but it was then that disaster struck. He fluffed two chips and in playing one of them he hit the ball in mid air, thereby incurring a two-stroke penalty on his way to an eight.

In an earlier round Chen had scored the first albatross in a US Open – a two at the par five second where he holed a three-wood shot – while the championship was further highlighted by an unusual penalty imposed on the South African, Denis Watson. On the eighth green in the first round his ball had hung on the lip of the hole for nearly 30 seconds before dropping into the hole for what he believed to be a par four. Such an interval was held to be excessive (10 seconds is the stated limit) and Watson was penalized two strokes. Cruelly he tied second, a stroke behind North.

Oakland Hills

Hole	Yards	Par	Hole	Yards	Par
1	436	4	10	454	4
2	527	5	11	411	4
3	199	3	12	560	5
4	433	4	13	172	3
5	457	4	14	465	4
6	359	4	15	399	4
7	405	4	16	409	4
8	439	4	17	201	3
9	217	3	18	453	4

Yards 6,996 Par 70

Above: *There are few better holes at Oakland Hills than the 16th, demanding as it does a most precise second shot over water to a well-bunkered green.*

Below: *When Ben Hogan won the US Open at Oakland Hills in 1951 he described himself, after a final round of 67, 'happy to have brought this monster to its knees'.*

Oakmont

Opposite top: *Arnold Palmer in trouble at Oakmont's 13th hole. It was on this course in 1962 that Jack Nicklaus announced, beating Palmer in a play-off for the US Open, his first victory as a professional.*

Opposite bottom: *Larry Nelson on his way to victory in the 1983 US Open, though it was slightly delayed – a storm during the last round meant that he had to go back the following morning to complete his last three holes.*

Below: *Oakmont has several distinctive features, not least its 'church pew' bunkers that come into play between the third and fourth holes.*

There are several unusual features about Oakmont which, together with Baltusrol, has staged more American Open championships than any other club – six. It boasts what are rated the most terrifying greens on the whole of the North American continent. Attempting to lag an approach putt close to the hole, Sam Snead once said, was 'like trying to stop a ball halfway down a marble staircase'.

William C. Fownes, a steel magnate from the nearby city of Philadelphia, who had been the force behind the building of the course in the early 20th century, once dropped a ball on the back of the second green and watched it roll all the way off the front.

Therein lies not the only terror of what is commonly regarded as the most testing of all the American championship courses. There is also the bunkering. Once there were more than 200 sand traps and though these have since been reduced to around 180, that is still three times as many as there are at Augusta.

Once, too, these bunkers were famed for their furrows, great channels through the sand almost like a ploughed field. The story goes that when Ted Ray was playing here, he once lost his ball in a bunker but was informed by one of the spectators that he would find it in 'row seven'.

Such a description could still apply on the third and fourth holes. While, with some reluctance by the club membership, the furrows have gone, the famous church pew bunkers that divide the third and fourth holes have not. They are lined, back-to-back, up the sides of the fairways of these two holes played in opposite directions. They invite in each case a hooked drive and it takes a lot of praying to get out of them again.

The golf course is also divided into two. Cutting through its middle is America's oldest highway, the Pennsylvania Turnpike, with its thundering traffic. Players cross it by a bridge behind the first green, continue for seven holes and then cross it again for the remainder of the round.

The ninth hole is a par five, not a long one but different in that the green is shared with the practice putting green, one of the largest in the world since it contains 72 holes of a putting clock. There are therefore 73 holes on the green at any one time but there is a special local rule that anyone who gets tangled up in the practice area can drop clear without penalty.

Johnny Miller's closing 63, which won him the 1973 Open in the most sensational and unprecedented style, has gone down for ever into the history of the game. Curiously, Oakmont has yielded not only the championship's lowest last round but also its lowest final 36 holes. In 1983 Larry Nelson finished 65,67

to beat Tom Watson by a stroke.

This was not the only disappointment Watson has suffered at Oakmont. In the 1978 PGA he was beaten in a play-off by John Mahaffey after holding a commanding lead going into the fierce finishing stretch that in 1953 saw Ben Hogan at his best.

The 15th is a long two-shotter and Hogan was so badly bunkered that he had to play out sideways, leaving him still with a big iron to the green. But he holed a long putt to save his par and then finished 3,3,3 – par, birdie, birdie – driving the green at the 17th and then hitting one of the best five irons to the middle of the 18th green.

A 17th hole measuring only 322 yards (294 m) does not sound menacing. In fact it is a classic, sharply dog-legged in the driving area and heavily bunkered to prevent, or at least challenge, those tempted to go for the green. But the temptation is always there. Hogan resisted it for three rounds but not in the fourth when, in any case, he had strokes to spare.

Oakmont

Hole	Yards	Par	Hole	Yards	Par
1	469	4	10	462	4
2	343	4	11	371	4
3	425	4	12	603	5
4	561	5	13	185	3
5	379	4	14	360	4
6	201	3	15	453	4
7	434	4	16	228	3
8	240	3	17	322	4
9	480	5	18	456	4

Yards 6,972 Par 71

Baltusrol

Baltusrol, in Springfield, New Jersey, has a special place in the hearts of the United States Golf Association. Together with Oakmont, it has now staged six American Open championships, its first in 1903 and its last in 1980 when Jack Nicklaus equalled the four wins of Willie Anderson, Bobby Jones and Ben Hogan. Nicklaus had also won over the same course in 1967 and this time he did it in even greater style, his 72-hole total of 272 being a championship record.

Baltusrol finishes with two par fives. This is the 18th.

Indeed, this was a year of records, for on the first day both Nicklaus and Tom Weiskopf opened with 63s, which stand as the lowest first round scores, equalling one other 63, by Johnny Miller in the fourth round when he won at Oakmont in 1973. Nicklaus indeed had a short putt on the last green for a 62 but confessed to 'chickening out' from a yard.

That first round had also been notable for a hole in one at the fourth by Tom Watson, which drew a smile from the golf course architect, Robert Trent Jones, who had a clear memory of the time when he was called in to toughen up the course for the 1954 Open, which was won by Ed Furgol.

One of the holes on which Jones concentrated was this short fourth and he turned it into one of the toughest in championship golf. It is an all-or-nothing hole, nearly 200 yards (183 m) from the back tee played over water to a green much wider than it is long and faced with a stone wall.

The members protested that it was too tough but Jones not only offered to pay for the changes out of his own pocket but agreed to demonstrate his convictions that it was still a fair hole by playing it with Johnny Farrell, the club professional at that time, the club president and the chairman of the Open committee. The last to play, Jones holed in one, remarking lightly after he had done so: 'As you can see, gentlemen, the hole is not too tough.'

There are two courses at Baltusrol, the Upper and Lower, laid out in the first instance by A.W. Tillinghast, one of the most respected of the early American architects.

The Lower is now regarded as the principal course and while it may bear little resemblance to the original, the flavour nevertheless remains. There is great variety and though the overall length is apparently severe at more than 7,000 yards (6,400 m), the impression is not one of brute strength. Bunkering is frugal but always strategically placed, while the greens are models of restraint, seldom demanding a massive approach putt or a 'knee trembler' down a wicked slope.

Unlike some American courses, there are few sharp dog-legs, the fairways instead gently bending to the contours of the land. There is nevertheless some imbalance: there is not a par five on the course until the 17th and then there are two, back-to-back. The 17th is quite enormous, 630 yards (574 m), the green, furthermore, elevated. It is about as genuine a three-shotter as you will find these days.

The existence of two courses enabled Furgol to win the US Open in 1954 by, in a sense, playing them both. At the last hole Furgol pulled his drive into the woods and he had no shot back onto the fairway. However, he did spy a narrow gap through which he could play to the 18th fairway of the Upper course, which runs parallel. Accordingly, he called for an official to ask whether the 18th of the Upper

was in bounds. The official did not know and second, third and fourth opinions were sought before it was finally ruled that since there were no defining stakes, Furgol could indeed take the alternative route. He won by a stroke from Gene Littler.

Furgol was a first-class example of someone who overcomes physical disability to reach the top. A childhood accident resulted in his breaking his left arm, which was then badly set. It became locked at a permanent angle of around 160 degrees and with the muscles wasting as well, was no more than a guide to the swing path of the club. Restricted though his movement was, Furgol devised a method that repeated and also prospered.

Baltusrol

Hole	Yards	Par	Hole	Yards	Par
1	465	4	10	454	4
2	377	4	11	428	4
3	438	4	12	193	3
4	194	3	13	393	4
5	388	4	14	409	4
6	470	4	15	430	4
7	470	4	16	216	3
8	374	4	17	630	5
9	205	3	18	542	5

Yards 7,076 Par 70

The 18th green and clubhouse of Baltusrol. Jack Nicklaus has won two of his four US Open championships here.

When Johnny Farrell won the US Open at Olympia Fields in 1928 it was the custom for golfers to wear a tie.

Founding Fathers: Ouimet and McDermott

For a number of romantic reasons Francis Ouimet is looked upon as the father of all United States Open champions. He was an amateur and only 20 years of age when he took the title at the Country Club, Brookline, on the outskirts of Boston in 1913. As his parents owned a house close by he was the local boy who made good, but he was also a veritable David against two Goliaths in that the men he beat in the play-off were the two greatest players in the world at that time, Harry Vardon and Ted Ray, who were on a tour of the States. A comparative performance today would be for some pimply youth to tie with and then defeat Greg Norman and Severiano Ballesteros.

In a sense there was an echo of this in the 1987 Masters when Larry Mize did defeat Norman and Ballesteros in a sudden death play-off, for Mize, too, was the local boy in that he came from Augusta and he unexpectedly saw off both these giants. However, as a professional of already some standing, he was much better known than Ouimet was all those years ago.

Francis Ouimet, an amateur whose victory over Harry Vardon and Ted Ray in a play-off for the 1913 US Open is regarded as the birth of American golf.

Adding further romanticism to Ouimet's remarkable victory was the fact that his caddie was the faithful 10-year-old, Eddie Lowery, who was not much bigger than the clubs he carried. Ten years old or not, he stubbornly refused in the play-off to accept 10 dollars in exchange for handing them over to someone else.

While Ouimet's performance is looked upon as the one which turned the American golfing tide, he was nonetheless not the first home-bred American to win a championship which, in its formative years, was the exclusive domain of immigrant Scots. Instead, that distinction fell to John McDermott, who won both in Chicago in 1911 and at Buffalo, New York, in 1912.

McDermott was undoubtedly one of the great players of that time. Of quiet disposition, he was a slave to practice and before opening the professional's shop in which he served, would invariably in summer rise at 5 a.m. and put in three hours on the practice ground. In the evening he would putt by lamplight. Sometimes he spread newspapers on the ground, using them as targets from 150 yards (137 m) distant. His mashie consequently became the master club in his bag.

McDermott was only 19 when he won at Chicago, again being involved in a three-way play-off. Such was the impetus he gave the game in the States that there was an immediate upsurge in the standard of play overall. A year later his total of 294 at Buffalo, at 6,236 yards (5,702 m) the longest yet used in a US Open, was two under par and also set a new 'low'.

The runner-up, Tom McNamara, broke 70 in the last round, which was in those days a mystical barrier. But all the talk was of McDermott, the feeling being that he was quite capable of equalling or even beating the record of Willie Anderson, who won the US Open four times in five years, beginning at the Myopia Hunt Club in 1901. McDermott was earning good money, clubs and balls were being marketed in his name, and he was investing his money wisely.

There was something of a set-back to his soaring confidence, however, when in 1912 he tried to win the British Open at Muirfield but failed even to qualify for the championship proper. It was said that his rather flowing

Francis Ouimet, with his caddy Eddie Lowery, on his way to victory at Brookline in the 1913 US Open.

swing was not suited to British conditions but in 1913 he finished equal fifth at Hoylake and that was the best performance yet by a visiting American.

Full of confidence, McDermott came home, won a tournament from a field that included Vardon and Ray in Pennsylvania only to spoil it all by saying in his victory speech: 'We hope our foreign visitors had a good time but we don't think they did and we are sure they won't win the US Open.'

Though he almost certainly meant it as a joke, McDermott was heavily criticized and he received a letter from the USGA saying that his entry for the Open might be rejected. In fact it was not but McDermott, worried already by some heavy losses in his stocks investments, withdrew more and more into himself.

Two further events hastened the end of his career. In the 1914 British Open at Prestwick, McDermott missed a train and consequently his starting time for the qualifying rounds. Though officials offered to let him in, McDermott would have none of it and booked his passage home on the *Kaiser Wilhelm II* but was shipwrecked when it collided with another ship in thick fog.

Though unhurt, McDermott never fully recovered and by the age of 23 his career was over. He spent most of the remaining 57 years of his life in and out of rest homes. But while he was good, he was very good.

Francis Ouimet discovered golf by discovering golf-balls. A short cut from school to his home took him across the Country Club course in Boston and by the age of seven he had accumulated quite a collection of balls found abandoned in the undergrowth. A club came later, one he shared with his elder brother, Wilfred who, between caddying duties at the Country Club, laid out a rough course in a pasture behind the Ouimet house.

The game fascinated the young Francis and

whenever he paused on his return from school to watch the members at play, he would afterwards hurry on home and try and emulate their shots. He also read everything he could find on the game and at the age of 11 followed his elder brother by caddying at the Country Club. He was then close at hand to observe the styles and methods of such as Walter Travis, Jerome Travers, Willie Anderson, Alex Smith and Tom McNamara. The owner now of two more golf clubs, Ouimet occasionally 'stole' a few holes at the Country Club when no one was looking, but most of his golf was played at Franklin Park, a public course in Brookline.

At the age of 16 Ouimet won the Boston Interscholastic championship and early in 1913 he added to it the Massachusetts Amateur. His goal immediately became the US Amateur championship at Garden City on Long Island and, having qualified with the second-best medal score just behind Chick Evans, one of the best amateur golfers in the land, his hopes were high.

However, in the second round he met Travers, already US Amateur champion three times, and Ouimet had no answer to the skill and experience of the older man. Having taken a week's leave from work for the Amateur championship, Ouimet decided that was 'it' for the year but his boss, having noticed his name in the entries for the US Open at the Country Club, told him to go ahead and play.

The favourites were naturally enough Vardon, who had already won the US Open at Chicago in 1900, and Ray, who a year earlier had won the British Open at Muirfield. This was long before the days of leaders out last in the final two rounds and Ouimet was only just going out when Ray, with whom he and Vardon were tied after 54 holes, finished with a 79 for a total of 304. If this was disappointing, Vardon was struggling too on the way to another 79 and Ouimet was left with a golden opportunity. Instead the American went out in 43 and the fact that he got into a play-off was due entirely to a sterling finish in which he played the last six holes in two under par. Home in 36, Ouimet too had finished with a 79 and was into a three-way play-off the following morning.

Ouimet was advised by Johnny McDermott to play his own game and take no notice of Vardon and Ray who, in turn, had eyes only for one another, never for a moment suspecting that the young American amateur held any sort of threat. It was a miserable wet day but there was a huge crowd, 10,000 or so strong it was said, and their allegiance lay very much with Ouimet. He did not let them down.

From the moment he sank a putt of around 4 feet (1.2 m) on the opening hole for a matching five, Ouimet's few nerves disappeared. His putting touch was better than that of either Vardon or Ray and if he hit a bad shot, such as his second out of bounds at the fifth, he simply shrugged before dropping another ball and playing the hole out as if nothing had happened.

All three were out in 38 and the first glimpse of a fairytale ending to the story came at the 10th. With the green now like a sponge in the continuing rain, both Vardon and Ray saw their tee shots spin back to the front of the green and from there each took three putts. Ouimet, on the other hand, pitched past the flag and then holed for a two.

It was only then that Vardon and Ray at last realized what they were up against and the strain of it showed when Vardon actually lit a cigarette, something he rarely did on the course. Ray was the first to capitulate but Vardon kept going until the 17th, where he desperately needed a birdie. Instead he hooked into a bunker and Ouimet, with a birdie himself, was three strokes clear. There was near pandemonium before a way was at last made clear for Ouimet to play to the last green and with a 72 the clean-cut, All-American boy had won by five strokes from Vardon and six from Ray. From that day golf in the United States was truly on the march.

Johnny McDermott, the first home-bred golfer to win the US Open which he did twice, in 1911 and 1912.

Arise, Sir Walter

Amid the euphoria that greeted Francis Ouimet's US Open victory at the Country Club, golf very nearly lost one of its most colourful characters. In the field for the first time was a certain Walter Hagen, who tied fourth three strokes behind. It was a championship he might have won.

Despite a miserable 6,5,7 start to the final round, Hagen was lucky enough to hole a full mashie shot for a two at the fourth and by the 14th he was right back in the hunt. A par five, he went for the green with his second but hit the ball right on the head, took seven and dropped out of sight.

Disheartened by his finish, Hagen decided that golf was not his game and he turned his thoughts to baseball, a lingering love. In the winter of 1913–14 he went to Florida and trained with the Philadelphia Nationals. He was allowed to pitch several times and was led to believe that he would get a full trial the following winter.

Consequently, he did not enter at first for the 1914 US Open at the Midlothian Club in Illinois and was only persuaded to do so by the editor of a newspaper who, as a close friend, also offered to pay Hagen's expenses. A lover already of the best things in life, especially when someone else was paying for them, Hagen accepted. But his taste for high living was nearly his undoing. In the best restaurant he could find he ordered and devoured the biggest lobster on the menu. In the early hours of the first morning of the championship he was taken ill and by breakfast time he could hardly stand.

A train journey to the course hardly improved either his health or his confidence but Hagen was determined to play. His driving was awful, his recovery play brilliant. Somehow he got to the turn in 35, his stomach began to settle, and with four birdies in the last five holes he was round in 68.

In those days the championship was played over only two days and Hagen had to go out again in the afternoon. He completed his second 18 holes in 74 and a total of 142 was good enough to keep him in the lead. There

Walter Hagen was known not only for his golf but also for his plus fours. But he did not wear them all the time.

were no exotic dishes for Hagen that evening.

The following day Hagen's golf was similarly conservative. He had a 75 in the morning, a 73 in the afternoon and his 72-hole total of 290 equalled the championship record, set by George Sargent five years earlier. There then followed an agonizing wait as an amateur, Chick Evans, launched the bravest of challenges. Evans went for everything but had no luck at all on the greens. Even so, he came to the last hole, a short par four, needing an eagle two to tie and drove the green. Hagen was there in the gallery watching and heaved a mighty sigh of relief as Evans's long putt drifted left. Having virtually decided to give the game up, Hagen was American Open champion and the game had gained one of its most colourful figures.

His style of play was as dashing as his dress and he quickly gained a huge following. He fought hard for the professionals to be given proper recognition and when in 1920 the Inverness club opened its doors to all the players, not just amateurs, he was the one who organized a collection and the gift of a grandfather clock.

Equally, he could stand on his dignity. When the British Open was played at Troon in 1923 Hagen, who had finished runner-up to Arthur Havers, declined to enter the clubhouse for the presentation because the professionals had been refused admittance all week. Instead, after politely thanking the officials, he walked back to his hotel and invited spectators to join him in a drink.

Walter Hagen drives from the 18th tee at Royal St. George's in his final round of 72 which won him the British Open for the third time, in 1928.

Hagen was a golfing showman though behind that debonair exterior lay a hard competitive edge. No shot, he felt, was ever beyond him and if the only way he could tie was to hole his second with a wood, then he would ask his caddie to go forward and attend the flag.

His forte was match-play and under this system he won the PGA five times. Conversely, but true to his manner of doing nothing by halves, Hagen once lost a challenge match to Archie Compston by 18 and 17. Travelling straight to Royal St. George's, Sandwich, he won the British Open, one of four victories in a land he loved as much as, in turn, he was loved by the people there.

Sadly, the Masters did not come into being until Hagen was at the very end of his career. The style of that tournament would have been ready-made for him but in his four appearances, by now well into his 40s, he never finished higher than 11th.

Surprisingly Hagen won only two US Opens. The other was in 1919 at Brae Burn in Massachusetts. The years of 1917 and 1918 had been lost because of the First World War but Hagen had been exempt military service and played instead exhibition matches in aid of war relief. He was the best golfer in America and deadly from 100 yards (91 m) and in.

Victory at Brae Burn had nevertheless looked unlikely when, after 54 holes, Mike Brady, very much an unknown, led him by five strokes going into the last round. However, Brady collapsed, taking 80 and Hagen was left needing par over the last nine holes to tie. He almost didn't even make that. Despite going out of bounds at one hole (only a one shot penalty then) he came to the last needing a three to win and had the audacity to summon Brady from the clubhouse so that he could watch Hagen putt for the birdie. It hit the hole but spun out which meant an 18-hole play off.

Hagen won it, though not without one late alarm that proved a test for his ingenuity. Two strokes ahead playing the 17th, Hagen cut his drive into a heavy, muddy lie from which it would have been difficult to advance the ball. After pondering the situation, Hagen claimed that a spectator must have trodden on his ball. But there were no witnesses and the appeal was refused.

Undeterred, Hagen then claimed that he must at least have the right to identify his ball. This was accepted and having wiped the ball clean, Hagen then replaced it so delicately that he could now get his clubhead to a second shot. The hole cost him a stroke but not the two it might have done. Hagen won with a 77 against a 78.

Men from Overseas

Though the early days of the US Open were dominated by immigrant Scots, the championship has fallen into the hands of true visitors from overseas only five times. Harry Vardon won at Chicago in 1900; Ted Ray at Inverness, Ohio, in 1920; Gary Player at Bellerive, Missouri, in 1965; Tony Jacklin at Hazeltine, Minnesota, in 1970; and David Graham at Merion, Pennsylvania, in 1981.

Through the 1890s Vardon had won the British Open three times and the Spalding manufacturing company introduced a ball called the Vardon Flier. To promote it they arranged in 1900 for Vardon to have an extensive tour of the United States which lasted most of the year and covered some 20,000 miles (32,000 km) with just a brief trip home for the Open at St. Andrews.

It was an enormous success and even though Vardon mostly played against the better ball of two opponents, he won 50 matches and lost only 13. Only two of these defeats were against one man alone. The easy grace of Vardon's swing captivated Americans still trying to learn the rudiments of the game. The arrival of J.H. Taylor gave that 1900 championship extra flavour and the title was always going to be between the two of them. Vardon's higher, slightly faded shots were the more suitable, for Taylor's lower right-to-left flight tended more to find the bunkers. Such differences in style still apply today for whereas golf on a British links often has to be kept under the wind and closer to the ground, in America it is more rewarding to 'fly the ball all the way'.

Vardon won by two strokes from Taylor, who was in turn seven strokes clear of the next man. But by 1920, the time of his last visit, Vardon was 50 and clearly at the end of his career. He had won the British Open for a record sixth time in 1914 but even now, six years on, he could still rekindle some of his old magic.

The US Open was being played that year at the Inverness club in Toledo and though no one was to know it at the time, it was the last to be won by an Englishman for 50 years. However, it was not Vardon who took the title but Ted Ray, in the midst of another long tour involving more than 100 matches.

For three rounds Vardon nevertheless played beautiful golf and with returns of 74,73,71 led by two strokes from Ray, who was as big and burly as Vardon was light and graceful. By the time he reached the turn in 36 in the final round Vardon had in three days played 99 holes (36 in the qualifying and 63 in the championship) in only 11 over par. For a man of 50 it was awesome stuff, not only for the quality of the golf but also for physical fitness.

Nothing it seemed at that point could stop Vardon and it was his misfortune that just as he came into the finishing stretch, the wind became a gale. Suddenly he found himself being stretched and the strain of it told on his putting, which so often happens to the older man. In these last years of his playing career, Vardon became a victim of the twitch and it was said that a jumping muscle in his right forearm could be seen from the gallery.

A shot dropped at the long 12th, a short putt missed at the 13th, and Vardon was in sad disarray. He took three putts on each of the next three greens and his step became as heavy

David Graham's finest hour came when he won the US Open at Merion. His last round of 67 was one of the most flawless of all time.

Above: *Another putt drops and David Graham takes a further step towards his US Open victory at Merion.*

Opposite top: *Gary Player, the 'man in black', watches an approach putt when he won the US Open at Bellerive in 1965.*

Opposite bottom: *Gary Player had no fear of bunker play. He was for a long time the best in the world.*

as it had previously been light. It was the 17th that finished him. A strong two-shotter with a stream crossing the front of the green, Vardon dared not rely on a pitch-and-single-putt four. He had to go for it, found the water and was done for.

For most of his career Ray had been overshadowed by the Triumvirate of Vardon, Braid and Taylor. He had won the British Open once, in 1912, and now he had the chance to conquer in the States as well. Though an unorthodox player, he was blessed both with strength and a delicate touch around the greens.

In the rising wind, which struck him earlier in his round than it had Vardon, it was his strength that became his ally. Holes that had troubled Vardon presented little difficulty to Ray. He cleared the water comfortably at the 17th and needed a four at the last to overtake Vardon; he got it.

Ray's 75 for 295 might still have been overhauled, most likely by Leo Diegel. However, just as the American was addressing himself to the needs of the last few holes, a friend rushed up to tell him of the score he needed to win. Slamming his club into the ground, Diegel snapped: 'I don't care what Ray did. I'm playing my own game.' He wasn't of course any longer. His concentration had gone and he tied second, along with Vardon, one behind.

It was another 45 years before the Americans again conceded their championship to a golfer from another country. Much had changed during that time, naturally enough, and by now golf was well into the era of Palmer, Nicklaus and Player, a second Triumvirate. Prize money had multiplied many times over and managers were multiplying it again. America was the place to play golf, if one wanted to get on in the world.

Gary Player wanted very much to get on. Born in South Africa without a silver spoon in his mouth, at the Old Killarney club in Johannesburg he caught the eye of a wealthy industrialist, George Blumberg, who was impressed by Player's devotion to practice. It was Blumberg's generosity that launched the greatest golfer South Africa has produced. Together with Gene Sarazen, Ben Hogan and Jack Nicklaus he forms an exalted quartet who have won (albeit in different years) the British Open, US Open, Masters and PGA.

To be blunt, Player was not much of a golfer when he first went to Britain in the late fifties. His grip was suspect and his swing often off-balance. It had to be. Being only 5 ft 7 in (170 cm) tall, Player had to put every last ounce he had into his shots just to keep up. But beneath his somewhat ugly method there lay a very large heart and a great deal of determination.

Player recognized at once the importance of physical fitness. Weight training, press-ups, jogging were all part of his daily routine and his strength became such that, between finger and thumb, he could pick up horizontally a driver lying on the ground when holding it at the very end of the grip.

He also had the gift of absorbing long flights from South Africa without disruption to his metabolism. He took to America as if he had never left home and he conquered it. He won his first British Open in 1959, the Masters in 1961 and the PGA a year later. At once the US Open became his goal and he reached it at Bellerive in 1965.

There were two particular qualities about Player's golf. He was probably the best bunker player the game has known and he was an inspired putter, just too as had been his fellow countryman, Bobby Locke. Player did not just sink putts; he willed them into the hole, his body, arms and legs seemingly locked together before he gave the ball a distinct rap.

Bellerive was a surprisingly new course on

which to stage a US Open. It had only been opened six years earlier and not even Robert Trent Jones, the architect, could persuade the grass to properly establish itself in that time. It was also an extremely long course, more than 7,000 yards (6,400 m), with no less than six par fours of more than 450 yards (411 m) each.

Against that the greens were large. It became a championship not of shot-making but one of putting and Player came into his own. Coming into the closing holes, outright victory seemed a formality. Instead, a three-stroke lead dwindled to nothing as Player took a double-bogey five at the 16th just as Kel Nagle, of Australia, was making a birdie ahead of him at the 17th. They consequently tied on a score of 282.

The championship therefore went into a fifth day for the first time, this also being the first time that only one round was played on each of the four designated days. Until then it had been staged over three days, 36 holes on the last. Player did not let his opportunity slip a second time. Five strokes ahead after eight holes in the play-off, he finished in 71 and beat Nagle by three. At the prize giving he made the grand gesture. He donated \$5,000 of his \$25,000 winnings to cancer relief and the remaining \$20,000 to junior golf in the United States. He had not forgotten his own beginnings.

Player was not the only man who appreciated the necessity of competing in America if he was to improve. In 1967 Tony Jacklin, a rising young British star, received an invitation to the Masters, played with Arnold Palmer and outscored him. Later the same year he became a member of the US Tour.

In 1968 Jacklin won the Jacksonville tournament and proved to himself that he could play with the best. A year later he was British Open champion, the first native of these islands to triumph since Max Faulkner in 1951. He was at once a sporting hero. With regular competition in America, the toughest school of all, his game had also improved immeasurably. He had learned the proper use of the legs and he had developed rhythm.

Even so, Jacklin was not among the favourites when the field assembled for the US Open at Hazeltine, on the outskirts of Minneapolis, in 1970. As with Bellerive, where Player had won, it was a relatively new course, long, prolific for its dog-legs and also its blind shots. From the first tee the players could see neither the fairway nor the green. The opening drive had to be played from memory and soon there were mutterings of discontent.

Jack Nicklaus was tactful. He said the course lacked definition. Dave Hill was less tactful. When asked what Hazeltine lacked, he replied: 'Eighty acres of corn and a few cows.' He was promptly fined \$150 for ill manners.

The only man who seemed unperturbed was Jacklin, who did not mind at all having to aim his drive by some distant chimney pot. He utterly destroyed the world's best; leading from first to last he was under par in every round, seven under for the 72 holes and the winner by seven from Hill. It was the biggest winning margin since Jim Barnes finished nine clear of the field at the Columbia Country Club, Washington, in 1921.

Jacklin's opening round of 71 was outstand-

Tony Jacklin, whose victory in the 1970 US Open at Hazeltine was the first by a British golfer for 50 years.

ing. Even those with long memories could not recall such a strong wind at a US Open. Sixty-nine of the 150 players failed to break 80, among them Nicklaus and Player, while Arnold Palmer only just managed it with a 79. On the second day the wind dropped and the scores came down; but Jacklin held his lead with a 70, still three ahead of Hill.

There were seldom any signs of Jacklin faltering, though the final crux of his victory is said to have been at the ninth hole in the final round. Beginning to look nervous for the first time, he had dropped strokes at the seventh and eighth and was in danger of three-putting the ninth. Instead his over-strong approach putt hit the very back of the hole, bounced 6 inches (15 cm) in the air and dropped back in for a birdie. The crisis, if crisis it was, had passed. Though Americans in particular were reluctant to acknowledge it, European golf took that day its first significant step on the long march that, by the mid-eighties, made it the equal of any in the world.

Improvement was not confined to Europe. Golf was taking hold in Japan as well while Australia was producing a whole crop of talented players. David Graham was just one and his victory at Merion in 1981 had gone down into history because it contained one of the finest last rounds of all time.

Graham had a troubled upbringing. He turned professional at the age of 14, falling out with his father and causing a rift between them that still exists. Early in his career he accumulated debts of $6,000 but he resolved to pay them back and did so, living on junk food for the best part of two years and never spending money on himself. Such self discipline lay at the root of the climb to the top.

Golf did not come easily to him. He began as a left-hander and, on switching to 'the other side', painstakingly developed a swing that seemed almost to have been built piece by piece. His back was unusually straight at the address and he would take the club back at a measured pace that hardly altered as he came through the ball. Just to add to this air of deliberateness he would glide more than walk down the fairways.

For three rounds at Merion, Graham could nevertheless only dog the footsteps of George Burns whose first three rounds of 69,66,68 set a 54-hole record of 203. The Australian was three strokes behind but in the last round he hardly put a foot wrong.

He missed only one fairway, the first, which he birdied in any case, and while strictly speaking he missed three of the 18 greens in regulation, so marginal were the errors that he was still able to use his putter from the fringes. His only dropped stroke came at the fifth, where he three putted.

Yet it was Graham's golf over Merion's last five classic holes that stand in the memory. At the 14th he was so full of confidence that he used his driver for the first time at this hole all week, dropped a seven iron 6 feet (1.8 m) away and holed for a birdie. A second shot with the same club at the 15th produced another three. At the 16th a third consecutive birdie was denied when his putt grazed the hole; the 17th he also two putted for his par three after a two iron to 20 feet (6 m). Now well clear of the flagging Burns, Graham reduced the 18th to a drive and four iron and all but holed again. Even so he had played the last five holes in two under par and his 67 stands alongside the best.

At his best Tony Jacklin, winner of the British Open in 1969 and the US Open in 1970, was blessed with a glorious freedom of movement and exquisite balance.

An Amateur Called Jones

Bobby Jones was born a weakling and died, 69 years later, not much more than a skeleton. In between he laid claim to being the greatest golfer of all time even if his record was subsequently surpassed by Jack Nicklaus. Jones's golfing career was much shorter and for an amateur its like will surely never be seen again.

Jones was 18 when he played in his first US Open at Inverness in 1920. By some almost divine intervention he was paired with the great Harry Vardon, who was then 50 and at the very end of his career. Jones was at the beginning and though no one was to know it at the time, during that match the baton of golfing immortality was passed from Vardon's weather-beaten hand into the firm grasp of the younger man.

Nicklaus never packed so much into so short a space of time. Jones played in 11 US Opens, won four, was second in another four (including losing a play-off) and had a worst finish of 11th. He tore up his card in his first British Open, played in three more and won them all. He won the US Amateur championship five times, reached the final on two further occasions, and the semi-finals twice more. He played in the British Amateur three times and won it once.

In those days these were the 'majors' for there was no Masters and as an amateur Jones could not play in the PGA. Between 1923 and 1930 he played in 21 of these championships and won 13. At that point and still only 28 he retired on the highest note of all, having in a single season won all four. There was nothing left. He had conquered what he called the 'Impregnable Quadrilateral'.

Bobby Jones teeing off at the 1930 US Open.

No golfer had previously so captured the imagination of the sporting public, on both sides of the Atlantic. He was twice accorded ticker-tape receptions in New York following triumphant visits to Britain, and in 1958, when captaining the American Eisenhower team, he was given the Freedom of the Burgh of St. Andrews.

In his speech of thanks Jones said: "I could take out of my life everything except my experiences at St. Andrews and still have a rich, full life.' He had come to love the place as nowhere else.

Such a reaction in the young Jones was not uncommon. He did not reach his ultimate standing in the game without a struggle and even in the years of his many triumphs, it still took a great deal out of him. He was often sick with the pressure of what was expected of him while the necktie he wore when playing frequently had to be cut from his throat because it had become soaked with sweat. After winning the British Open in his Grand Slam year – there were still the US Open and Amateur to come – he vowed that he would 'never, never do this again'. He was as good as his word.

So frail was Jones as a baby that he was not expected to survive. But by the time he was five his parents moved to a house bordering the second fairway of the East Lake course for their summer holidays. Young Bobby was given a sawn-down cleek and he fell under the influence of the newly appointed professional, Stewart Maiden, upon whose flowing, graceful swing he modelled himself.

Though there was no history of golf in the family, Jones was a natural. He won the Georgia Amateur championship at 14 and made his first appearance in the US Amateur in the same year, 1916, losing in the third round. During the war years his reputation increased in some fund-raising matches in aid of the Red Cross and when the war was over, Jones promptly reached the final of the US Amateur, but lost.

With a more experienced head on his shoulders, Jones could have got into contention in his first US Open in 1920. He hit some shots that made even Vardon blink, and finished eighth. A year later he improved to fifth at Columbia, though he was a long way behind Jim Barnes.

However, Jones knew only one way to play golf and that, as he said, was to hit every shot 'for all there is in it'. It was just such a stroke that took him to his first US Open at Inwood, New York, in 1923. A year earlier he had finished a stroke behind Gene Sarazen at Skokie, Illinois, and now he was in a play-off against Bobby Cruickshank, who had made up three strokes in the last 18 holes.

Though Jones looked pale and gaunt – a foreshadow of the stress that he was to feel in the years ahead – he played the better golf, but Cruickshank hung on and they were still level as they came to the 18th. Once again, Jones was far ahead off the tee but he found a bare lie and it seemed he might have to lay up short of the water, as Cruickshank had already done. Barely hesitating, Jones pulled out his long iron and went for the green nearly 200 yards (183 m) away. It was a perfectly struck shot and the title was his at last.

This did not immediately open the flood-gates, however, for it was another three years before Jones won again, at Scioto, Ohio, in 1926. A few weeks before, he had taken his first British Open at Royal Lytham and come home to his first ticker-tape reception. Tired physically as well as mentally, Jones apparently dropped out of contention with a second round of 79 but he came back with a third of 71 to challenge Joe Turnesa.

There were three strokes between them going into the last round but Turnesa, out in 37, was four strokes clear with only seven to play. However, the pressure began to tell and a succession of dropped strokes gradually allowed Jones, with an equal succession of pars, to catch up and then lead with only the 18th to play. Jones was playing behind and ahead of him Turnesa at last recaptured some form with a fine pitch and single putt for a birdie four. So now it was Jones who needed a birdie, this time to win. The hole measured 480 yards (439 m) and just as at Inwood, he had the class when needed. A perfect drive and there he was pouring into another long iron, his ball soaring against the sky and coming to rest 10 feet (3 m) from the flag. Two putts and he was champion again. He was the first man to hold the Open championships of Britain and America in the same year.

Jones had a poor US Open in 1927, which was won at Oakmont by Tommy Armour after a tie and then an 18-hole play-off with Harry Cooper. A year later there was another tie, this time at Olympia Fields, Illinois. Jones rather backed into it with Johnny Farrell after Roland Hancock, a 20-year-old from Wilmington, North Carolina, needing two fives to win, instead finished with two sixes.

For some reason the USGA had decided that 18 holes was not a true test for a play-off and changed it to 36. Jones had been some way below his best in the four designated rounds, finishing indeed with a 77. He then trailed by three strokes at lunch in the play-off, caught up in the afternoon but fell behind again when he dropped a stroke at the second 16th. Only a very long putt kept his interest alive at the 17th and it seemed he might force yet another 36 holes when he hit the last green in two for a sure birdie. However Farrell, a long way short and in the rough for two, pitched to 8 feet (2.4 m), holed the putt and gave Jones a dose of his own medicine.

Everything comes in threes, so the saying goes, and sure enough the 1929 US Open at Winged Foot resulted in yet another play-off, again involving Jones but this time against Al Espinosa, a descendant of one of the Spanish families that had settled in California. Espinosa began the final round four strokes behind Jones but he played the last six holes in two under par for a 75 and 294. Some way behind him Jones began playing like a rabbit and ran up two sevens which left him needing a four at the last to tie. Furthermore he was short and wide of the 18th green in two but, having pitched to 12 feet (3.6 m), he holed a very difficult side-hill putt for his second successive play-off. He dominated it, the

Bobby Jones' looks in his youth were as handsome as his golf.

Bobby Jones at Interlachen where he won his fourth US Open.

winner by a massive 23 strokes with 72,69 as Espinosa failed to break 80 in either round.

As the year 1930 dawned, Jones had a dream. He was by then unquestionably the best golfer in America. He had won the US Open three times and the US Amateur on four occasions. He had not contested the British Open in either of the last two years but he had won it in both 1926 and 1927. He would be going this time because the Walker Cup was at Royal St. George's, Sandwich, and that would mean he would be taking in the British Amateur as well. This was the one 'major' he had not yet won and the one he also felt was the hardest to win.

Since the Amateur was that year being played at St. Andrews, it was at least his favourite venue but he did have one narrow escape. Cyril Tolley, the well known British Walker Cup player, had a putt to beat him on the 18th green, missed it and was beaten himself at the 19th where Jones laid him a stymie. This practice of a player having the option of leaving his ball in the way of his opponent on the green has since been abandoned.

The Amateur title safely under his belt, Jones moved on to Hoylake for the Open. This he won despite playing some way below his best. On the train journey to Southampton prior to the voyage in the *Europa* to New York, Tolley, who was a close friend, asked him if he had ever played so poorly for so long. Jones replied that he had not. Nevertheless, it was a measure of him that he was now halfway to his Grand Slam and it was now or never. He had already announced that he would not contest the British Open again.

After a hero's welcome down Broadway and a banquet in his honour, Jones headed west to Interlachen just outside Minneapolis for the US Open. It was at once clear that he was a different man, confidence flooding through his every shot. He opened with a 71 but the lead was shared first between Macdonald Smith and Tommy Armour on 70 while Horton Smith took it over at the halfway stage with 72,70, two ahead of Jones.

It was in the third round that Jones broke loose. He played beautifully and needed two pars for a 66, which would have been the lowest round ever in the championship's history. Instead he finished in 68 but it was good enough for a lead of five strokes and as he waited to tee off in the afternoon, an estimated crowd of 15,000 thronged the opening holes.

After a nervous beginning Jones had his lead cut to a single stroke but he steadied in the face of a mounting crisis and was helped by the most controversial decision of his career. At the 17th he lost his ball. It hit a tree and rebounded, it was thought, into a dried up water hole, covered in reeds and tall swamp grass.

Unsure what to do, Jones turned to the referee, who declared that the ball had gone into the water hazard and that Jones could therefore drop out onto the fairway. This he did, and made a five.

However, as no one had actually seen where the ball finished there was a substantial body of opinion that felt the ruling was wrong; that Jones should have been sent back to the tee instead of being allowed to play a simple pitch to the green. That could have put a whole new slant on things and some suggested that it even tainted his ultimate victory. However, there was no argument about Jones's closing hole. Thinking he might now need a birdie, for Macdonald Smith was closing in, he got it, holing from 40 feet (12 m).

As it happened, Jones finished two strokes clear and within a few weeks he carried all before him in winning the US Amateur at Merion. The Grand Slam, or the Impregnable Quadrilateral, was complete.

Bobby Jones in 1930, the year he won the Grand Slam of the British and American Open championships as well as the two amateur championships. He called it the Impregnable Quadrilateral.

Sarazen, Guldahl and Snead

Gene Sarazen was only 20 when in 1922 he burst upon the golfing scene. In the space of a few months he won the US Open at Skokie, Illinois, and then the PGA at Oakmont. Twelve months later he successfully defended the PGA, beating none other than Walter Hagen at the 38th at Pelham, New York. It took him another 10 years to win the US Open a second time and to win the PGA a third. In between, Sarazen, who was born Eugene Saraceni but changed his name because he thought it made him sound like a violinist, very nearly lost his way.

Hardly anyone watched Sarazen at Skokie. A former caddie at Apawamis, he had been a professional for only two or three years. Players like Hagen, Jim Barnes, the defending champion, the rising Bobby Jones and those two fine visitors from England, George Duncan and Abe Mitchell, were much more in the public eye.

Horton Smith, the first winner of the Masters in 1934. He scored 284 and won by a stroke from Craig Wood.

But Sarazen, who shared a dormitory with other young players, was confident almost to the degree of being cocky. His final round of 68 was by three strokes the lowest winning round in a US Open, and the way he played the 18th was very much the stuff of a champion. He had an idea that a par five and a 69 might be good enough but he could not be sure what was going on behind him. His drive was good but with the wind in his face, not even a brassie could get him home in two. Such was the lie that instead he risked his driver, hit a tremendous shot onto the green and got his four. It was just as well. Jones and John Black, playing some way behind him, finished in 72 and 73 respectively and he beat them by a stroke each.

Overnight, or certainly after he had added the PGA, Sarazen became a star. He was in constant demand for exhibition matches and he was even lured to Hollywood, having visions of becoming a film star. Eventually some good sense returned for he was only 5 ft 4 in (163 cm) tall and hardly a Rudolph Valentino figure. Golf, he realized, was his life but though he continued to win tournaments, that early spark was missing.

His driving, once his strength, became unreliable and for a time he changed his grip from the interlock to the overlap. It did not work but he did build a 30 oz (850 g) driver (more than twice the normal weight) which he swung for an hour each day to strengthen his hands at the top of the backswing. The making of him, however, was the sand wedge, which he designed himself and which became the prototype of the wide-soled club that is now a part of every golfer's armament.

Still the major prizes remained elusive until in 1932 his many voyages across the Atlantic were at last rewarded; at Prince's in Kent he won his only British Open. But Sarazen was tired by the time he got back home again for the US Open at Fresh Meadow, New York. As the British champion, he found that he was now favourite, a responsibility he did not savour.

For two rounds he played conservatively (74,76) to lie five strokes behind the leader. Over the first eight holes of the third round on the last day, that deficit became seven. There followed the finest spell of sustained golf the game had known for Sarazen played the next 28 holes in 100 strokes. It began when he hit a seven iron at the ninth to 12 feet (3.6 m) and he holed the putt for a two. The inward half he played in 34 to be round in 70 and in the afternoon he was out in 32, back in another 34

Gene Sarazen, one of the few golfers to have won all four of the major championships.

for a 66. Once again his winning round set a record.

Over lunch, at which he was joined by Bobby Jones, who had by then retired, Sarazen sipped a couple of beers and estimated that he needed a 68 in the final round to win. It was an exact calculation but he did better than that. His golf was totally inspired. Apart from a dropped shot at the second, where he was bunkered, he was all pars and birdies. He had three birdies in four holes starting at the third and his second two of the day at the ninth. His 'Calamity Jane' putter seemed unable to miss.

There was only one birdie coming home, at the 15th, while his sand wedge, the club that made him, rescued his par at the last. As it happened, Sarazen had three strokes to spare and with a Masters victory in 1935 he became the first man to win at different times the recognized four majors.

Other than Bobby Jones, only one man won the US Open in successive years between the wars. He was Ralph Guldahl, who had his cherished moments at Oakland Hills in 1937 and at Cherry Hills in 1938. A big, lumbering man, he also took the Masters in 1939 and yet somehow he was not the sort of player who captured the imagination.

At Oakland Hills he had looked out of the running early in the final round after tieing the 54-hole lead. Two things got him going. He

Sam Snead on one of his visits to Britain.

badly needed a birdie at the long eighth and used his considerable power to hit the green with a two iron second shot. For a slow-moving and deliberate man, he was surprisingly quick about his putt and holed it from 35 feet (10.5 m).

Instead of a birdie he had made an eagle and his next inspiration came at the turn when the announcer's voice carried across the course declaring 'Snead 283'. Guldahl therefore knew what he had to do to win and that was a 70. Despite quickly dropping two shots, he made them up and with a 69 won by two strokes; comfortable but not as comfortable as the six he had to spare at Cherry Hills 12 months later.

Splendid though Guldahl's finish was at Oakland Hills, there was wide sympathy for Sam Snead, who had come strolling out of the hills of Virginia with an assortment of ill-matched clubs and taken golf by storm. The story goes that when still an assistant, he was nearly sacked for driving into the members playing ahead of him. A complaint was lodged but the plaintiff had mistakenly thought it was Snead's second shot. When he heard that it was Snead's drive he did an immediate about turn and instead offered sponsorship on the circuit. It was the best investment he ever made.

Snead made his professional debut in 1936 and though at first an erratic driver, a heavier club with little loft worked wonders. He never parted with it, his hitting becoming such an attraction that he brought new life to professional golf. Surprisingly in one so raw, he was made favourite for his first Open at Oakland Hills and received a preferred starting time.

Nor did Snead let his admirers down. He began with a 69, tied Guldahl for the 54-hole lead, and finished in the grandest manner of all with an eagle three at the last. It was not to be, however, and, as the years passed, so the US Open remained the one trophy on which he could never lay his hands, close though he repeatedly was.

Most agonizing of all was the disaster Snead suffered at the Philadelphia Country Club in 1939, in an Open which was won by Byron Nelson after a play-off with Densmore Shute and Craig Wood. Nelson was the first man to finish on 284 but it never looked enough, for Snead had only to play the last two holes in par (4,5) for 282. Nor was it particularly serious when he ran through the 17th green. What may have rattled him was the 5-foot (1.5 m) putt he left short to save his par.

At all events, Snead lashed into his drive off the 18th tee and hooked it. His lie in the rough was not good but he chose to have a go at it with his brassie and it was perhaps the worst choice of club in his whole career. He topped it into a bunker and was now fighting for distance. A wedge would have got him out safely, but instead he risked an eight iron in an attempt to reach the green and slammed his ball into the face of the bunker. From there he stumbled into another and what had appeared on the tee to be a straightforward five became an eight. He finished sixth, two strokes behind the three who played off.

Nor was that the end of Snead's frustration. Playing some of his finest golf when it was needed most at the St. Louis Country Club in 1947, he gradually ate away at the target Lew Worsham had set half an hour before him. With two holes to play, Snead needed a birdie to win. Instead he dropped a stroke at the comparatively easy 17th. So now what he needed was a birdie just to tie. And the 18th was a much more difficult hole. He got it like a man with two fine shots and then a putt of no more than 18 feet (5.5 m).

It was the fourth play-off in five US Opens and Snead was in clear sight of the promised land when the following day he stood two strokes clear with three to play. But Worsham made a two at the 16th with a very long putt and drew level at the next when Snead drove into the rough and went through the green with his second.

The odds were nevertheless still on Snead after the second shots to the 18th for while he was on the green, Worsham was off it and then chipped a yard past. So Snead had a putt of 18 feet (5.5 m) or so for the championship but struck it badly and left his ball short, about the same distance away as Worsham's.

He was convinced that it was his turn again but just as he was about to putt, Worsham queried it with the referee, who had to measure out the distances. Snead was indeed right, by 2 inches (5 cm), but, his concentration now broken, he missed. Worsham holed and won with a 69 against a 70. It was perhaps Snead's bitterest moment of all.

Ralph Guldahl, US Open champion twice, Masters champion once.

Curtains for Hogan and Palmer

Jack Fleck celebrates the holing of another putt during the 1955 US Open. His defeat of Ben Hogan in a play-off was one of the biggest shocks the game has known.

If a poll were to be taken to determine the three men considered to have had the greatest influence on American golf since the war, there is little doubt that the three names most favoured would be Ben Hogan, Arnold Palmer and Jack Nicklaus. By a coincidence, two of them – Hogan and Palmer – met their Waterloo on the same golf course, the Olympic Club at San Francisco, in the US Open championships of 1955 and 1966 respectively.

Hogan had won his fourth championship at Oakmont in 1953 by his most commanding margin of all, six strokes from Sam Snead, and though 42 when he headed west towards the Golden Gate Bridge he was still the most formidable player of that time.

Again he plotted his strategy and so satisfied was he that he did not even bother to play the course on the two last practice days, fiddling about instead on the twin Ocean course. By contrast, a little-known professional by the name of Jack Fleck, who ran two public courses in Davenport for his main income, played 44 holes every day. Had anyone read a letter Fleck sent to a friend, they would have laughed. He considered the odds against his winning were no worse than 10–1.

Less than half the field broke 80 on the opening day. Tommy Bolt chipped and putted his way to a 67, Hogan took 72, Fleck 76. Penal rough and narrow fairways had taken their toll and despite a 73 in the second round, Hogan still moved up to a share of second place. It was Fleck who joined him with a 69.

All eyes remained on Hogan and sure enough he took another seemingly safe step towards a record fifth title with a 72 in the third round, one stroke ahead of Snead. Fleck fell away with a 75. Out early after lunch for

Arnold Palmer was a masterly bad-weather golfer. He proved that when winning the 1961 British Open at Royal Birkdale.

his last round, Hogan cruised round the difficult course in 70 and so invincible did his total of 287 appear that he was proclaimed on television as being the winner.

Hogan pointed out that there were players still on the course who could beat him but even so he presented his ball to the USGA's Golf Museum. Thus was fate tempted. Away down the hill Fleck was putting as he had never putted in his life. He was out in 33, got news of Hogan's total and knew that he would have to come home in 34 for a 67 to tie.

With four holes to play he was still two behind; he made a two at the 15th and came to the last needing a birdie to tie. Though driving into the rough, Fleck found a good lie, hit a seven iron to 8 feet (2.4 m) and judged the break of a fast putt perfectly. Hearing the crowd roar, Hogan, who was packed and ready to leave, ordered his clubs to be returned to his locker.

No one gave Fleck any hope at all in the play-off. But it was Hogan who suffered the reaction. He was unable to assert himself early and Fleck responded with ever more purposeful golf. Out in 33, he led by two strokes and only became nervous towards the end, twice dropping shots. But he was still a stroke ahead as they stood on the 18th tee and Hogan did not have a final ace up his sleeve. He pulled his drive into a terrible place in the cloying rough and it took him another three undignified heaves to reach the fairway. Fleck, with a straightforward four, was round in 69, won by three strokes and set golf on its ear. Though Hogan was second again a year later at Oak Hill, New York, his curtain had fallen.

If this seemed at the time the end of an era, another was about to begin. Cary Middlecoff won in 1956 at Oak Hill; Dick Mayer, Tommy Bolt and Billy Casper succeeded him, but none had quite the aura of Hogan. Someone had however and that was Arnold Palmer. In fact it was the Masters that was the making of him for in 1958 he had thrilled the galleries with his aggressive golf and particularly with an eagle three he had made at the 13th in the final round when it was badly needed. Two years later he won again, even more dramatically, with birdies at each of the last two holes to overtake Ken Venturi.

By now Palmer was the major force in golf, the carelessly tossed cigarette before he putted, the glove stuffed casually in his hip

pocket, and the hitch of his pants all being eagerly imitated. He was in a purple patch in that summer of 1960, winner of the Masters and four other tournaments when he arrived at Cherry Hills in Colorado for the Open.

Though the favourite, Palmer did not play like it. He had opening rounds of 72,71,72 and trailed Mike Souchak by seven strokes. Fourteen players altogether were in front of him and over lunch Palmer idly speculated as to what a 65 might do. When he was told 'nothing' since he was out of the hunt, Palmer exploded: 'Like hell, it would give me 280 and 280 wins Opens.'

He strode to the first tee and drove the green 346 yards away for the first time all week. He had birdies at each of the first four holes, six in the first seven and was out in 30. By so doing Palmer scattered most of those ahead of him, though two remained stubborn. One of them was the ageing Hogan and the other a young amateur by the name of Nicklaus. But Nicklaus missed a short putt rather hastily at an important moment while Hogan, needing at least a 4,4 (birdie, par) finish, was twice in the water and could do no better than 5,7. Palmer, home in 35, got his 65 and his 280 and won by two from Nicklaus. He was right after all; 280 does win Opens.

Holder now of both the Masters and the US Open, Palmer immediately flew the Atlantic for the Centenary Open at St. Andrews. He finished second to Kel Nagle but liked what he found, returned and won the British title in both 1961 and 1962, in the latter year also taking his third Masters. In 1964 he triumphed at Augusta a fourth time. A second US Open had eluded him in a play-off against Nicklaus at Oakmont in 1962 but at the Olympic Club in 1966, a golden opportunity beckoned again.

By now the US Open was being played over four days and not three, and, helped by a 66 that could easily have been less in the second round, Palmer went into the last day three strokes clear of Billy Casper.

When he then went through the turn in 32 Palmer had a lead of seven strokes and his thoughts were now not of winning but lowering the championship record of 276 set by Hogan at Riviera in 1948. He only needed 37 home to do it and with six holes to play he was still six shots in front.

There followed a collapse from which Palmer never recovered. He lost those six strokes in the space of five holes and indeed had to sink a putt of about 6 feet (1.8 m) even to get himself into a play-off. He had come home in 39 for his 71, Casper in 32 for a 68.

The play-off was in some ways a repetition. At the turn Palmer was two ahead again, 33 against 35, but a birdie by Casper at the 11th, where Palmer bogeyed, shifted the balance and with a run of 4,3,6 against Palmer's 5,5,7 from the 14th, Casper had won his second US Open by four strokes.

Courage of Ken Venturi

The United States Open Championship has had its multiple champions and its single, once-off winners. Some of the latter could not now even tell you how they did it. Once they had done it, however, the achievement could never be taken away from them; their name was on the cup for ever. Even so, some are half forgotten. One who is not is Ken Venturi.

Behind his victory at the Congressional Club, Washington, in 1964 lies the story of a golfer born to stardom, dragged to the depths of despair and then rising again for one shining moment that owed more to courage than anything else.

Venturi was 33 when he had to qualify for that particular Open and he very nearly tore up his card before making the championship itself. He was only dissuaded from doing so by his two partners, Mike Souchak and Billy Collins.

As an amateur Venturi was a golfer apparently destined for greatness. He had a distinguished international career and when in 1956 he received his second invitation to play in the Masters, he soon appeared likely to become the first amateur to win it. After opening rounds of 66 and 69 he led by four strokes going into the fourth and last. He took 80 and his first dream was shattered.

Under the guidance of Byron Nelson, however, Venturi's swing became a thing of beauty. He turned professional and in 1960 he rose to second in the US money list.

One day, however, he went to pick his ball out of the hole and got a stabbing pain in his back. Despite treatment and rest, it did not go away. He flattened his swing to compensate but his golf deteriorated. By 1963 his winnings had dropped to less than $4,000 from $41,000 in 1960. He was as low as a golfer can get.

But a week or two before the Open in 1964, he managed third place in the Thunderbird Classic and his morale received its first boost in a long time. He qualified for the Open and in the heatwave that was then enveloping Washington, he managed to get round Congressional, the longest course yet for a US Open, in 72,70 to be six strokes behind Tommy Jacobs at the halfway stage. Even better was to follow. In the morning of the third day, the last time the final 36 holes were played on the one day, Venturi went out in 30.

By then, however, a hot sun was climbing to its zenith and the humidity was nearly unbearable. The temperature rose steadily towards 100 degrees and Venturi, dehydrated, began to wobble on his feet. He dropped two strokes in his last two holes but with a 68 had closed the gap on Jacobs to two strokes.

In the clubhouse he half collapsed and there were severe doubts that he could go on. Iced tea and salt tablets partly revived him and 50 minutes after leaving the 18th green, Venturi was back on the first tee, a doctor at his side carrying a bag of ice and more salt tablets. He played steadily through to the turn in 35 and news reached him that he had passed Jacobs. Now it was a case of pure endurance as dehydration once again overcame him.

Venturi hardly dared look at a scoreboard, even if indeed he could focus his eyes sufficiently to read it. The 13th was a strong par four but Venturi's drive ripped down the middle, a six iron floated to the green and his putt dropped. As he raised his head, his eyes caught sight of a nearby scoreboard. He was four strokes clear and only five to play.

The battle was almost over, all the anguish a thing of the past. Par followed par and soon Venturi, his head still bowed, was making his weary but triumphant journey up the 18th fairway. As the crowd rose to greet him, Joe Dey, then Commissioner for the USGA, moved to his side and said quietly: 'Hold your head up, Ken, you're a champion now.'

Above: *Ken Venturi won the 1964 US Open against all the odds, including a severe heatwave and illness.*

Opposite: *Cary Middlecoff, US Open champion in 1956 at Oak Hill, once said that he always had 'difficulty in getting my game past the airport' in that he never seemed able to play well abroad.*

Ben Hogan: a Golfing Colossus

Ben Hogan played golf like Steve Davis plays snooker. He did not put his mind solely to his next shot but also to the shot after that and even the one after that. He was as clinical a player as there has ever been, as meticulous in his preparation as he was in the execution of his strokes. He had the same control over the golf ball that Davis has over the snooker ball.

Hogan became a legend, however, not only because of his long list of major championships. Only Jack Nicklaus, Bobby Jones and Walter Hagen have won more. His four US Opens have not been surpassed, equalling the record of Willie Anderson and Jones and in turn later equalled by Nicklaus. But it was the winning of one of them, at Merion in 1950, that created the awe that still surrounds him.

A long and often frustrating apprenticeship that began in 1936 was only rewarded finally when, ten years later, he won the PGA. Two years after that he took the US Open at Riviera in California, promptly regained the PGA and was seemingly safely launched. But on a grey February morning in 1949 his broken body lay in a tangled mass on an American highway after a head-on collision. It took an hour to cut him free and X-Rays revealed a broken collarbone, a broken pelvis, a broken ankle, a broken rib and internal injuries. He then developed a blood clot and his life hung by a thread.

Hogan was unable to play competitively for the whole of that year but he went to England as non-playing captain of the American Ryder Cup team and by December was playing golf again, albeit from within the comfort of a caddie-cart. It was the only way he could get round for his legs never truly healed, swelling painfully after exercise.

But Hogan had always been a man of steel and it was this icy determination that carried him through, not only at Merion but also in the succeeding years as he became an even more formidable player after those crippling injuries than he had been before.

As always, Hogan's preparation at Merion was thoroughness itself, and so sure was he of where he would hit the ball on every hole that he discarded his seven iron. He knew it would not be needed. What he was less sure of was how, or indeed whether, he could physically stand up to 72 holes.

The 1953 US Open over, Ben Hogan is all smiles at the presentation ceremony at Oakland Hills with his wife, Valerie.

So fast were the greens that Hogan decided not to ground his club before a downhill putt; even so, at one point his ball did indeed trickle another 4 feet (1.2 m) nearer the hole as he prepared to strike. There was no penalty, and with opening rounds of 72 and 69 he stood in fifth place. But his legs ached despite all the careful bandaging from ankle to groin and a long, hot bath only partly alleviated the pain. Furthermore, Hogan had to face 36 holes on the last day.

Again he returned a 72 and now he was in third place, two behind Lloyd Mangrum. All continued to go well after lunch and after 12 holes of the final round Hogan had taken a commanding three-stroke lead. It was then that his legs gave out and he almost fell. As he leaned against a friend he confided that he did not think he could finish.

Cary Middlecoff, his partner, would mark his ball for him on the greens while his caddie would pick it out of the hole. Hogan was like a distressed runner at the end of a marathon. He was by now hitting the ball by instinct, each painful step a battle in itself. Somehow the shots still flowed but his putting left him. Twice he three putted and then lost a third shot at the 17th.

Merion's 18th is a real tiger of a par four and Hogan knew it better than he knew what score he had to beat. Standing on the 18th fairway, eyes narrowed beneath his familiar white cap, he faced two options. He could try and cut a four wood to get a birdie or hit a safe one iron and settle for a four. Fred Corcoran, who pioneered golf management and looked after the affairs of Sam Snead, assured him that a four would get him into a play-off. Hogan took his one iron and from a slighty hanging lie struck a perfect stroke. He took two putts and tied Lloyd Mangrum and George Fazio.

He had sounded the depths of his reserves and as he lay in his bath that evening he knew he had to go through it all again the following day. Not only did Hogan survive it, he triumphed, though not without one late moment of drama. On the 17th, Mangrum, then two strokes behind, unthinkingly picked up his ball to blow away a fly. In those days the ball could not be cleaned as it is today and the referee had to inform him that he had taken six and not four. For a moment Mangrum stood motionless and then, with a shrug, said: 'Oh well, I guess we'll all eat tomorrow.'

If this for Hogan was his storybook US Open, his successful defence a year later at Oakland Hills was the one that had the purists purring in satisfaction. This was the championship in which the USGA decided on the toughest examination paper there has ever been, Robert Trent Jones, the architect, creating changes that made strong men wince. Hogan was not an admirer for it was his belief that the course lacked strategy from the tee. The fairways were so narrow that it was possible only to aim for the middle of the fairway. It was not therefore possible to open up the green and the flag for the second shot.

After opening rounds of 76 and 73, defensive golf had nevertheless failed to pay dividends. He went onto the attack the next day, made the turn in 32 and with five holes to play he seemed set for a 67. Instead it all dribbled away into a 71 and he trailed Lloyd Mangrum by two.

But over lunch Hogan resolved that a score in the 60s was possible even if no one had yet done it. In the afternoon, and particularly down the homeward stretch, he unleashed a whole succession of peerless strokes and with a 67 beat Clayton Heafner by two strokes, Heafner indeed being the only other man to break 70 during the week and that was with a 69. Hogan, as he said afterwards, had subdued the monster.

Ben Hogan heads for one of his most celebrated triumphs, his US Open victory at Oakland Hills in 1953.

The Golden Years of Nicklaus

In Bob Sommers's admirable *History of the US Open* he describes how, immediately after Arnold Palmer's only victory at Cherry Hills in 1960, Ben Hogan, who had himself been in contention for 70 of the 72 holes, slumped in the locker room and said to anyone who cared to listen: 'I played 36 holes today with a kid who should have won this thing by 10 strokes.'

That kid was Jack Nicklaus who, at the age of 20 and still an amateur, had just finished runner-up two strokes behind. Had he not been playing with Hogan, it might have been different. Facing a short putt towards the end, Nicklaus noticed a badly repaired pitch mark between his ball and the hole. Normally he would have asked if it could be repaired but shy of upsetting the intimidating Hogan, Nicklaus said nothing. His putt caught the pitch mark and was deflected wide of the hole.

Nonetheless, he had made a profound impression with three 71s and a 69, and a year later, at Oakland Hills, still an amateur, he finished equal fourth three strokes behind Gene Littler, one of the sweetest swingers the game has known. Later in that summer of 1961 Nicklaus won the Amateur championship a second time and a considerable golfing force was on its way. There was some hesitation about his turning professional but once he had done so his impact was immediate. His first professional victory was in nothing less than the US Open – at Oakmont in 1962.

More than any of the summits he subsequently climbed, the impact of that first victory was felt around the world. Palmer was then at the height of his powers, with an inborn magnetism that made him adored wherever he went. More people, it was said with some truth, were prepared to watch Arnold Palmer haul his clubs from the back of his car on arrival at the course than see another, lesser known individual complete a round of 66.

'Arnie's Army' was made up of young and old alike and that army was at its strongest in '62 for Oakmont lies in Pennsylvania and Pennsylvania is Palmer's home State, born and bred not far away in Latrobe. There was for them therefore only one possible winner that year, wide though the interest also was in the rather beefy newcomer, Nicklaus.

They were paired together on the first two days and the whole world went out to watch them. The first reverberations were not long in coming. Nicklaus began the first round birdie, birdie, birdie; Palmer started par, bogey, bogey and was at once five strokes behind. Sanity, though, was restored. By the end of

Jack Nicklaus often became an almost statue-like figure as he locked himself over a putt, but he was deadly at holing out. Here he is on his way to a record-equalling fourth US Open in 1980.

Arnold Palmer putting during his US Open play-off with Jack Nicklaus at Oakmont in 1962. Nicklaus won by three strokes with a 71 against Palmer's 74.

the day Palmer had retrieved a 71 to Nicklaus's 72, and after 36 holes Palmer was three strokes ahead, with a 68 to the younger man's 70 on the second day.

Though he missed a fairly short birdie putt on the 18th green in the third round, Palmer's 73 nevertheless advanced him into a share of the lead with Bobby Nichols, both now two ahead of Nicklaus. The vast whooping and hollering crowds were ever more convinced that this was again to be Palmer's year and after lunch they stampeded as he threatened to get away from the field with two birdies in his first four holes. With an eagle three at the ninth he could be out in 32 and his drive had certainly put him within range. It was a difficult second shot with a three wood but it was worth a crack.

Nor did it matter particularly when it did not quite come off, for though the shot found rough on the right, the lie was good and a birdie was still likely. Instead, Palmer fluffed his chip only a yard or so and took six. At once the momentum was gone, though even so he still had his chances. He was kept informed of Nicklaus's progress a few holes ahead of him and though this turned out to be a 69, Palmer knew that a birdie at either of the last two holes would give him a 70 and victory by a stroke. He pitched to 8 feet (2.4 m) at the teasing 17th but missed for his birdie, hit a glorious mid-iron to 10 feet (3 m) at the last and missed that putt as well. They had tied.

It has been claimed that only the putting saved Nicklaus just as it savaged Palmer. While Nicklaus had only once three-putted in 72 holes, Palmer had three-putted 13 times. Yet, as Nicklaus has since pointed out, he had only 11 single putts whereas Palmer had more than double that number. The play-off was an anti-climax. Palmer was four strokes behind after only six holes and though he got it back to one with six to play, his recovery ended at the 13th, which he again three putted. Nicklaus, with a 71, won by three.

Yet Nicklaus was not immediately acclaimed king. The following year he missed the cut at the Country Club, Brookline, where Palmer lost another play-off to Julius Boros; he was nowhere in 1964 or 1965 and it was not until 1967, at Baltusrol, that he won again. By then he was beginning to outstrip Palmer in the major championships with three Masters, one US Open, one British Open and one PGA in his first five years as a professional.

Palmer's US Open record was nevertheless the more consistent and after 36 holes he was again in the lead, rounds of 69 and 68 putting him one ahead of Nicklaus. Paired together on the third day, they both played poorly and Marty Fleckman, an amateur, overtook them. Paired again on the final day, Nicklaus and Palmer played probably the finest golf they have ever done together when the stakes were high. There was nothing between them for a while as they left a floundering Fleckman far behind and it all turned at the seventh, a fiendish par four of 470 yards (430 m).

Palmer played a thrilling one iron to 10 feet (3 m), Nicklaus a safer one to 40 feet (12 m). But it was Nicklaus who holed, Palmer who missed and the floodgates were opened as Nicklaus proceeded to birdie seven out of the last 12 holes. One supreme stroke followed another and with a 65 to Palmer's 69, he won by four strokes. His total of 275 was a record,

Above: *Jack Nicklaus (left) and Arnold Palmer on the final green at Baltusrol during the 1967 US Open. Nicklaus won by four strokes after a last round of 65.*

Below: *A grim looking Jack Nicklaus. But all was well. He went on to win the 1972 US Open at Pebble Beach. It represented a double triumph. Nicklaus had won the US Amateur championship on the same course in 1959.*

beating Hogan's 276 which had been set 19 years earlier. Baltusrol therefore became a special place to Nicklaus, though it was not the last time his path was to cross Palmer's.

First, however, there was another bridge to be negotiated. For more than 40 years the 13 major championships of Bobby Jones had stood on a lofty pinnacle. In 1972 at Pebble Beach, out on the Californian coast overlooking the Pacific, Nicklaus equalled it. Pebble Beach had not staged a US Open before and if anything it was the golf course that won. Nicklaus was two over par for the 72 holes and won by three from the Australian, Bruce Crampton.

He never once broke 70 and on the last day, when the wind was so strong that a regatta out on Carmel Bay was cancelled, only one player equalled the par of 72. Twenty-six of the 70 players failed to break 80. The sun nevertheless shone and the greens were like glass. There were two telling moments for Nicklaus, whose 74 was matched by only two other players in the top 20.

Having taken six at the 10th, where he drove down the cliff, he went through the green at the short 12th and fluffed a chip. But he scrambled a four by holing a wickedly difficult putt just as Palmer, a few holes ahead, was missing an important putt for a birdie that, had he sunk and Nicklaus missed, would have reversed the leadership. Then at the 17th, with the flagstick bent almost double, Nicklaus hit it with his tee shot, his ball stopping dead. It was the culminating moment.

When the US Open returned to Baltusrol in 1980, Nicklaus had long since passed Jones's 13 majors. Now he was looking for a record-equalling fourth US Open. There had never been such a beginning, for Tom Weiskopf straightaway equalled the championship record with a 63 and then Nicklaus equalled it too, missing indeed from a yard on the last green for a 62.

But it was not Weiskopf who threatened Nicklaus to the end but Isao Aoki, of Japan, whose three 68s tied him for the lead with 18 holes to play. On that last tumultuous afternoon, Nicklaus gained an early lead of two strokes and then played some of the greatest golf of his life. But Aoki, with an unorthodox swing and an individual putting stroke, hung on, and when he pitched to 5 feet (1.5 m) at the long 17th, his inevitable birdie looked like cutting the margin to only a stroke. But Nicklaus holed from 24 feet (7.3 m). That was it. Both birdied the last and Nicklaus, with a 68 for 272, had set by three strokes a new US Open record as well as equalling the four titles of Willie Anderson, Bobby Jones and Ben Hogan.

The Lowest Score of the Lot

Jack Nicklaus resisted in his time a number of assaults by young pretenders to his throne. One of the more sustained was that by Johnny Miller, a lithely built, fair haired Californian who gave his every shot everything he had and, on his day, had a reputation for knocking the flagsticks right out of the holes. As an amateur in 1966, he had finished equal eighth in the US Open and in 1974, by then a professional, he won no less than eight American tournaments, a tally no one else has approached since.

Miller's finest hour was nevertheless in 1973 when, with a final round of 63, he won the US Open at Oakmont. It is the lowest winning round in any of the four major championships and that is its hallmark. Certainly there have been other 63s but none in the last round and none by the champion.

That it was done at Oakmont, one of the toughest of all the US Open venues, even further boggled the imagination and for that there had to be some explanation. Perhaps there was, though no one ever got to the bottom of it. Oakmont had several defences that year. It was more severely bunkered than when Nicklaus had won here in 1962, the average width of the fairways was down to 35 yards and the rough was tough. The greens had been tuned to be at their famous fastest and the 17th had been lengthened to 322 yards (294 m) so that no one could possibly drive it – until Nicklaus did in the first round and then holed the putt for an eagle two! Gary Player nevertheless led with a 67 and was at pains to tell the world how good that round had been. No one else broke 70.

But they did the next day, whole clusters of them, including a course record 65 by a club professional from Long Island by the name of Gene Borek. The reason was that the greens were no longer like marble, when spin and position was everything. Somebody, it seems, had left the sprinklers on though nobody ever owned up to it. Horror of horrors, as far as the USGA was concerned, the US Open became dartboard golf.

On the third day it rained and the course became softer still. Fewer broke 70 but that was because the flags were hidden away. Jerry Heard had a 66 and shared the lead with John Schlee, Julius Boros and Arnold Palmer, three veterans. No one paid any attention to Miller. A 76 in the third round had put him out of it, six strokes behind, 12 players in front of him. He told his wife to be ready to leave as soon as he had finished.

In such circumstances, of course, there is nothing to lose and Miller was nothing if not an attacking player. He had a birdie at the first, another at the second, another at the third and another at the fourth. Only one of those putts was more than a tap in. True to character, he was knocking the flagsticks out of the holes, and, an hour though he was ahead of the leaders, it began to cross his mind that perhaps he could yet win.

No one else thought so and in any case Miller came off his 'high' with some pars and then took three putts at the eighth. He got the stroke back with a raking two iron second to the long ninth for his four and was out in 32. Behind him the lead was chopping and changing when Miller got a second wind.

He holed a putt of 15 feet (4.6 m) for a birdie at the 11th and had his biggest break at the next, a monster of 603 yards (551 m). Having driven into the rough, he could only play out safely to the fairway but he rifled his third with a four iron to 15 feet (4.6 m) and holed the putt. The news of his progress was now spreading like wildfire and panting spectators arrived just in time to see Miller lash another

Two of Andy North's three professional victories have been in the US Open. Here he heads for his first, at Cherry Hills in 1978.

four iron to 5 feet (1.5 m) at the 13th for a third successive birdie. He had caught up.

The harder Miller hit the ball, the straighter it flew, particularly with that four iron. His drive at the 14th covered the best part of 300 yards (274 m), his four iron another 180 or so (164 m) and in went the putt for his last birdie. He played the final three holes in par for 31 home and was round in 63.

The shock waves reverberated down the course and one by one those who might have caught Miller fell away. John Schlee had to birdie the last and Tom Weiskopf had to eagle it. Neither did and the total brilliance of Miller that day as he missed only one fairway and not a single green had prevailed. It was a final round to rank with Hogan's 67 at Oakland Hills and Palmer's 65 at Cherry Hills. Both, with respect to Miller, were regarded as more difficult courses.

Johnny Miller was one of the most brilliant attacking players the game has known. He demonstrated it best when he had a last round of 63 at Oakmont to win the 1973 US Open.

Watson Has His Moment

At first they called Tom Watson a choker. He might have won the US Open in 1974 and he might have won it again in 1975. Each time the pressure of the last round got to him. In 1977 he got rid of that image by twice holding off Jack Nicklaus, first to win the Masters and then the British Open, in which his five victories have been exceeded only by Harry Vardon. But Watson still had his critics, who now latched on to his driving, which they said was too erratic for him ever to win the US Open.

In 1982 he laid that ghost, too, and in my opinion Watson has unquestionably been America's second-finest golfer since the Second World War, behind Nicklaus. He has also been wonderfully unaffected by his many successes – leading money winner for four consecutive years beginning in 1977 and five times in all – which reflects a most modest disposition.

Watson's victory at Pebble Beach was also one of the most dramatic there has been and once again it was with Nicklaus that he shared centre stage, denying the great man the record fifth championship he so craved. The course was one he knew well, having played it many times when at Stanford University, only a 90-minute drive away.

His plan was to make his birdies early and then hang on. It did not work out and at the halfway stage he was five strokes off the lead. A 68 in the third round changed all that, taking him to the front of the pack alongside Bill Rogers. Nicklaus, struggling with his putter, was three strokes behind, but then, after a dull beginning to his last round, he caught fire with five consecutive birdies to join a pack of five hunting the outright lead. One by one they fell away until Watson and Nicklaus were the only ones left, two holes apart.

Playing the 12th, Watson was two ahead but he dropped a stroke there just as Nicklaus

Tom Watson, perfectly balanced, as he follows the flight of a fairway wood during his 1982 US Open victory at Pebble Beach.

A proud moment for Tom Watson as he receives the US Open trophy from Bill Campbell (right), president of the United States Golf Association, while President Gerald Ford looks on.

was about to make a birdie at the 15th. This made them level again until Watson sank a monster at the 14th for a birdie and took the lead once more.

At almost the precise moment Nicklaus was finishing in 69 for 284, Watson was hitting his one poor drive down the 16th. It cost him a stroke for he could not go for the green and he was therefore back to level pegging, two holes to play, one a par three, the other a par four.

Ten years before, Nicklaus had hit the flag on the 17th dead centre, tapped the putt in for a two and made off with the championship. Luck had been with him then and now Watson needed one birdie at either of these last two holes to win. As his two iron tee shot drew more than he had intended, his thoughts were more of tieing than winning. His ball ran off the green into ankle-high rough.

Watson was grim faced as he walked from the tee but he was in luck. His ball was sitting up and he knew he ought to save his par. No one at this time had a better short game than Watson and he had room in which to work his sand wedge under the ball. Always quick to play his shots, he sized the situation up, went through a brief rehearsal, popped the ball out and was off and running, arms aloft in exultation even before the chip rolled into the hole.

Behind the 18th green Nicklaus was watching on a television monitor and his face fell. He knew he would lose and lose he did for Watson was able to play the 18th safely away from the treacherous sea-shore. It did not matter that he made another birdie to win by two. It was the chip at the 17th that had done it.

US Open

Players from US unless otherwise stated
An asterisk (*) denotes an amateur
Prize money unchanged unless shown

1895 Newport, Rhode Island ($335)
173 Horace Rawlins 45,46,41,41 ($150)
175 Willie Dunn 43,46,44,42
176 James Foulis 46,43,44,43
A.W. Smith* 47,43,44,42

1896 Shinnecock Hills, New York
152 James Foulis 78,74
155 Horace Rawlins 79,76
158 G. Douglas 79,79

1897 Chicago, Illinois
162 Joe Lloyd 83,79
163 Willie Anderson 79,84
168 James Foulis 80,88

1898 Myopia Hunt Club, Massachusetts
328 Fred Herd 84,85,75,84
335 Alex Smith 78,86,86,85
336 Willie Anderson 81,82,87,86

1899 Baltimore, Maryland ($750)
315 Willie Smith 77,82,79,77 ($150)
326 George Low 82,79,89,76
Val Fitzjohn 85,80,79,82
W.H. Way 80,85,80,81

1900 Chicago, Illinois
313 Harry Vardon (GB) 79,78,76,80
315 J.H. Taylor (GB) 76,82,79,78
322 David Bell 78,83,83,78

1901 Myopia Hunt Club, Massachusetts
331 Willie Anderson 84,83,83,81 ($200)
Alex Smith 82,82,87,80
333 Willie Smith 84,86,82,81
Anderson won play-off 85, Smith 86

1902 Garden City, New York ($870)
307 Laurie Auchterlonie (GB) 78,78,74, 77 ($200)
313 Stewart Gardner 82,76,77,78
Walter Travis* 82,82,75,74

1903 Baltusrol, New Jersey
307 Willie Anderson 149,76,82
David Brown 156,75,76
315 Stewart Gardner 154,82,79
Anderson won play-off 82, Brown 84

1904 Glen View, Illinois
303 Willie Anderson 75,78,78,72
308 Gilbert Nicholls 80,76,79,73
309 Fred Mackenzie 76,79,74,80

1905 Myopia Hunt Club, Massachusetts
314 Willie Anderson 81,80,76,77
316 Alex Smith 81,80,76,79
317 Peter Robertson 79,80,81,77
P.F. Barrett (Canada) 81,80,77,79

1906 Onwentsia, Illinois ($900)
295 Alex Smith 73,74,73,75 ($300)
302 Willie Smith 73,81,74,74
305 Laurie Auchterlonie (GB) 76,78, 75,76
James Maiden 80,73,77,75

1907 Philadelphia, Pennsylvania
302 Alec Ross 76,74,76,76
304 Gilbert Nicholls 80,73,72,79
305 Alex Campbell 78,74,78,75

1908 Myopia Hunt Club, Massachusetts
322 Fred McLeod 82,82,81,77
Willie Smith 77,82,85,78
327 Alex Smith 80,83,83,81
McLeod won play-off 77, Smith 83

1909 Englewood, New Jersey
290 George Sargent 75,72,72,71
294 Tom McNamara 73,69,75,77
295 Alex Smith 76,73,74,72

1910 Philadelphia, Pennsylvania
298 Alex Smith 73,73,79,73
John McDermott 74,74,75,75
Macdonald Smith 74,78,75,71
Alex Smith won play-off 71, McDermott 75, M. Smith 77

1911 Chicago, Illinois
307 John McDermott 81,72,75,79
Mike Brady 76,77,79,75
George Simpson 76,77,79,75
McDermott won play-off 80, Brady 82, Simpson 85

1912 Buffalo, New York
294 John MacDermott 74,75,74,71
296 Tom McNamara 74,80,73,69
299 Alex Smith 77,70,77,75
Mike Brady 72,75,73,79

1913 Brookline, Massachusetts
304 Francis Ouimet* 77,74,74,79
Harry Vardon (GB) 75,72,78,79
Ted Ray (GB) 79,70,76,79
Ouimet won play-off 72, Vardon 77, Ray 78

1914 Midlothian, Illinois
290 Walter Hagen 68,74,75,73
291 Charles Evans Jnr.* 76,74,71,70
297 George Sargent 74,77,74,72
Fred McLeod 78,73,75,71

1915 Baltusrol, New Jersey
297 Jerome Travers* 148,73,76
298 Tom McNamara 149,74,75
300 Robert MacDonald 149,73,78

1916 Minikahda, Minnesota
286 Charles Evans Jnr.* 70,69,74,73
288 Jock Hutchison 73,75,72,68
290 Jim Barnes 71,74,71,74

1917–18 No championship

1919 Brae Burn, Massachusetts ($1300)
301 Walter Hagen 78,73,75,75 ($500)
Mike Brady 74,74,73,80
306 Jock Hutchison 78,76,76,76
Hagen won play-off 77, Brady 78

1920 Inverness, Ohio ($1,745)
295 Ted Ray (GB) 74,73,73,75
296 Harry Vardon (GB) 74,73,71,78
Jack Burke 75,77,72,72
Leo Diegel 72,74,73,77
Jock Hutchison 69,76,74,77

1921 Columbia, Maryland
289 Jim Barnes 69,75,73,72
298 Walter Hagen 79,73,72,74
Fred McLeod 74,74,76,74

1922 Skokie, Illinois
288 Gene Sarazen 72,73,75,68
289 John Black 71,71,75,72
Bobby Jones* 74,72,70,73

1923 Inwood, New York
296 Bobby Jones* 71,73,76,76
Bobby Cruickshank 73,72,78,73
302 Jock Hutchison 70,72,82,78
Jones won play-off 76, Cruickshank 78

1924 Oakland Hills, Michigan
297 Cyril Walker 74,74,74,75
300 Bobby Jones* 74,73,75,78
301 Bill Mehlhorn 72,75,76,78

1925 Worcester, Massachusetts ($2,145)
291 Willie Macfarlane 74,67,72,78
Bobby Jones* 77,70,70,74
292 Johnny Farrell 71,74,69,78
Francis Ouimet 70,73,73,76
Macfarlane won play-off 147, Jones 148

1926 Scioto, Ohio
293 Bobby Jones* 70,79,71,73
294 Joe Turnesa 71,74,72,77
297 Bill Mehlhorn 68,75,76,78
Gene Sarazen 78,77,72,70

US Open

Leo Diegel 72,76,75,74
Johnny Farrell 76,79,69,73

1927 Oakmont, Pennsylvania
301 Tommy Armour 78,71,76,76
Harry Cooper 74,76,74,77
302 Gene Sarazen 74,74,80,74
Armour won play-off 76, Cooper 79

1928 Olympic Fields, Illinois ($5,000)
294 Johnny Farrell 77,74,71,72 ($1,000)
Bobby Jones* 73,71,73,77
295 Roland Hancock 74,77,72,72
Farrell won play-off 143, Jones 144

1929 Winged Foot, New York
294 Bobby Jones* 69,75,71,79
Al Espinosa 70,72,77,75
296 Gene Sarazen 71,71,76,78
Densmore Shute 73,71,76,76
Jones won play-off 141, Espinosa 164

1930 Interlachen, Minnesota
287 Bobby Jones* 71,73,68,75
289 Macdonald Smith 70,75,74,70
292 Horton Smith 72,70,76,74

1931 Inverness, Ohio
292 Billy Burke 73,72,74,73
George Von Elm* 75,69,73,75
294 Leo Diegel 75,73,74,72
Burke won play-offs 149/148, Von Elm 149/149

1932 Fresh Meadow, New York ($4,950)
286 Gene Sarazen 74,76,70,66 ($1,000)
289 Bobby Cruickshank 78,74,69,68
Phil Perkins 76,69,74,70

1933 North Shore, Illinois ($4,990)
287 Johnny Goodman* 75,66,70,76
288 Ralph Guldahl 76,71,70,71
290 Craig Wood 73,74,71,72

1934 Merion, Pennsylvania ($5,000)
293 Olin Dutra 76,74,71,72
294 Gene Sarazen 73,72,73,76
295 Wiffy Cox 71,75,74,75
Bobby Cruickshank 71,71,77,76
Harry Cooper 76,74,74,71

1935 Oakmont, Pennsylvania
299 Sam Parks Jnr. 77,73,73,76
301 Jimmy Thomson 73,73,77,78
302 Walter Hagen 77,76,73,76

1936 Baltusrol, New Jersey
282 Tony Manero 73,69,73,67
284 Harry Cooper 71,70,70,73
287 Clarence Clark 69,75,71,72

1937 Oakland Hills, Michigan ($6,000)
281 Ralph Guldahl 71,69,72,69
283 Sam Snead 69,73,70,71
285 Bobby Cruickshank 73,73,67,72

1938 Cherry Hills, Colorado
284 Ralph Guldahl 74,70,71,69
290 Dick Metz 73,68,70,79
292 Harry Cooper 76,69,76,71
Tony Penna 78,72,74,68

1939 Philadelphia, Pennsylvania
284 Byron Nelson 72,73,71,68
Craig Wood 70,71,71,72
Densmore Shute 70,72,70,72
Nelson won play-off 138, Wood 141, Shute eliminated

1940 Canterbury, Ohio
287 Lawson Little 72,69,73,73
Gene Sarazen 71,74,70,72
288 Horton Smith 69,72,78,69
Little won play-off 70, Sarazen 73

1941 Colonial Club, Texas
284 Craig Wood 73,71,70,70
287 Densmore Shute 69,75,72,71
289 Johnny Bulla 75,71,72,71
Ben Hogan 74,77,68,70

1942–1945 No championships

1946 Canterbury, Ohio ($8,000)
284 Lloyd Mangrum 74,70,68,72 ($1,500)
Byron Nelson 71,71,69,73
Vic Ghezzi 71,69,72,72
Mangrum won play-offs, 72/72, 72/73, 72/73

1947 St. Louis, Missouri ($10,000)
282 Lew Worsham 70,70,71,71 ($2,000)
Sam Snead 72,70,70,70
285 Bobby Locke (S. Africa) 68,74,70, 73
Porky Oliver 73,70,71,71
Worsham won play-off 69, Snead 70

1948 Riviera, California
276 Ben Hogan 67,72,68,69
278 Jimmy Demaret 71,70,68,69
280 Jim Turnesa 71,69,70,70

1949 Medinah, Illinois
286 Cary Middlecoff 75,67,69,75
287 Clayton Heafner 72,71,71,73
Sam Snead 73,73,71,70

1950 Merion, Pennsylvania ($14,900)
287 Ben Hogan 72,69,72,74 ($4,000)
Lloyd Mangrum 72,70,69,76
George Fazio 73,72,72,70
Hogan won play-off 69, Mangrum 73, Fazio 75

1951 Oakland Hills, Michigan ($14,800)
287 Ben Hogan 76,73,71,67
289 Clayton Heafner 72,75,73,69
291 Bobby Locke (S. Africa) 73,71,74, 73

1952 Northwood, Texas ($14,900)
281 Julius Boros 71,71,68,71
285 Porky Oliver 71,72,70,72
286 Ben Hogan 69,69,74,74

1953 Oakmont, Pennsylvania ($20,400)
283 Ben Hogan 67,72,73,71 ($5,000)
289 Sam Snead 72,69,72,76
292 Lloyd Mangrum 73,70,74,75

1954 Baltusrol, New Jersey ($23,280)
284 Ed Furgol 71,70,71,72 ($6,000)
285 Gene Littler 70,69,76,70
286 Dick Mayer 72,71,70,73
Lloyd Mangrum 72,71,72,71

1955 Olympic, California ($25,480)
287 Jack Fleck 76,69,75,67
Ben Hogan 72,73,72,70
292 Sam Snead 79,69,70,74
Tommy Bolt 67,77,75,73
Fleck won play-off 69, Hogan 72

1956 Oak Hill, New York ($24,000)
281 Cary Middlecoff 71,70,70,70
282 Julius Boros 71,71,71,69
Ben Hogan 72,68,72,70

1957 Inverness, Ohio ($28,560)
282 Dick Mayer 70,68,74,70 ($7,200)
Cary Middlecoff 71,75,68,68
283 Jimmy Demaret 68,73,70,72
Mayer won play-off 72, Middlecoff 79

1958 Southern Hills, Oklahoma ($35,000)
283 Tommy Bolt 71,71,69,72 ($8,000)
287 Gary Player (S. Africa) 75,68,73,71
289 Julius Boros 71,75,72,71

1959 Winged Foot, New York ($49,200)
282 Billy Casper Jnr. 71,68,69,74 ($12,000)
283 Bob Rosburg 75,70,67,71
284 Claude Harman 72,71,70,71
Mike Souchak 71,70,72,71

1960 Cherry Hills, Colorado
($62,020)
280 Arnold Palmer 72,71,72,65 ($14,400)
282 Jack Nicklaus* 71,71,69,71
283 Dutch Harrison 74,70,70,69
Julius Boros 73,69,68,73

1961 Oakland Hills, Michigan
($68,300)
281 Gene Littler 73,68,72,68 ($14,000)
282 Bob Goalby 70,72,69,71
Doug Sanders 72,67,71,72

1962 Oakmont, Pennsylvania
($81,600)
283 Jack Nicklaus 72,70,72,69 ($17,500)
Arnold Palmer 71,68,73,71
285 Phil Rodgers 74,70,69,72
Bobby Nichols 70,72,70,75
Nicklaus won play-off 71, Palmer 74

1963 Brookline, Massachusetts
($96,350)
293 Julius Boros 71,74,76,72
Jacky Cupit 70,72,76,75
Arnold Palmer 73,69,77,74
Boros won play-off 70, Cupit 73, Palmer 76

1964 Congressional, Washington D.C.
($95,400)
278 Ken Venturi 72,70,66,70 ($17,000)
282 Tommy Jacobs 72,64,70,76
283 Bob Charles 72,72,71,68

1965 Bellerive, Missouri
($131,690)
282 Gary Player (S. Africa) 70,70,71,71 ($26,000)
Kel Nagle (Australia) 68,73,72,69
284 Frank Beard 74,69,70,71
Player won play-off 71, Nagle 74

1966 Olympic, California
($155,290)
278 Billy Casper 69,68,73,68 ($26,500)
Arnold Palmer 71,66,70,71
285 Jack Nicklaus 71,71,69,74
Casper won play-off 69, Palmer 73

1967 Baltusrol, New Jersey
($177,800)
275 Jack Nicklaus 71,67,72,65 ($30,000)
279 Arnold Palmer 69,68,73,69
281 Don January 69,72,70,70

1968 Oak Hill, New York
($188,800)
275 Lee Trevino 69,68,69,69
279 Jack Nicklaus 72,70,70,67
281 Bert Yancey 67,68,70,76

1969 Champions, Texas
($205,300)
281 Orville Moody 71,70,68,72
282 Deane Beman 68,69,73,72
Al Geiberger 68,72,72,70
Bob Rosburg 70,69,72,71

1970 Hazeltine, Minnesota
($203,500)
281 Tony Jacklin (GB) 71,70,70,70
288 Dave Hill 75,69,71,73
289 Bob Lunn 77,72,70,70
Bob Charles (NZ) 76,71,75,67

1971 Merion, Pennsylvania
($200,000)
280 Lee Trevino 70,72,69,69
Jack Nicklaus 69,72,68,71
282 Bob Rosburg 71,72,70,69
Jim Colbert 69,69,73,71
Trevino won play-off 68, Nicklaus 71

1972 Pebble Beach, California
($202,400)
290 Jack Nicklaus 71,73,72,74
293 Bruce Crampton (Australia) 74,70, 73,76
294 Arnold Palmer 77,68,73,76

1973 Oakmont, Pennsylvania
($227,200)
279 Johnny Miller 71,69,76,63 ($35,000)
280 John Schlee 73,70,67,70
281 Tom Weiskopf 73,69,69,70

1974 Winged Foot, New York
($227,700)
287 Hale Irwin 73,70,71,73
289 Forest Fezler 75,70,74,70
290 Lou Graham 71,75,74,70
Bert Yancey 76,69,73,72

1975 Medinah, Illinois ($244,000)
287 Lou Graham 74,72,68,83 ($40,000)
John Mahaffey Jnr. 73,71,72,71
288 Bob Murphy 74,73,72,69
Hale Irwin 74,71,73,70
Ben Crenshaw 70,68,76,74
Frank Beard 74,69,67,78
Graham won play-off 71, Mahaffey 73

1976 Atlanta, Georgia ($268,000)
277 Jerry Pate 71,69,69,68 ($42,000)
279 Al Geiberger 70,69,71,69
Tom Weiskopf 73,70,68,68

1977 Southern Hills, Oklahoma
($284,990)
278 Hubert Green 69,67,72,70 ($45,000)
279 Lou Graham 72,71,68,68
281 Tom Weiskopf 71,71,68,71

1978 Cherry Hills, Colorado
($310,200)
285 Andy North 70,70,71,74
286 Jesse Snead 70,72,72,72
Dave Stockton 71,73,70,72

1979 Inverness, Ohio ($330,400)
284 Hale Irwin 74,68,67,75 ($50,000)
286 Jerry Pate 71,74,69,72
Gary Player (S. Africa) 73,73,72,

1980 Baltusrol, New Jersey
($356,700)
272 Jack Nicklaus 63,71,70,68 ($55,000)
274 Isao Aoki (Japan) 68,68,68,70
276 Keith Fergus 66,70,70,70
Tom Watson 71,68,67,70
Len Hinkle 66,70,69,71

1981 Merion, Pennsylvania
($361,730)
273 David Graham (Australia) 68,68, 70,67
276 Bill Rogers 70,68,69,69
George Burns 69,66,68,73

1982 Pebble Beach, California
($385,000)
282 Tom Watson 72,72,68,70 ($60,000)
284 Jack Nicklaus 74,70,71,69
286 Bobby Clampett 71,73,72,70
Dan Pohl 72,74,70,70

1983 Oakmont, Pennsylvania
($506,184)
280 Larry Nelson 75,73,65,67 ($72,000)
281 Tom Watson 72,70,70,69
283 Gil Morgan 73,72,70,68

1984 Winged Foot, New York
($596,000)
276 Fuzzy Zoeller 71,66,69,70 ($95,000)
Greg Norman (Australia) 70,68,69, 69
281 Curtis Strange 69,70,74,68
Zoeller won play-off 67, Norman 75

1985 Oakland Hills, Michigan
($654,000)
279 Andy North 70,65,70,74 ($103,500)
280 Denis Watson 72,65,73,70
Dave Barr (Canada) 70,68,70,72
Tze-Chung Chen (Taiwan) 65,69, 69,77

1986 Shinnecock Hills, New York
($700,000)
279 Raymond Floyd 75,68,70,66 ($115,000)
281 Lanny Wadkins 74,70,72,65
Chip Beck 75,73,68,65

1987 Olympic, California
($825,000)
277 Scott Simpson 71,68,70,68 ($150,000)
278 Tom Watson 72,65,71,70
282 Severiano Ballesteros (Spain) 68,75,68,71

1988 Brookline, Massachusetts
($1,000,000)
278 Curtis Strange 70,67,69,72
Nick Faldo (GB) 72,67,68,71
280 Steve Pate 72,69,72,67
Mark O'Meara 71,72,66,71
D.A. Weibring 71,69,68,72
Strange won play-off 71, Faldo 75

BRITISH OPEN CHAMPIONSHIP

The Open championship is by some way the oldest of golf's four majors. It was first played in 1860 at the instigation of the Prestwick Club close to Ayr on the west coast of Scotland. A year before, a famous Scottish golfer, Allan Robertson, had died. He was looked upon as the finest player in the land and the game felt the need to find a new champion.

The club presented a wide leather belt, much in the style of those worn by a prize fighter, for annual competition with the proviso that anyone who won three times in a row should keep it permanently. Young Tom Morris did win it three times in a row (1868–70) and that was very nearly the end of the Open; there was no championship in 1871.

However, the idea was too good to let drop altogether and Prestwick, which until then had staged every Open, got together with the Royal and Ancient Golf Club of St. Andrews and the Honourable Company of Edinburgh Golfers, whose headquarters were then at Musselburgh, and in 1872 revived the championship. They replaced the leather belt, which now resides in the R & A clubhouse, with a silver claret jug and this has remained the trophy ever since.

For another 22 years these three clubs took it turn and turn about to host the Open before widening its scope by taking the championship to Royal St. George's on the Kent coast in 1894. It was the first step into the future. Management of the Open was taken over by the R & A alone in 1919.

Fourteen different courses have now staged the Open at different times but Prestwick, though it has not been re-visited since 1925, has still held the most, with 24. The latest to join the roster was Turnberry in 1977. It immediately yielded the lowest winning aggregate, 268, by Tom Watson.

Harry Vardon's six victories between 1896 and 1914 are still the most, closely followed by James Braid, J.H. Taylor, Peter Thomson and Watson, all of whom have won five times. The Morris family hold two distinctions. The father, Old Tom, is the oldest winner at 46, the son, Young Tom, the most junior at 17.

Taylor, Vardon and Gary Player have all won in three different decades, the biggest span between first and last victories being the 19 years by Taylor, covering the period 1894 to 1913. Only three amateurs have been Open champion: Bobby Jones three times, Harold Hilton twice and John Ball once.

Left: *Other than Harry Vardon, who won the title six times, only four golfers have won the Open championship five times. One of them is Tom Watson, here on the way to his victory at Royal Troon in 1982.*

Right: *A dream comes true for Nick Faldo as he holds the famous silver claret jug after his Open championship victory at Muirfield in 1987.*

Prestwick

Prestwick was the birthplace of the Open championship. It was held there for 12 consecutive years beginning in 1860 and then on another 12 occasions until 1925 when it became clear that it could no longer cope with the ever increasing crowds. Prestwick's 24 Opens nevertheless are still a record, one more even than St. Andrews, which has come to be regarded as its spiritual home.

These days, Prestwick is a place of curiosity to visiting golfers, like an ancient monument; a reminder of the terrain on which golf used to be played when luck and skill were in equal proportion.

Originally, in 1851, there were only 12 holes with the first a par six of 578 yards. A stone cairn still marks the siting of the first tee. In 1883 these 12 holes were increased to 18 and little, if anything, has changed since. A hundred years have passed as if in the twinkling of an eye.

There is consequently a great 'feel' about Prestwick, sensed as soon as one ducks under the little railway bridge before turning into the car park by the low greystone clubhouse. Hard by the first hole stretches on its right the little stone wall over which a million and more golf balls must have been driven onto the railway line running through Prestwick Station. Beyond, stretching out towards the international airport and Royal Troon, lie the hillocks and dunes of a true links.

Within the clubhouse, with that special aroma that goes with wooden lockers and old leather, the feeling of history is ever stronger. Records of Opens long since forgotten are mere slips of ragged paper and fading writing. In the main lounge, with its leather armchairs and a round table thick with magazines and newspapers, the talk is not of the golf but the 'goff'.

Nowhere does a sense of well-being pervade more than in the dining room. On the wall are arranged a century of past captains' portraits as lunch is taken on a long, highly polished table. The soup is hot, the main course cold, great sides of beef and ham waiting to be carved by the diners themselves. To go with it is the claret, afterwards the cheese and port, and of course kümmel to help the putting.

At 6,631 yards (6,083 m) the course is not

The approach back to the clubhouse at Prestwick, home of the first Open championship in 1860.

long, though long enough in 1987 to stage the British Amateur championship. Then its neatly trimmed fairways and fine greens illustrated that the modern methods of golf course

upkeep are very much a part of Prestwick.

Perhaps its most famous hole is the Cardinal, the third, a par five of 500 yards (457 m), so named because of the great bunker, railway sleepers shoring up its face, which runs the full width of the fairway. It is a formidable obstacle over which the second shot has to be played. There is no sight of the green for that, like many others, lies in a little dell among the humps and the hollows.

The fourth, a dog-leg left to right, is a fine two shotter skirting the Pow Burn; the short fifth is eccentric and known as the Himalayas for the towering ridge that lies between the tee and another hidden green.

From then on the course becomes more conventional until it reaches the bottleneck of its last four charming holes. The tee shot to the narrow 15th fairway is played over a slim saddle, the 16th almost driveable and the 17th, the Alps, plunging up and down like a roller coaster. Even in 1925 it was hopeless trying to control the galleries and even that custodian of tradition, Bernard Darwin, was moved to write: 'I gravely doubt that a championship should be played there again.'

The broad sweep of Prestwick's 10th fairway, beyond it the Firth of Clyde and in the distance the Isle of Arran.

Prestwick

Hole	Yards	Par	Hole	Yards	Par
1	346	4	10	453	4
2	168	3	11	194	3
3	500	5	12	515	5
4	382	4	13	461	4
5	206	3	14	363	4
6	400	4	15	348	4
7	431	4	16	296	4
8	431	4	17	391	4
9	458	4	18	288	4

Yards 6,631 Par 71

St Andrews

Considering the minimal changes that have been made to it, not so much over the years as over the centuries, it is a wonder that the Old Course at St. Andrews has stood up so long to the more sophisticated armoury of the modern game and the increasing expertise of those at the top.

The extension of one or two tees, none of them by much, has increased the course's overall length to not far short of 7,000 yards (6,400 m) but there are still so many vulnerable holes on it that the 'Old Lady' seems bound to yield one day.

Once, in the 1970 Open Championship, she was insulted when Tony Jacklin began his defence of the title by going out in 29. But a violent storm, which meant that Jacklin could not complete his round until the following day, saved her respect and for a long time the record stood at no lower than 65, held jointly by Neil Coles, Greg Norman and Nick Faldo.

But the weather, so often her ally, was no longer there, so to speak, in the Dunhill Cup, the international team competition, in October 1987, and it was then that America's leading money winner of the year, Curtis Strange, at last struck the inevitable blow. He

There is no more celebrated view than that down the first and 18th fairways at St. Andrews, the clubhouse of the Royal and Ancient on the left and the 'auld grey toon' so close to the links.

Shared greens are a feature at St. Andrews. Here players wait on the 14th while another putts on the fourth.

went round the Old Course in 62, just two days after an Australian, Rodger Davis, had done it in 63.

Strange's score was *343* 454 *323* (31) and *323* 45*3* 44*3* (31), the figures in italics being the birdies. Strange's 62 was achieved without an eagle but with five birdies on either nine. It was indeed a marvellous round but when the weather was overcast, the wind absent and the Old Course on the soft side, it has to be said that the challenge is not quite the same as in high summer when the flags are fluttering and the fairways and greens fast running.

It is then that the art of playing the Old Course lies not in finding the greens but finding them in such places as make it possible to putt. The greens are enormous, for only four holes, the first, ninth, 17th and 18th have their own putting surfaces. The remaining 14 holes are all played to double greens, the second sharing with the 16th, the third with the 15th, and so on, with every combination, as it happens, adding up to 18.

Yet it is not only the huge size of the greens that makes putting a game within a game, but also their violent borrows over miniature hills and dales. There is scarcely ever a straight putt at St. Andrews and from the wrong place the golfer is looking not at three putts but perhaps four. A recent past captain and still a most capable player once came in maintaining that he had hit every green in the correct number of strokes but had taken in excess of 50 putts!

However this is only part of the challenge – and indeed frustration – of the most famous golf course in the world. The other lies in the bunkers which, in many cases, were created by the hand of nature, sheep, it is said, having once burrowed into them for protection against the savage gales.

A great many have names, for example Hell, which guards the route to the long 14th; the Principal's Nose, in the middle of the 16th fairway; Strath, which fronts the 11th green; and Cockle, which awaits a mis-hit approach to the seventh. In some, Bernard Darwin once observed, 'there is scarcely room for an angry man and his niblick', and even those who play the course regularly are said always to be

Above: *The 'Home of Golf', the clubhouse of the Royal and Ancient Golf Club of St. Andrews. The deep windows of the Big Room look directly down the first fairway and above it is the balcony to the office of the secretary. In the foreground is the 18th green.*

Below: *For centuries little has changed to the Old course at St. Andrews. No links has so endured the passage of time.*

coming across an 'unknown' bunker.

For all the vulnerability of some holes, particularly round what is known as the 'Loop', which begins at the seventh and ends at the 12th – it was here that Strange had his six consecutive birdies – there are some great holes and none more challenging than the 17th, otherwise known as the Road Hole.

Once the drive was played over a low line of black railway sheds. Now they are gone, as indeed has the railway itself, but the challenge is still there even if in the different form of the unprepossessing Old Course Hotel (Golf and Country Club). However, it is the second shot to the slightly raised and angled green that poses the problem. Eating into its near left side is the Road Bunker, a devilishly deep but small hazard while beyond is the road itself off which those whose ball runs onto it can never make up their minds whether to chip or putt if they are to negotiate the steep little bank. This is a 'horror hole' if ever there was one.

It was nevertheless the scene in 1971 of 'the shot that won the Walker Cup', a three iron by Dr. David Marsh, just as it was also the hole that cost Tom Watson the 1984 Open when his two iron second finished hard against the little stone wall beyond the road.

The great charm of the Old Course is nevertheless St. Andrews itself, that 'Old Grey Toon' that stretches right down to the broad acres of the first and 18th fairways with its constant stream of onlookers.

Dominating it is the Royal and Ancient clubhouse with the deep windows of the Big Room looking right down on the first tee, behind it the members briefly lowering their newspapers for a critical assessment of those opening drives.

Open champions from Old Tom Morris to Nick Faldo have stood on that same ground and no golfer's education is complete until he has done the same, for this is the very Home of Golf, its own Houses of Parliament.

St. Andrews

Hole	Yards	Par	Hole	Yards	Par
1	370	4	10	342	4
2	411	4	11	172	3
3	398	4	12	316	4
4	463	4	13	425	4
5	564	5	14	567	5
6	416	4	15	413	4
7	372	4	16	382	4
8	178	3	17	461	4
9	356	4	18	354	4

Yards 6,960 Par 72

Muirfield

Muirfield, which looks out across the Firth of Forth just downstream from the noble city of Edinburgh to the west, was the first course on which the Open championship was played over 72 holes. That was nearly 100 years ago, in 1892, an amateur, Harold Hilton, being the winner.

The actual name of the club is the Honourable Company of Edinburgh Golfers and Muirfield is their third home. They played first at Leith and then at Musselburgh before moving to their present site in 1891. In the beginning, the Honourable Company being founded in 1744, its members even wrote the first rules of golf and very much to the point they were too, since they numbered only 13.

Perhaps of all the clubs which play host to the Open – Muirfield's 13 to date having been exceeded only by Prestwick and St. Andrews – this club defends tradition the most fiercely. It does not even have a professional's shop, golf balls and tee pegs either being bought in the clubhouse or down the road in Gullane or, slightly further afield, North Berwick. It is an area thick with golf courses.

Foursomes is still the most popular form of golf at Muirfield and the members meet over dinner to arrange their matches, then going on to negotiate handicaps. The waiting list for membership is long and anyone over 50 years of age is advised not to apply in case he never makes it!

Part of the mystique of Muirfield was created of recent years by its former secretary, Captain Paddy Hanmer RN ret., whose bark was undoubtedly worse than his bite. The hesitant visitor from distant parts, having presented his credentials, would be accompanied outside by the Captain carrying a pair of field glasses through which he would scan an invariably deserted golf course. The visitor would then be advised that it would probably be all right for him to go off the 10th if he was quick about it!

To do the job properly, the best place to stay at Muirfield is the Greywalls Hotel, an elegant country house hotel looking straight down the

The 12th green at Muirfield and beyond the little huddle of the 13th. This picture was taken during the 1980 Open.

10th fairway and a great favourite with the Americans.

As a test of golf, the course is very highly regarded and far from being an 'old water meadow', as Andrew Kirkaldy, one of the best players never to have won the Open, described it after the move from Musselburgh. It is also a comfortable watching course in that its circular design, with first a clockwise outer ring and then an anti-clockwise inner ring, lead to innumerable short cuts and never too long a walk back to the clubhouse.

Only the third, fourth and fifth holes successively follow the same direction and the good players must therefore always have their wits about them since the wind is constantly coming from a different quarter.

The links fall gently towards the Forth and a chief feature is the bunkers. They are not only so deep that a player disappears from sight but the ground around them tends to gather the ball, punishing therefore a shot that is only marginally mis-hit.

After a relatively gentle start, the first stiff examination comes at the sixth, a long dog-legged par four with an awkward dip in the fairway. The eighth, with its minefield of bunkers to the right of another bending fairway, leads to further trouble while the ninth, with its famous greystone wall all along the left side threatens out of bounds.

Favourite holes on the inward half are the 10th, stretching straight up into the dunes, the tiny 13th, with its tilting green and encircling bunkers, the long 17th with its fierce cross-bunkering and then the 18th which is rated among the finest finishing holes in championship golf.

Muirfield

Hole	Yards	Par	Hole	Yards	Par
1	447	4	10	475	4
2	351	4	11	385	4
3	379	4	12	381	4
4	180	3	13	152	3
5	559	5	14	449	4
6	469	4	15	417	4
7	185	3	16	188	3
8	444	4	17	550	5
9	504	5	18	448	4

Yards 6,963 Par 71

The 18th green at Muirfield. It was from the bunker on the right that in 1987 Paul Azinger, of America, failed to get up and down in two, leaving Nick Faldo Open champion.

Mussleburgh

Musselburgh, one of the early homes of the Honourable Company of Edinburgh Golfers who now reside at Muirfield, is the only one of the original Open championship golf courses that has been lost in the passage of time and is no longer a golf course.

East of Edinburgh and indeed on the coast road to Muirfield, it is now a racecourse and children's playground, though relics of the old holes can still be seen. The club itself has moved a mile or so away to Prestongrange where it has a most handsome clubhouse and 18 holes, which it did not have before.

The old course originally had only seven holes but by the mid-1800s two more were added, giving it an overall length of 2,850 yards (2,606 m), and it was over these that the Open championships of 1874, '77, '80, '83, '86 and '89 were played.

In those days the links were shared by not only the Honourable Company but also the Bruntsfield Links and the Royal Burgess. All three departed in the 1890s but it was the move of the Honourable Company that caused the most acrimony for with it went the Open championship. However, by then the ground was much too cramped and there was also some trouble with the local authorities because of the proximity of the road and the danger to the public of flying golf-balls.

Musselburgh was not a long course but three of the holes were listed as par fives even though not much more than 400 yards (366 m) in length. This gives some idea of the limited flight of the golf-ball of those days, the rubber-cored ball not coming into full use until the early 1900s.

Musselburgh nevertheless played an important part in the development of the Open, which from 1860 until 1872 was played exclusively at Prestwick. For the next 19 years it circulated between St. Andrews, Musselburgh and Prestwick before then expanding to wider fields.

Of the six winners at Musselburgh, Jamie Anderson and Bob Ferguson had the most distinction. Their victories in 1877 and 1880, respectively, were the first of three consecutive victories in each case. Apart from Young Tom Morris, Peter Thomson, of Australia, is the only other man to have recorded three wins in a row.

In fact, Anderson might have gone on to win the championship four times in a row but in 1880, when the Open went back to Musselburgh, he did not enter. His absence was put down, so it is said, 'to the shortness of notice given of the championship'. How times have changed; now the date for the Open is set at least three years in advance.

Mungo Park was the first winner at Musselburgh in 1874 and his score of 159 for the 36 holes was the lowest since Young Tom Morris's three years earlier. A sailor, Mungo took the game up when he was past his prime and was overshadowed by his brother, Willie. Together with their father, Willie senior, the Parks won the Open seven times.

Anderson, on the other hand, began his golf at an early age and while he was not known as a long hitter, he was very accurate with his approach shots, often played so quickly that he hardly seemed to give the flag a glance. His winning score at Musselburgh was 160, including one nine holes of 37.

The less strenuous demands of Musselburgh were illustrated by Bob Ferguson in 1880. His nine hole scores are not recorded in the Royal and Ancient's Championship Records but 81, 81 for 162 was rather better than his 170 at St. Andrews and 171 at Prestwick the two following years. This is understandable. Musselburgh was his home links, within sight of the house in which he was born.

A powerful man, Ferguson was at his best with the cleek and iron and few were better at coping with a strong wind or heavy ground. He and Anderson were the dominant figures in succession to the Morrises.

Ferguson's attempt to win the championship a fourth successive year at Musselburgh in 1883 was foiled by Willie Fernie, one of the great St. Andrews professionals. This was undoubtedly a disappointment to the home crowd, particularly since the championship went to a play-off, both players scoring 159 for the 36 holes.

Ferguson, in fact, led by a stroke with one to play but Fernie drove the green, holed for a two against a four and won by a stroke. It was his only Open win although he was runner-up four times. A sound teacher, he also helped in the original design of Turnberry.

David Brown, another Musselburgh man, seldom travelled far afield in his early golfing days. He was a slater by trade but his victory in 1886 with 79,78 for 157 must have inspired him. He later went to America and tied for the US Open in 1903, losing in a play-off to Willie Anderson at Baltusrol.

Willie Park junior, whose father had won the first Open championship of all in 1860, was in 1889 the last winner at Musselburgh, suitably by the lowest score, 155, which tied Andrew Kirkaldy. It was a dramatic finish for Park had been two behind with three to play.

In those days play-offs were not considered a matter of any urgency and it was another three days before they went out to settle things. Park was always in control, three strokes ahead at half way and the winner by five with 158 against 163. Something of a gambler in that he would take challenges from anyone, Park was at his deadliest on the greens. That well-known phrase 'a man who can putt is a match for anyone' is attributed to him.

JOHN HENRY TAYLOR
Open Champion
1894.1895.1900.1909.1913.TIED 1896.
JAMES BRAID
Open Champion
1901.1905.1906.1908.1910.
HARRY VARDON
Open Champion
CLEMENT FLOWER

Royal St George's

There are two schools of thought in golf. On the one hand there are the traditionalists who will argue that it was never meant to be a fair game and that the run of the ball, be it for or against you, is an indispensable factor of play. On the other hand there are those, mostly of a younger generation, who maintain that every good shot should be properly rewarded and not made the victim of some capricious bounce.

It is for this reason that Royal St. George's, on the flats between the little town of Sandwich and the shingle beach of the Kent coast, is the least popular site of the Open championship among the professionals. While there are all the facilities in the world necessary to hold the Open, from space for a tented village, to car parking, to practice grounds, to ease of spectator movement, it is still looked upon by the players with distrust.

The reasons are not hard to analyse. Royal St. George's, which celebrated its centenary in 1987, having been founded, so it is said, by Dr. Laidlaw Purves and Henry Lamb when they spotted the land from the Sandwich church tower, is old fashioned. It even has some of the eccentricities of Prestwick.

Set amid some towering dunes and whispering grass, it is for much of its 6,800 yards (6,218 m) all humps and hollows and unusual lies. This is not at all to the liking of the modern professional who, when having hit what he believes to have been a perfect drive, finds himself addressing his next shot with one foot several inches above the other.

A combination of this and the wind, which is an almost constant factor in these parts, makes St. George's a very tough examination. The modern par is 70, or 280 for four rounds, and in the 11 Opens held here that aggregate has been beaten only once, by the American, Bill Rogers, in 1981 with a total of 276.

This was in fact the first Open to be played at Sandwich since 1949, the lengthy interval being caused by the difficulty of access through the narrow streets of the ancient town. A new by-pass eased congestion and meanwhile the course had also been altered.

Two short holes, the blind third and the eighth, were abandoned. The third was rebuilt slightly to the left with a view of the green and the eighth re-routed as well as being made into an attractive par four. Conversely, the 11th, previously a par four, is now a par three.

Otherwise, always accepting some new tees to cope with the greater distances the ball is hit these days, the course is substantially the same as it was when the likes of J.H. Taylor, Walter Hagen, Henry Cotton and Bobby Locke were variously in their primes.

Opposite: *Known as the Great Triumvirate, J.H. Taylor, James Braid and Harry Vardon (left to right) dominated golf at the turn of the century.*

Ian Woosnam successfully negotiates 'Duncan's Hollow' beside the 18th green at the Open championship, Royal St George's in 1985.

Above: *Royal St. George's first staged the Open in 1894.*

Below: *Harold Hilton drives from the third tee at Royal St. George's during the 1914 Open.*

Scoring to the turn is generally thought to be easier than coming home. There is a great trinity of holes through the 13th, 14th and 15th, which form a triangle close to Prince's and the 18th is one of the hardest finishing holes, dead straight but to a difficult green with an awkward swale just to its left. It very nearly cost Sandy Lyle the 1985 Open.

That year there was a good example of how important a part the changing weather can play. One morning Severiano Ballesteros could not reach the 17th green with two woods, but in the afternoon Lyle played it with a drive and a nine iron.

Royal St. George's has hosted many other events besides the Open including, in 1988, the Curtis Cup. There is irony in this for the club does not have any women members, though they are allowed to play. It is an arrangement that has worked quite satisfactorily and the gabled clubhouse has an atmosphere that makes the golfer feel instantly at home.

Royal St. George's, Sandwich

Hole	Yards	Par	Hole	Yards	Par
1	445	4	10	399	4
2	376	4	11	216	3
3	214	3	12	362	4
4	470	4	13	443	4
5	422	4	14	508	5
6	156	3	15	467	4
7	529	5	16	165	3
8	415	4	17	425	4
9	387	4	18	458	4

Yards 6,857 Par 70

Hoylake

Hoylake, like Carnoustie, has lost favour for the moment as an Open championship venue. It has not been used since 1967 when that tall and distinguished Argentine, Roberto de Vicenzo, proved among the most popular winners. The fault is not that of Hoylake, officially entitled the Royal Liverpool Golf Club. Again it is a victim of the popularity of the Open for there is no longer the space to house the attendant paraphernalia that goes with it. This is a pity for Hoylake is not only a genuine championship golf course, but it has played such a prominent part in the game's history that it is sometimes referred to as the 'St. Andrews of England'.

Of the seaside courses it is junior only to Westward Ho!, dating back to 1864. A year later it was responsible for launching the Amateur championship. Hoylake also staged the first ever international match, between England and Scotland in 1902, and in 1921 another between Britain and the United States that led to the birth of the Walker Cup.

Among its most famous sons are John Ball and Harold Hilton. Ball won the Amateur championship eight times, which it is safe to say will never be repeated. In 1890 he became not only the first amateur but also the first Englishman to win the Open and only Bobby Jones himself has subsequently held these two titles at the same time – 40 years later. This was the year of Jones's Grand Slam and appropriately the Open championship leg of the quadrilateral was achieved at Hoylake.

Hilton is the solitary Englishman to have won the American Amateur championship, in 1911, the only other non-Americans to have done so being two Canadians. He also won the Open championship twice and the Amateur four times. The two men were born within eight years of one another and died within two: twin careers of rare distinction.

From the red-brick Victorian clubhouse looking out towards the Dee estuary and, beyond, the mountains of North Wales, it is hard to believe how majestic are the links. It appears flat with few distinguishing landmarks, just a line of houses on its far side. But away to the left there is a sprawl of dunes close to the estuary where at low tide the sands stretch seemingly to Wales itself.

This is the best of the golf with some splendid and quite spectacular holes from the eighth to the 13th, pretty well all along the shore. Yet a feature of Hoylake is the practice ground to the right of the first hole and, coming the other way, to the right of the 16th.

A feature of a British links is the depth of the bunkers around the greens. Unlike for Greg Norman here at Hoylake, it is sometimes not even possible to see the flag.

The Royal Liverpool Golf Club at Hoylake. It is sometimes called the 'St. Andrews of England'.

Though, therefore, in the middle of the golf course, it is nevertheless out of bounds.

At the first it protrudes into the line of the drive, the fairway then turning right and skirting the very edge of the practice ground all the way to the green. A small bank known as 'the kop' is the demarcation line. Though only a few feet high, it presents a considerable threat to the second shot and many have been the red faces as a ball sails out of bounds. As a 19th hole, with the prospect of sudden death, there is no more intimidating factor.

At the 16th, a par five, the practice ground comes into play again, for only the very longest drives will give an uninterrupted view of the green. Often, therefore, it is a case of the golfer taking his life in his hands and firing his second shot, invariably with a wooden club, clean over the corner of the out of bounds.

Most controversial of all is the seventh, known as the Dowie. A short hole of 200 yards (183 m), the narrow green abuts another small bank or kop on its left and beyond it again is out of bounds. It is therefore quite possible to hit a tee shot to within a few yards of the flag but still be out of bounds.

Soon one is up into the dunes, dipping and turning before emerging again into the broad acres of the last five holes that, for all their flatness amid the swaying grass of the rough, pose many a problem before the finishing post comes in sight. The analogy is not inappropriate. Once the course was shared with a racecourse, the 18th indeed still being called 'Stand'.

Hoylake

Hole	Yards	Par	Hole	Yards	Par
1	428	4	10	409	4
2	369	4	11	200	3
3	505	5	12	454	4
4	195	3	13	157	3
5	449	4	14	512	5
6	423	4	15	460	4
7	200	3	16	533	5
8	479	5	17	418	4
9	393	4	18	395	4

Yards 6,979 Par 72

Royal Cinque Ports, Deal

Royal Cinque Ports, on the edge of the little town of Deal which overlooks the English Channel to the faint outline of the French coast, has staged only two Open championships, the last of them in 1920. Like Prince's, which with Royal St. George's and Cinque Ports forms a trinity of splendid Kent courses, it has been overtaken by the demands of the attendant circus that now accompanies the championship.

At 6,407 yards (5,859 m) it is also probably on the short side but whenever the Open is staged at St. George's and one of the qualifying rounds is played at Cinque Ports, the players invariably come away extolling the virtues of the greens.

Deal, as it is more commonly known, is nevertheless not forgotten as a venue for the more important amateur events, both the British and English championships having been held here in recent years. It is still a good test of golf, made tougher by the flat countryside to the west and sea to the east with nothing therefore to break the seemingly permanent wind.

It has come to be regarded as the headquarters of the annual Halford Hewitt tournament in which the old boys of 64 public schools, 10 men to a team and all playing foursomes, fight it out to the death. There are not many tournaments, if indeed any at all, in which there is a starting field of 640 players but its popularity is undiminishing. Deal is also the perfect stage, for the gleaming white clubhouse, its verandah frequently overflowing with spectators, offers a grandstand view of the 18th and 19th holes.

The 19th is of course the first hole but it is as the first of any necessary extra holes that are needed that it comes into its own. Though not, at 325 yards (297 m), a demanding hole in terms of length, it does have a burn crossing the fairway just short of the green and it is this that attracts disaster. Many a pair and many a school have foundered in its depths.

Though the English Channel is mostly out of sight behind the sea wall, which has more than once collapsed in the face of high tides, the tang of salt is always in the air and while Deal can be a vile and inhospitable place it can also, on the right day, be a quite heavenly links on which to play golf.

There is a spring to the turf which encourages good play and if there is some lack of definition, that is understandable with the sea so near. Yardage charts mean little, for a hole

One of the most delightful holes at Deal is the short fourth, nestling among the dunes.

The first green at Royal Cinque Ports, Deal, and beyond it the clubhouse. One Open championship, in 1920, was held here but more recently it has been used as a qualifying course for Sandwich.

that plays a drive and eight iron in the morning can easily become a drive and two iron when the tide turns and the wind springs up.

It is from the 12th that Deal comes into its own. It is a long run home from there with four par four holes in excess of 400 yards (366 m) and a par three of more than 200 yards (183 m), all in the same direction and all into the prevailing wind.

The greens then can be elusive indeed and those who win their matches early can heave a sigh of relief, not least because it avails them the opportunity of stopping off at that little inn, the Chequers, either to quench their thirst or for something a little stronger.

Royal Cinque Ports

Hole	Yards	Par	Hole	Yards	Par
1	325	4	10	362	4
2	364	4	11	382	4
3	453	4	12	418	4
4	153	3	13	400	4
5	494	5	14	215	3
6	304	4	15	420	4
7	358	4	16	456	4
8	164	3	17	360	4
9	383	4	18	396	4

Yards 6,407 Par 70

Prince's

In 1923, when Gene Sarazen first competed in the Open championship at Troon, he failed to qualify. Since a year earlier Sarazen had won both the United States Open and the PGA, this was a severe disappointment and he vowed there and then that he would not rest until he had won this oldest title.

It took him another nine years before he finally succeeded in 1932, in the one and only Open to be played at Prince's, a close neighbour of the more celebrated Royal St. George's on the Kent coast overlooking Pegwell Bay to the distant white cliffs of Ramsgate.

The two courses directly abut one another at one point close by what used to be the old Prince's clubhouse and the 14th hole at St. George's. Certainly, the latter has had its changes over the years but it is still possible there to follow much of the path of the old champions.

It is more difficult to do so at Prince's, for though the old clubhouse still stands as a reminder, the new clubhouse is at the other end of the course and the old championship lay-out has become entwined within the present 27 holes.

The equally demanding three nines have also been renamed: Shore, Dunes and Himalayas, their respective yardages being 3,455 (3,159 m), 3,492 (3,193 m) and 3,321 (3,037 m). Each can play every inch of them for there is a bleakness about Prince's that takes one back to the days when golf was not about yardages but a challenge between man and the elements.

There is a sense of almost uncharted territory here, for Prince's is not a heavily

The old clubhouse at Prince's with the flag to the then 18th green in the foreground. It was here in 1932 that Gene Sarazen won his only Open championship.

bunkered course, relying more on the naturalness of its terrain and precise judgement of distance against a landscape of gentle dunes and greens that are sometimes hard to define amid the general flatness.

Over the years Prince's has been a victim of flood, wars and financial crises. High tides in spring and autumn have been a constant threat. In the First World War the course was used for coastal defence and in the Second World War it was a battle training ground. The links were well known by P.B. 'Laddie' Lucas, son of P.M., a former secretary who had a hand in its design, and when his Spitfire was shot up over the Channel, he made use of one of the flatter fairways for an emergency landing.

Sir Aynsley Bridgland was instrumental in restoring the course after the war and in 1956 it was the scene of a rare British victory in the Curtis Cup. However, it may be for Sarazen's victory that it is best known – a step along the way to his becoming the first man to win at different times the four majors.

A panoramic shot of Prince's rugged links with the power station on the horizon.

Prince's

Shore			*Dunes*			*Himalayas*		
Hole	**Yd**	**Par**	**Hole**	**Yd**	**Par**	**Hole**	**Yd**	**Par**
1	457	4	1	430	4	1	386	4
2	167	3	2	511	5	2	415	4
3	491	5	3	176	3	3	184	3
4	414	4	4	410	4	4	355	4
5	418	4	5	386	4	5	400	4
6	498	5	6	408	4	6	580	5
7	373	4	7	562	5	7	195	3
8	208	3	8	184	3	8	415	4
9	429	4	9	425	4	9	391	4
Yd 3,455			Yd 3,492			Yd 3,321		
Par 36			Par 36			Par 35		

Royal Lytham & St Anne's

It is one of the peculiarities of golf courses that many of them seem to be adjacent to railway lines. Royal Lytham, on the Lancashire coast just south of Blackpool, is no exception. The Preston–Blackpool railway runs parallel to the second, third and eighth holes, its very presence being an intimidating factor with any player who has a tendency to slice.

Though very much a links, there is no awareness of the sea at Lytham. It has long since been enclosed on all sides by suburbia and from that point of view does not have the instant appeal of somewhere like Turnberry, all unspoiled magnificence.

For all the spread of red brick, however, Lytham is a very fine test and there is little of any consequence in the British golfing calendar that has not been held there. It has now seen eight Open championships and two of them, those of 1969 and 1979, are particularly notable. In the first, Tony Jacklin brought the silver claret jug back to Britain after an absence of 18 years; ten years later Severiano Ballesteros became the first continental winner since Arnaud Massy in 1907.

Like the many fine courses that stretch along the Lancashire coastline, Lytham is a constant victim of strong westerly winds, evidence of which can be seen from the manner in which the scrub-like trees lean to the east, as if pushed there by some giant hand.

The prevailing wind makes the last five holes one of the supreme tests in championship golf. The 14th may be straight but in a cross-wind the fairway can be elusive and the 15th, not far short of being a par five, can be quite brutish. It takes a long drive to give a sight from the slightly climbing, curving fairway of the green protected by a horseshoe of bunkers.

There is some relief at the 16th, which has become known as Ballesteros's car-park hole, since in 1979 it was there that the Spaniard drove under the wheels of a parked car but still got an important birdie in his last round. The 17th was made famous in 1926 by the bunker shot Bobby Jones played from the scrub on the left of the fairway when he won the first of his three Opens. The club he used, a mashie iron, the equivalent of today's four or five iron, still hangs in the substantial Victorian clubhouse which is similar to many in the north of England.

This redbrick clubhouse looks directly down on the 18th hole with its diagonal line of fairway bunkers, and is so close to the green that in 1974, the first Open in which the larger 1.68 inch (4.27 cm) ball became mandatory, Gary Player had to chip to the green left handed after his second shot had finished close to one of the clubhouse walls.

Earlier, Player had faced a desperate search for his ball beside the 17th green after hooking his second shot and the many trouble spots Lytham has are illustrated by a story in *The*

Angled cross bunkers bar the way to the 18th green at Royal Lytham where in 1969 Tony Jacklin broke a run of 18 years without a British winner.

Lytham Century, by Tony Nickson, one of the club's past captains:

'Each of the local clubs', he wrote, 'mans one section of the course as stewards. Knott End take the area by the seventh and 11th holes. In 1969, when they appeared on duty, they were surprised to find 17 new golf balls of various makes scattered in the spinney to the left of the long 11th, where one might expect a pulled second shot to land. It could have been a coincidence but the suspicion must remain that some of the caddies, who had walked the course in the early morning to check the pin positions, had put down an insurance policy against a wayward shot by their masters.'

Unusually for a championship course, Lytham begins with a par three. First appearances could hardly be more deceptive. 'It's a beast,' wrote Bernard Darwin.

Royal Lytham

Hole	Yards	Par	Hole	Yards	Par
1	206	3	10	334	4
2	420	4	11	485	5
3	458	4	12	189	3
4	393	4	13	339	4
5	188	3	14	445	4
6	486	5	15	468	4
7	551	5	16	356	4
8	394	4	17	413	4
9	162	3	18	386	4

Yards 6,673 Par 71

Below: *Royal Lytham's second green and the bunkers to be negotiated with the second shot.*

Royal Birkdale

There are a few richer pastures for golf than on that wonderful stretch of duneland just south of Southport on the Lancashire coast. Side-by-side in quick succession, almost like Siamese triplets, lie Royal Birkdale, Hillside, and Southport and Ainsdale. A few minutes drive further on and one comes to Formby, different in character from the other three with all its pines, but a joyous place nonetheless.

Senior among this illustrious quartet – though not in years since Formby is in fact the oldest – is Royal Birkdale. Conversely, it did not make its entrance as an Open championship venue until 1954, when Peter Thomson won the first of his five titles. But it has now staged six and is in constant demand for both professional and amateur events, women's as well as men's.

This is not difficult to understand for as soon as one drives out of Southport on the Liverpool road and catches a glimpse of the golf course, narrow blotches of green fairway weaving their way through an almost moon-like landscape of mighty dunes, there is the inescapable feeling that this is going to be quite 'something'.

Indeed it is, and from atop the highest points one can look beyond the boundaries of the course to more land on which another half dozen courses could be built. Whether any of them could surpass Royal Birkdale is another matter and it is acclaimed by professionals and amateurs alike.

For this the credit lies initially with the architect, George Low, and then with Fred Hawtree and J.H. Taylor, who were subsequently called in for some re-designing when the old clubhouse was pulled down and the new one re-sited.

Not for them the traditional blind shots over dunes and ridges. Instead, the holes were laid out amid the valleys between the dunes, the bordering sandhills perhaps inadvertently

Opposite top: *This plaque marks the spot from which Bobby Jones played his celebrated mashie iron to Royal Lytham's 17th green in the 1926 Open championship. Though lying in sand, Jones found the green some 150 yards away and the four he got enabled him to overtake Al Watrous.*

Though lying in spectacular duneland, Royal Birkdale is a great favourite with the professionals because the fairways tend to follow the line of the valleys with few eccentric stances.

becoming natural grandstands and the fore-runner of the 'stadium golf' now so fashionable in America.

Within these winding valleys, the fairway lies are generally even with none of the eccentric stances associated with links golf. If this is one bonus for those who believe golf should be a fair game, there is also another in that there is scarcely an exposed green. They nestle instead in the lee of encircling sandhills, protected to some extent from the elements. Against such back-drops it is also easier to judge the distances to the flag.

For all that, Birkdale can throw up some rough weather and when Arnold Palmer won his first Open here in 1961 his 73 amid the tempest of the second round is still recalled with a sense of wonder.

Over the years the course has undergone changes, notably the building of a classic short 12th across a valley to a green in the saddle of two dunes, and also the abandonment of the short 17th. For a time there was uncertainty whether the 18th should be a par five or a par four. It was the former when Lee Trevino won his first Open in 1971 and the latter when Tom Watson triumphed in 1983. A strong four is in fact better than a weak five, particularly since the 13th, 15th and 17th are all genuine par fives.

There has been tampering, too, with the sixth, a long par four or short par five, spoiled for many years by a cross bunker that caught too many long drives. Now there is some room to the left which helps.

Thomson in fact won both his first and last Opens here but of all the modern golfing history written at Birkdale, nothing surpassed the 1969 Ryder Cup match when a purely British side tied with the United States.

Throughout, the two sides had been locked in the closest of duels and in the end it all boiled down to Tony Jacklin and Jack Nicklaus, all square and one to play, the two teams level. Appropriately they halved the hole and even more appropriately Nicklaus conceded Jacklin's second putt, acknowledging that it would have been too awful had he missed it. Such spirit is typical of golf and golfers.

Royal Birkdale

Hole	Yards	Par	Hole	Yards	Par
1	448	4	10	395	4
2	417	4	11	409	4
3	409	4	12	184	3
4	203	3	13	506	5
5	346	4	14	199	3
6	490	5	15	543	5
7	154	3	16	414	4
8	458	4	17	525	5
9	414	4	18	472	4

Yards 6,986 Par 72

Royal Birkdale provides some of the best viewing for spectators.

Royal Troon

If anyone unfamiliar with the game of golf needs an explanation for a player going 'out in 36' and 'back in 35', he need look no further than Royal Troon, one of the many fine courses along the Ayrshire coast. As with a number of the famous seaside links, the first nine holes go 'out' to the furthest extremity of the course while the second nine are played 'back' to the clubhouse.

To be sure, there is the occasional hole which switches direction (in Troon's case the eighth and 12th) but with the prevailing wind here from the north west, which is at the golfer's back on his way to the turn, the battle is almost always on the home journey.

No one knows this better than the South African, Nick Price. In the 1982 Open championship he frittered away a three-stroke lead going into the last six holes and lost by a shot to Tom Watson.

It is undoubtedly a mark of the standing of Troon – the 'Royal' prefix was bestowed on the occasion of their centenary in 1978 – that their five Open champions have all been players of distinction. The 1923 winner, Arthur Havers, was the last British winner of the Open for 12 years, while the other winners at Troon, until Watson in 1982, were Bobby Locke (1950), Arnold Palmer (1962) and Tom Weiskopf (1973).

The club motto is 'Tam Arte Quam Marte', which means 'as much by skill as by strength' and nowhere does this apply more aptly than at the sixth and eighth holes. The former is at 577 yards (528 m) the longest on the Open championship circuit, and the latter, at 126 yards (115 m), the shortest.

In fact the eighth is hardly known as 'the eighth' at all. It is always referred to as the 'Postage Stamp' because of its tiny green between a hill on the left and a steep drop into a bunker on the right. Herman Tissies, a German competitor in the 1950 Open, remembers it well.

It took him 15 strokes to hole out; five shots in one bunker, five more in another before landing back in the first one again. This is the second highest score for a hole ever recorded in the Open championship.

Gene Sarazen, on the other hand, has reason to recall the Postage Stamp with much greater

Royal Troon, where Tom Watson won his fifth Open title in 1982, is one of the toughest championship courses.

A feature of the modern Open championship is the big stands around the 18th green. This one is at Royal Troon, the roof of the Marine Hotel beyond.

pleasure. In 1973, by way of celebrating the 50th anniversary of his first appearance in the Open, he entered again at the age of 71. It was intended to be a purely nostalgic appearance but instead he made the headlines.

In the first round, partnered by Max Faulkner and Fred Daly, Sarazen holed in one at the eighth with a five iron and briefly was even on the leader board. Twenty-four hours later at the same hole he sank a bunker shot for a two. So that was a total of three strokes for the same hole in successive days which had to be suitable economy of effort for a septuagenerian.

When Palmer won at Troon in 1962 he did so by a street, six strokes clear of the runner-up, Kel Nagle. He was then at the height of his powers and such an attraction that the course was overrun by spectators, many of them coming in through what was known as the 'Aberdeen gate', which meant off the beach without paying.

It was at about this time that the Open was finally taking off as the great sporting spectacle it is today, and Troon continues to be very much a part of it. In some ways it may lack subtlety while its proximity to Prestwick Airport down by the ninth and 10th can have players and spectators alike almost ducking for cover for fear of being hit by approaching aircraft. But there is no doubting its quality as a test of golf.

Royal Troon

Hole	Yards	Par	Hole	Yards	Par
1	362	4	10	437	4
2	391	4	11	481	5
3	381	4	12	432	4
4	556	5	13	468	4
5	210	3	14	180	3
6	577	5	15	457	4
7	400	4	16	542	5
8	126	3	17	223	3
9	419	4	18	425	4

Yards 7,067 Par 72

Carnoustie

There is no greater victim of the Open championship's success than Carnoustie. It is certainly among the most severe tests of golf in the British Isles and at more than 7,000 yards (6,400 m) it is the longest. Yet much more than that is now needed successfully to stage the championship.

It is the lack of suitable hotel accommodation, practice facilities, an area for the tented village and access that have all combined to remove Carnoustie, temporarily it is hoped, from the Open rota. It has not been played there since 1975 when Tom Watson won the first of his five titles.

Nor is Carnoustie at once the most appealing of sites; the square and basic clubhouse, which is the home of the oldest artisan club in the world (1839), would hardly win a design award while there is a certain grey drabness to the immediate surroundings.

First appearances in this case however are deceptive, for stretching out towards the rifle range and the frequent crack of gunfire lie the noblest of links within sound if not sight of the North Sea breaking on the Angus coast.

One of its main features is the Barry Burn, which plays a particularly prominent part in a tough finishing stretch that begins at the 14th with twin cavernous bunkers, known as the Spectacles, blocking the entrance to the green.

At least it is a par five but the 15th, almost as long, is a severe par four to a green partly hidden in a small depression. Immediately there comes a long par three, nearly 250 yards (229 m) long to a green not unlike an upturned dish. Next the Barry Burn awaits.

It winds like a vast snake all around the 17th so that the drive has to be hit to an island fairway. Anything mis-hit, hooked or even too long is liable to find the depths and the burn is there again at the 18th, most dangerously in front of the green. Always there in the mind is the difficult decision of whether to 'go for it' or just to lay up.

Only golf of the highest order suffices, as earlier, notably at the long sixth, where there is out of bounds to the left and a bunker dead centre. As at the 18th there is a choice – right of the bunker to be on the safe side or between the fence and the bunker, in the hope of putting the green in range. This gap is known as Hogan's Alley because in 1953 Ben Hogan aimed down it every time as a means to winning the Open.

Unfortunately, the triangle of woodland between the third, fourth and fifth holes has become rather threadbare of recent years, though this has not affected the golf, and it is the fervent ambition of everyone in the district to get the Open re-instated.

Carnoustie's link with golf from overseas is strong for not only have Hogan, Gary Player in 1968 and Watson been winners there but on

Ben Hogan won his celebrated Open at Carnoustie in 1953. The course has not been used for the championship since 1975. The clubhouse is not its most endearing feature.

the three occasions of staging the Amateur championship two Americans, Willie Turnesa and Steve Melnyk, and a South African, Bobby Cole, were the winners.

Furthermore, a great many men of Carnoustie emigrated to the United States at the turn of the century to make their fortune. One of them, Stewart Maiden, had a great influence on the career of Bobby Jones and thereby on the game of golf itself.

Carnoustie

Hole	Yards	Par	Hole	Yards	Par
1	406	4	10	455	4
2	464	4	11	370	4
3	345	4	12	482	5
4	381	4	13	167	3
5	391	4	14	482	5
6	575	5	15	463	4
7	395	4	16	248	3
8	172	3	17	432	4
9	475	4	18	440	4

Yards 7,143 Par 72

Royal Portrush

The Open championship has only once been played in Ireland, at Royal Portrush in 1951. It was won by Max Faulkner, a most colourful man, in character as well as dress, and though no one knew it at the time, it was to prove the beginning of a most barren passage so far as British winners of the title were concerned. Another 18 years were to pass before a successor to Faulkner was found in the figure of Tony Jacklin.

Though Portrush could no longer cope with the attendant circus of a modern Open, it remains a jewel of a course, one that can be mentioned very much in the same breath as Ballybunion, Royal County Down and Portmarnock, to name but three more of Ireland's prized golfing possessions.

As soon as one turns the corner on the coast road from Portballantrae and catches below a glimpse of the links, lying like a crumpled green sheet, there is a feeling of something special. To the west lie the hills of Donegal, to the north the open sea, the Skerries and Islay, to the east a rugged coastline leading to the Giant's Causeway.

No one can fail to be uplifted by such a panorama and the links themselves add further stimulant. There are two main courses, the Dunluce (so named after the ancient castle on the cliffs a mile or so away to the east) and the Valley. Dunluce is the championship course and it was here, amid the mighty dunes, that Faulkner won.

Years earlier, in 1895, Lady Margaret Scott had won here as well the first British Ladies Championship to be staged outside England and through all the years the women golfers have been the more faithful visitors. This reveals a certain hardiness for the winds from the Atlantic can be, to say the least, invigorating.

If Portrush has a weakness it lies in its two rather ordinary par five finishing holes, which seem to have been added on almost as an afterthought, the 17th away from the clubhouse and the 18th back to it again. However, to balance it are 16 strengths, high among them the fifth, or White Rocks, from its high tee to a threading fairway and then a green so close to the cliff edge that it was once in danger of falling down. Happily, and at a great deal of expense, this has now been saved.

Perhaps the most renowned hole however is the 14th, called Calamity Corner. At 213 yards (195 m), the shot can vary from a full drive to a mid iron. The direct line to the flag demands a long carry over a deep ravine on the right, the slope descending some 50 feet (15 m). From down there even a bogey four is something of a bonus.

A more prudent line is to the left and in the 1951 Open, Bobby Locke, who was then going for the hat-trick since he had won at Sandwich and Troon the previous two years, deliberately aimed for a small swale tucked into the side of the green. He found it in every one of his four rounds, chipped and single putted each time for his par three and ever since it has been known as 'Bobby Locke's Hollow'.

Locke's bid for a third successive championship did not materialize. The ball did not run kindly for him, though his start was promising enough with a 71, the same as Faulkner. The leaders were Jimmy Adams and the little Australian, Norman Von Nida, both round in 68 in a stiffish wind the locals rated as a mere breeze.

It was some inspired putting that gave Faulkner his first glimpse of the trophy. On the second day he took only 26 putts in his round of 70 which lifted him three strokes clear

Opposite top: *One of the defences of any links is the weather, as a wild sky broods over Carnoustie.*

Opposite bottom: *The eighth green at Carnoustie where, in 1968, Gary Player won his first Open championship.*

Below: *The 13th green at Royal Portrush. In the background is the Skerries, a hazard for shipping.*

Max Faulkner watches with baited breath as he plays a pitch during his Open championship victory at Royal Portrush in 1951.

of Fred Daly and Harry Weetman. However, in those days the final two rounds were played on the Friday so that the professionals could get back to their shops by Saturday morning and the burden of the lead was half expected to be too much for Faulkner.

Faulkner himself, on the other hand, was full of confidence, out to prove that his reputation of being a natty dresser was no barrier to winning golf. In horizontal striped shirt and primrose coloured plus-fours he had the unmistakable air of the champion elect.

His morning 70 for a 54-hole aggregate of 211 took him six strokes clear of the popular Argentine, Antonio Cerda, and Norman Sutton, while Peter Thomson, Weetman and Locke were all further strokes adrift.

From this position Faulkner could now only lose the title rather than win it, though by now the rain had set in, which did not make his task any easier. He went through the turn in 37 but kept his head when further strokes were lost in sand at the 12th, 15th (which is called Purgatory) and 16th, and finished in 74 for a total of 285.

There was no such thing then as the leaders going out last and as Faulkner sat in the clubhouse drinking a succession of cups of tea, it became evident that only Cerda could catch or overtake him. The Argentine went out in an inspired 34 to make up three strokes and then made further birdies at the 12th and 13th.

That left Cerda needing one more birdie in his last five holes to tie. He could not manage it, taking four at Calamity Corner and six at the next. His challenge had been brave but a closing 70 left Faulkner the winner by two.

He was a popular champion, as colourful in his way as the two Americans, Walter Hagen and Gene Sarazen, in the years preceding him. This was also one of the last old-style Opens with the crowds still on the fairways. It was a free-and-easy atmosphere typical of Portrush.

Royal Portrush

Hole	Yards	Par	Hole	Yards	Par
1	389	4	10	480	5
2	497	5	11	166	3
3	159	3	12	395	4
4	455	4	13	371	4
5	384	4	14	213	3
6	198	3	15	366	4
7	432	4	16	432	4
8	376	4	17	517	5
9	475	4	18	481	5

Yards 6,786 Par 72

Looking back from the first green towards the clubhouse at Royal Portrush.

Turnberry

On a summer evening, the sky clear and the sun an orange ball dropping into the sea, there is no better place to have dinner than in the Turnberry Hotel, though it is the view that takes precedence over the excellence of the fare. Outside, the colours are for ever changing as the outlines of the Isle of Arran and the Mull of Kintyre become for ever darker and then, shifting the gaze to the left, that rising hulk of rock from the very depths of the sea somewhere between the Scottish coast and the Irish mainland, Ailsa Craig, moves seemingly ever closer.

Immediately below, almost lost now in the ground mists and lengthening shadows, lie two golf courses, the Ailsa and the Arran. The first of these is the championship course on which two Opens, the first in 1977 and the second as recently as 1986, have now been held. More, it is safe to say, will come for Turnberry is the most enchanting of all its venues.

For this, golf will be for ever in the debt of a man by the name of Frank Hole, who, just after the Second World War, was chairman of British Transport Hotels, the owners then of Turnberry. For the second time in its life, Turnberry had played its part in the war effort. In 1914–18 it was used as a training school for the Royal Flying Corps and then in 1939–45 it was commandeered by Coastal Command as a convenient base from which to protect the Atlantic convoys.

This second upheaval led to the digging up of fairways and greens and the laying of massive concrete runways, the remnants of which can still be found between the two courses. There was a strong fear that Turnberry could never be properly restored as a golf course but Frank Hole was convinced otherwise and under the guiding hand of that celebrated architect, Mackenzie Ross, there blossomed possibly an even greater masterpiece.

On such summer evenings Turnberry can be a place of the utmost tranquility. But it can also be wild and inhospitable, the sea thundering on the rocks around the perilous ninth tee, close by which stands the gleaming white lighthouse which is seemingly there as a warning as much to golfers as it is to shipping.

It was on this very stretch of Ayrshire coast that Robert the Bruce began his conquest of the Isle of Arran that was to lead to victory at Bannockburn, and invariably, too, the golfer faces a battle of a different sort. Perversely, two of the lowest ever rounds in the Open have been played at Turnberry, 63s by the American, Mark Hayes, in 1977, and by Greg Norman in 1986. It was here, too, that Tom Watson set the championship record, 268 for the 72 holes in 1977.

Gene Sarazen once remarked that the mark

Spectators ring the eighth green at Turnberry during the 1986 Open championship.

Above: *All eyes were on Tom Watson and Jack Nicklaus over the last two days of the 1977 Open at Turnberry.*

Below: *An aerial view of Turnberry, the ninth tee and lighthouse prominent.*

of a great hole is one you start worrying about long before you reach it. There are a number of these at Turnberry, beginning perhaps at the short fourth, aptly named 'Woe Be Tide' because of its lofted green and danger on all sides.

Then there is another short hole, the sixth, all of 222 yards (203 m), and one at which it is sometimes necessary to use a forward tee in the interests of fair play. Most famous of all is the ninth: from the rock-perched tee one must drive across sea and coves to the fairway on which a small stone cairn indicates the way.

There is splendour too about the 10th to a dropping fairway hugging the shore. The 14th is always difficult if the wind is against one, though it appears straightforward. There is peril to the right of the short 15th and the 1963 Walker Cup was largely lost at the 16th where the British kept underclubbing and putting their second shots in Wilson's burn at the foot of the steep slope fronting the green.

For all the narrowness of the long 17th, the best in the game are looking to get on the green in two and there are holes at Turnberry that offer something in return for the tougher examinations elsewhere, which is only fair.

Turnberry

Hole	Yards	Par	Hole	Yards	Par
1	350	4	10	452	4
2	428	4	11	177	3
3	462	4	12	441	4
4	167	3	13	411	4
5	441	4	14	440	4
6	222	3	15	209	3
7	528	5	16	409	4
8	427	4	17	500	5
9	455	4	18	431	4

Yards 6,950 Par 70

Vardon Breaks the Deadlock

It was appropriate that Harry Vardon should have won in 1914 his sixth Open championship at Prestwick, as he did two earlier ones. It is a record that has stood unequalled for more than 70 years and his name is as synonymous with golf as Prestwick is with the early days of the Open. The Vardon grip, in which the little finger of the right hand overlaps the forefinger of the left, is still considered the most orthodox.

Vardon had two contemporaries, J.H. Taylor and James Braid, and between them they won the Open 16 times in 21 years, beginning in 1894. They were known as the Triumvirate and no other three golfers have been so dominant over so long a spell.

Historians have called this the Golden Age of Golf and it was as the war clouds were gathering in 1914 that it drew to a close. By then both Vardon and Braid were 44, Taylor was 43, and with each of them having five Open victories to his credit, there was an undoubted sense that this was going to be the 'decider'.

Consequently, the climax could not have been better orchestrated as Vardon and Taylor were paired together for the whole of the last day, Vardon ahead by two strokes overnight, Taylor ahead by two with 18 holes to play. With Braid out of it, the huge crowds had eyes only for these two men.

Spectators in those days roamed loose over the course and the players were repeatedly jostled. Vardon claimed that often he would finish a round with his shins black and blue for once he had played his shot and handed back his club to his caddie, he was virtually indistinguishable from anyone else in his Norfolk jacket.

Allowing for some exaggeration, it was often said that a greater hazard to Vardon in

James Braid (left) *and J.H. Taylor* (below), *two of golf's famous triumvirate at the turn of the century.*

his afternoon rounds were his divot holes of the morning, so repetitive was his striking! The two holes which virtually assured him of his sixth championship were the third, the Cardinal, where he got a birdie four, and the fourth, where Taylor had a seven after visiting the burn.

Only one more Open was played at Prestwick, in 1925, its unsuitability in coping with big crowds being confirmed as Macdonald Smith, who had been born in Carnoustie but emigrated to America, came home to stand on the verge of a most popular victory – too popular.

A course record 69 in the second round had given him a lead of two strokes and even as the trains were arriving from Glasgow, Kilmarnock, Irvine, Troon and Ayr bearing his many supporters, so he increased his lead in the third round to five strokes. It was estimated that between 10,000 and 15,000 battled for vantage points for his triumphant march to victory, though all they did was destroy his concentration. In total disarray, Smith took 82 in his final round and Jim Barnes, already a winner of the US Open, was left to take the title in relative solitude.

And so Prestwick was left with its ghosts, the most prominent of whom had been Young Tom Morris, whose very excellence had almost stifled the championship in its infancy. The year it was revived, with the silver claret jug as the new trophy, Young Tom promptly triumphed again, making it four consecutive victories. But his supreme moment had been in 1870 with his record score of 149 for the 36 holes, three rounds of 12 holes each.

In one of them he scored 47, which represented an average of under four shots per hole and was therefore quite phenomenal golf given the equipment of the time. At the first, which then measured 578 yards (529 m), he had a three and he won by no less than 12 strokes. Sadly Young Tom was only 24 when he died but his four victories lit a flame that has never been extinguished.

*It was not uncommon for golfers to play with a pipe clenched firmly between their teeth: Ted Ray (*below*), after whom the famous British comedian took his name; and Harry Vardon (*below, right*), Open champion on a record six occasions.*

Nicklaus Survives the Old Course

Around the 18th green of the Old Course at St. Andrews on a grey and overcast July afternoon of 1970 the proverbial pin might have been heard drop. From every vantage point spectators hung, holding their breath as a slight, colourfully dressed American, Doug Sanders, surveyed a putt of about a yard to win the Open championship.

It does not sound the most difficult of lengths but when so much hinges upon it and the green is notorious for its subtle breaks, the mind plays strange tricks. Sanders's uncertainty was first evident when, just as he was about to putt, he thought he saw a stray piece of grass on his line.

He bent to pick it up but his concentration had been broken and almost inevitably the putt was missed, which meant a tie with Jack Nicklaus, waiting anxiously and hardly daring to look in the recorder's hut.

Sanders would have been the first champion to have emerged from the ranks of prequalifiers and 24 hours later, in the first Sunday finish, he paid the ultimate price. He had nevertheless just about kept pace with Nicklaus through the first 17 holes of their play-off, just a stroke behind and one to play.

But Nicklaus, with a nice sense of theatre, removed his sweater before driving and launched himself into such a massive shot that his ball ran through the green, from where he had to chip off the bank. Sanders, from a shorter drive followed by a fine pitch, seemed likely to get his three but Nicklaus beat him to it, holing from 8 feet (2.4 m) and hurling his putter so high that no one seemed certain where it might come down as there was a general ducking for cover.

To win at St. Andrews is the crowning moment in the career of any golfer and it is fitting that the most successful of them all, Nicklaus, should have won two of his three here at the Home of Golf. The other was in 1978, which was no less popular since only 12 months earlier he had played some of his finest golf at Turnberry only to be denied by Tom Watson.

For his many supporters it would have been too much to bear had Nicklaus been thwarted again but his prospects were not good as he trailed the slim New Zealander, Simon Owen, by a stroke with three to play. However, sheer class usually tells at such moments and sure enough the birdie Nicklaus got at the 16th while Owen was taking five was the telling blow.

Moreover, Nicklaus's long memory and attention to detail reminded him of the pace of the 17th green from years before in a following wind and the beautifully judged long putt he laid dead for his first four while Owen was taking five again gave him the necessary cushion for a second triumphant homecoming.

Just as it was at the 17th that Nicklaus was able to breathe easily again, so it was at the 17th that in 1984 Tom Watson saw a dream perish. All day he had stood on the threshold of a sixth Open championship which would have equalled the record of Harry Vardon.

But in front of him Severiano Ballesteros was scenting victory too, sharing the lead and safely through the 17th with a par four after playing a six iron second shot to the green. The clubbing is important for behind him Watson, having taken the braver line off the tee and skirting therefore the Old Course Hotel, opted for a two iron for a shot estimated to be 190 yards (174 m).

It was much too much and his ball skipped

One of Jack Nicklaus's proudest moments, winner of the Open championship for the first time in 1966 at Muirfield. It was on the same course in the 1959 Walker Cup match that he had made his first appearance in Britain.

Right: *Tony Lema had never played in Britain before but he still won the Open at St. Andrews in 1964.*

across the green against the stone wall from where he had to play an awkward chip. The five he took left him a stroke behind but already he knew it was too late for drifting down on the evening air was the mighty roar from the 18th green as Ballesteros holed from 15 feet (4.6 m) for a birdie. So it was by two strokes that the Spaniard won but the mere record of it tells little of the suspense that surrounds it.

Unashamedly, it is these modern Opens that command the most attention out of the 23 that have been played at St. Andrews. There seems to have been some drama at every turn, while in 1964 there was the satisfaction of seeing, just once, a very considerable player at his peak.

Two years later Tony Lema was to be killed in an air crash and a rare and graceful talent for the game was lost. Lema, moreover, made nonsense of the belief that to win the Open it was necessary to come over days in advance and learn the course off by heart. Lema had never played the Old Course before and he got in only 27 holes of practice.

But by sensible application and the eyes of a good caddie, Tip Anderson, who had also worked for Arnold Palmer, Lema's wonderful touch on and around the greens put him in increasingly firm control and despite a typical late assault from Nicklaus (66,68 in the last two rounds) Lema's 73,68,68,70 provided a winning margin of five strokes.

Below: *Australian Kel Nagle, winner of the 1960 Open at St. Andrews*

It was the arrival of Arnold Palmer for the Centenary Open at St. Andrews in 1960 that proved to be the launching pad of the championship as it is known today though, unlike Ben Hogan who in 1953 had similarly arrived as holder of both the Masters and US Open, Palmer did not win at his first attempt (he won it the next year).

Instead it was the rather underrated Kel Nagle, of Australia, winner the previous year of the Canada Cup with Peter Thomson, who played the best golf. He opened powerfully with rounds of 69 and 67 and though Palmer then made up four of the five strokes by which he had trailed at that point, his closing 68 fell just one short.

No one, of course, had graced the earlier years of the Open more than Bobby Locke, a courteous South African who played the game at what might be termed a gentlemanly pace. He never varied from it any more than he would vary the draw with which he hit the ball, even his putts.

It was fitting that the last of his four Open championship victories should be at St. Andrews in 1957, though its end was unusual. The championship had been moved from Muirfield at the last minute because of the petrol shortage during the Suez crisis and Locke, with rounds of 69,72 and 68 behind him, had to hole only a short putt on the last green to win by three strokes from Peter Thomson.

There is a tradition, if possible, for the new champion to hole the last putt of all and Locke marked his ball to allow Thomson to hole out, this being the first time that the leaders went out last. However, in marking his ball Locke had to move the marker a putter blade to one side. When replacing his ball he forgot 'the blade' and therefore holed out for a 70 from the wrong place. Technically, Locke could have been penalized.

Thomson, second this time, had already won in 1955 over the Old Course while the first post-war Open went, on a rare visit to these shores, to Sam Snead. At a time of austerity he compared it to 'camping out'.

Between the wars there had been only four Opens at St. Andrews and Bobby Jones's win in 1927 on a course he had loathed when first he had played it six years earlier became love at second sight.

Above: *In front of not the biggest gallery he has ever faced, Jack Nicklaus displays a delicate touch around the greens of St. Andrews in the 1970 Open.*

Left: *Jack Nicklaus 'lets it all out' as he drives during the Open championship at St. Andrews in 1978.*

Trevino's Good Fortune

Of all the golfers who have brought colour as well as consummate skill to the Open championship, none has been more popular than Lee Trevino. Mexican by birth, the son of a gravedigger, he is not what you would regard as a conventional golfer. He stands very open at the address position and gives the appearance that he is going to slice everything. Of course he does not.

Trevino has an instinct for the game born of a hard school in which he had to back himself at hitting a ball with everything from a bottle to a golf club one handed, just to pay for the next meal. Never was this nerve for survival more valuable than in the Open championship of 1972, which still stands as one of the most gripping and enjoyable of all.

All week the sun shone. Trevino was defending the title he had won at Royal Birkdale the previous year. Tony Jacklin was still at the height of his powers and Jack Nicklaus was on course for the Grand Slam since he had that year already won both the Masters and the US Open. All three remained the central figures, right until the last putt dropped.

If Nicklaus could have his time over again, he once told me, he would begin it on the 16th tee in the final round. He played those last three holes in one over par (4,5,4) when he was looking for 3,4,4, which would have been one under, but even so he had a marvellous 66 and it was very nearly good enough.

Disappointing though this was for him, it was Jacklin who tasted frustration at its worst. In the third round he seemed certain to lead until Trevino made birdies at each of the last five holes, holing from a bunker at the 16th and chipping in from off the back of the green at the 18th. Yet worse was to come.

On that final pulsating afternoon there was nothing between them until at the 17th Trevino took too bold a line from the tee and was badly bunkered. He could only just get the ball out, falling over backwards as he did so and was at that moment so resigned to defeat that he said to Jacklin: 'It's all yours Tony', which it appeared to be since Jacklin was only just short of the green in two.

When Trevino then pitched through the green in four, the position was even more hopeless but a chip over which he did not appear to take a great deal of care went in for a five while Jacklin of all things took six, three putting. And with a five at the last, Jacklin did not even finish second, falling behind Nicklaus who had lost by a shot.

By 1987 all the talk was of Ian Woosnam, who had just won the Scottish Open by a street and was already Europe's leading money winner in a season he was to dominate. No one paid too much attention to Nick Faldo, who had spent two years reconstructing a swing that had already served him well enough.

A British winner was in any case still something of a novelty, only Sandy Lyle having triumphed at Royal St. George's in 1985 since Jacklin had broken the ice in 1969. But Faldo was much closer to the sort of game he had long been seeking than he cared to admit publicly and for three days he dogged the footsteps of a young American, Paul Azinger.

There were two unusual features. Faldo did not lead on his own at any stage while he was playing. It was only after he had finished and could therefore do no more about his destiny that Azinger, needing a four at the last to tie, took five. The other presumably unique statistic was that Faldo played each of his last 18 holes in par.

But what are the feelings of man so close to the most glittering prize of all as he comes to the last hole? Faldo, with a rare turn for the descriptive, encapsulated it all in his account of his second shot, a five iron.

'Then comes this vital shot and you can't

Lee Trevino gets a warm embrace from 'Mr. Lu' after his Open victory at Royal Birkdale in 1971.

think about it. You have to hit it from memory. Then I had hit it and it was straight at the flag and I just wanted to shout "Cor, look at that." In its way it was like driving a car and you nearly have an accident. I went hot and cold all over at the same time and then it was all over.'

It was at Muirfield in 1966 that Nicklaus won his first Open championship, a happy homecoming since it was here in the 1959 Walker Cup match that he had first played golf in Britain. This was also the first time the championship was played over four days.

So deep was the rough that Doug Sanders said beforehand that he would like a concession on all the hay when it was cut! Nicklaus quickly recognized the perils that lay within it and preferred driving with his one iron rather than his driver.

It paid off and despite two closing 69s from David Thomas, who was therefore finishing runner-up for the second time (in this case shared by Sanders), Nicklaus got home by the stroke he clawed back with a birdie at the 17th hole.

To win the Open in three different decades, as Gary Player has done (1959, 1968 and 1974) is an exceptional performance and the 15 years which span his first and last victories is the third longest. J.H. Taylor's five championships spanned 19 years and Harry Vardon's six titles 18 years.

In fact Player won at Muirfield in 1959 from a modest field and with one of the worst opening rounds by a champion, a 75. But the great heart the golfing world came to know so well never faltered and with 71,70 and 68 he had the distinction of scoring progressively lower.

Henry Cotton's second victory in 1948 was the result of some of the most masterly driving the championship has seen while his second round of 66, with equal halves of 33, was as regal as his audience since among the gallery was King George VI, a keen golfer.

Between the wars there were only two Opens at Muirfield, victory by Walter Hagen in 1929 being gained by a large margin in awful weather, but for all the 13 championships that have come to these treasured links, only one man has won there twice and that was James Braid, one of the Triumvirate.

Above: *The putt that won him the 1987 Open. Nick Faldo on the 18th green at Muirfield as he holes out for his 18th successive par.*
Below: *A smartly dressed Gary Player holds the Open championship trophy after his first victory at Muirfield in 1959.*

Hagen, Cotton and Lyle

Henry Cotton was in the 1930s the supreme British golfer.

By common consent two golfers, one American and the other British, did more for the standing of their profession than any others. One was Walter Hagen and the other Henry Cotton. Both bore a similar outlook on life though it was Hagen who put it into words when he said that it was not necessary to be a millionaire, 'only to live like one'. By a coincidence, both won their first Open championships at Royal St. George's, Sandwich, Hagen in 1922 and Cotton in 1934.

When Hagen first played in the Open at Deal in 1920, he was told that the clubhouse was out of bounds to professionals and that instead he would have to use the pro's shop. Undeterred, he rented a limousine, parked it right outside the club's main entrance and had his chauffeur serve him lunch there.

In all respects Hagen was a showman but in between the banter and his apparent excesses he was able to turn his concentration on and off as if by a switch. He compelled attention whether you liked or disliked him and it was almost impossible to be indifferent.

Hagen finished far down the field at Deal, three times failing to break 80, but he improved the following year at St. Andrews and was confident enough at Sandwich in 1922 to spend one evening at his Ramsgate hotel putting on the carpet with some friends until 2 a.m. It was then that he claims he made his famous remark, on being told that most of his opponents were in bed: 'Maybe, but they are not sleeping.'

The man Hagen most feared that year was Jock Hutchison, the defending champion, who indeed led by two strokes going into the last round. Hagen had the services of some runners to keep him informed of Hutchison's progress and when his seemingly main rival had a 76 to his own 72, Hagen believed he was home and dry.

Instead, George Duncan was in the midst of one of the great last rounds, out in 34 and needing a four at the last for a 68 and a tie. Hagen had gone out to watch and it was with bated breath that he saw Duncan just miss the 18th green on the left from where he failed to give his chip quite enough to climb the steep little slope and took five. Ever since, this has been known as 'Duncan's Hollow' and many years on it almost brought about the downfall of Sandy Lyle.

There was none of Hagen's flamboyance about Cotton. A public schoolboy, his background was more upper middle class but he brought to the game a singlemindedness and determination that few have matched. His inspiration was his wife, Toots, whose own private means meant that he was able to enjoy a lifestyle that was the envy of his contemporaries.

Even so, Cotton would spend long hours on the practice ground and while it was his victory at Carnoustie in 1937 that gave him much technical satisfaction, it was that at Royal St. George's in 1934 that carried the greater significance.

It became known as the 'turning of the tide' after many years of American dominance and was built on two quite brilliant opening rounds of 67 and 65 for a 36-hole 132 that still stands as a record. Moreover, the 65 led to the naming of the Dunlop 65 ball that for 40 years had the biggest sales in Britain.

Above: *Bill Rogers enjoyed his finest hour when he won the 1981 Open at Royal St. George's, four strokes clear of Bernhard Langer.*

Left: *Walter Hagen putting out for his Open championship victory at Royal St. George's in 1928. Hats were then very much the fashion.*

Sandy Lyle has an abbreviated follow-through as he watches a tee shot in the 1985 Open at Sandwich.

No one could live with that sort of golf but for all his ability, Cotton was also an emotional man and the prospect of at last landing the great prize told on his nerves. He had to wait to tee off for his last round while stomach cramps left him nauseated and pale.

Suddenly his progress was much less assured than had ever seemed likely, and at one point it even began to appear that he might lose. But Cotton pulled himself together over the last six holes and though his final round of 79 hardly looks good on paper, he still won by five strokes from Sid Brews.

If the last six holes saved Cotton, it was the last five that were the making of Sandy Lyle. In 1985 the championship had appeared a straight fight between Bernhard Langer of West Germany, and David Graham of Australia, since they shared the lead three strokes ahead of the field with 18 holes to play.

Both, however, made a series of mistakes and Lyle, jogging quietly along in his usual manner, gradually found himself drawn into contention. It was the unexpected birdies he got at the 14th, where he had been in deep rough off the tee and short of the Suez Canal in two, and then at the always difficult 15th, that suddenly put him on top of the leaderboards.

A four at the last seemed almost certain to be good enough to secure the championship but Lyle, a strapping fellow of great natural strength, found Duncan's Hollow with his second shot and sank to his knees in despair when his chip did not quite mount the crest in the green and rolled back almost to his feet again. He still got a five, however, and, after an agonizing wait, saw the bids of Graham and Langer to catch him just fail. So ended 16 years without a British champion.

Bill Rogers, of America, had won rather easily at St. George's in 1981, bringing to an end an interval of 32 years during which the course, or rather the venue as a whole, was considered unsuitable for a modern championship. The previous one had been in 1949 when Bobby Locke, of South Africa, won the first of his four Opens after a tie with that genial Irishman, Harry Bradshaw, who was the victim of a most unusual incident.

At the fifth hole in the second round Bradshaw had driven into the rough and found his ball lying in a broken bottle. Not quite knowing what to do and this being an age when players were much more inclined to play the ball as it lay rather than ask for a ruling as they do now, Bradshaw simply swung at the bottle and hoped for the best. The hole cost him a six and but for that, who knows?

The story of the 1938 Open, won by Reg Whitcombe, one of three brothers, was all about the last day. Whitcombe scored 71,71 in the first two rounds and 75,78 in the third and fourth when the lowest score of the day was 74 by Cotton. Many were the returns in the 80s and two even in the 90s.

It was the weather of course that did it, a savage gale ripping down the exhibition marquee and making golf almost impossible. Whitcombe twice took four putts but his clipped swing was eminently more suitable than that of the more flowing Jimmy Adams in such conditions and a high total of 295 was still low enough.

Jones en Route for Grand Slam

It was at Hoylake in 1930 that Bobby Jones, whom some believe to have been the greatest golfer of all time, completed the second leg of the Grand Slam. A few weeks earlier he had survived what always seemed to him to be the most difficult hurdle, the Amateur championship at St. Andrews. Now he added to it the Open championship. Soon, after a ticker-tape reception in New York, he was to add the United States Open at Interlachen and the US Amateur at Merion.

In those days there was nothing like the same number of tournaments as there is now and amateurs were much more the equals, or nearly so, of the professionals. No amateur has won the Open chamionship since Jones and only one, Johnny Goodman, in 1933, the US Open.

Jones's record speaks for itself. In the Open he played four times and won three of them. In the US Open he made 11 appearances and won it four times; indeed, between 1922 and 1930 there was only one year (1927) in which he wasn't either winner or runner up. He won the US Amateur five times in 13 attempts, was twice beaten in the final and was twice a semi-finalist. He made three attempts at the British Amateur and won it once.

The strain of it all nevertheless told very much on him. He was often sick with tension and always lost weight during a championship. While he awaited the outcome of the Open at Hoylake, he had to use both hands to hold a glass of whisky and declared there and then 'never again'. He kept his word and retired after conquering what he always referred to as the Impregnable Quadrilateral.

Though Jones had some difficulty with the opening holes at Hoylake he still led by a stroke at half-way; but just as he was going out for his last round, the mighty Archie Compston came storming through like a whirlwind with a 68 to edge in front by a stroke.

It was an unnerving time for Jones, especially at the second when a wayward drive hit a steward on the head. No damage was done however, either physically or in golfing terms, for Jones still made a birdie. However, it was the seven he took at the eighth, five of them from just short of the green, that pulled him up dead in his tracks.

For a while it seemed that he could not even think straight, and he played on as if in a daze. It was the 16th that became his crucial hole. Going for the green in two, he instead found a difficult lie in the left-hand bunker. He had to stand with one foot in the sand and the other on the bank behind him but with a massive concave wedge Horton Smith had given him, Jones manufactured a stroke of genius for his

Bobby Jones at Hoylake in his Grand Slam year of 1930. His balance is perfect as another drive finds the centre of the fairway.

birdie and at that moment the championship became his.

It was this same 16th hole that was to play a key part in the last Open to be played at Hoylake, in 1967. The winner was Roberto de Vicenzo, from Argentina. He was one of the most popular visitors to these shores, as both his grace as a golfer and the gentle humour of his disposition appealed very much to the British public. He also had a fine record in the Open, second to Locke in 1950 and seven other finishes in the top four. But at the age of 44, his time was running out.

Jack Nicklaus and Gary Player were the favourites and though Nicklaus, the defending champion, led at half-way, Vicenzo overtook him with a third round of 67. Clive Clark headed the British challenge until he had a disastrous start to his final round of 6,5,5 (out of bounds at the first!) and gradually it developed into a straight fight between Vicenzo and Nicklaus.

Vicenzo was still ahead as he came to the 16th but his second shot, which had to be played over the corner of the out-of-bounds that is the practice ground, was a crucial shot in the circumstances. However, the ball flew straight and true and I can recall it still climbing against a blue sky before coming to rest on the green. The final corner had been turned and soon Vicenzo, a tall, erect, beam-

ing figure came home to a standing ovation.

The most significant Open victory at Hoylake was that by Sandy Herd in 1902. It changed the whole face of the game because Herd was the first man to use the new-fangled rubber-cored ball, known as the Haskell after its inventor. Ironically, Herd had earlier been outspoken in his condemnation of the ball, saying: 'It drives all right but that is about all I can say about it.'

Harry Vardon was of the same opinion, neither of them liking its more lively characteristics when putting as opposed to the established gutta percha. However, while practising for the Open with John Ball, Herd was handed one to try again and clearly had second thoughts. When he won by a stroke from Vardon and Braid, demand for the ball became so great that, until supply improved, they were selling at around £1–10 shillings, the equivalent today of £45!

At about this time golf was beginning to spread to the Continent, taken there by British amateurs enjoying exotic holidays in such places as Biarritz. There the local youths earned money as caddies and one of them, Arnaud Massy, became not only a professional but Open champion at Hoylake in 1907.

Massy had first played in Herd's Open, gained instant respect and took a club-making appointment with Ben Sayers at North Berwick. A finely built man with broad shoulders, he also married a Scottish girl. Experience of playing golf amid the Atlantic winds at Biarritz stood him in good stead, particularly on the first day when many scores were in the 80s, and a measure of Massy's two-stroke victory was that he eclipsed Vardon, Braid and Taylor, the famous Triumvirate who all finished close behind.

Peter Thomson's victory in 1956 was also notable, for it was his third in succession, the only time this has been done since the championship went to 72 holes in 1892. The Open was not then attracting much of an American entry but one who was there was the mighty hitting Mike Souchak.

Thomson never had to rely on strength. He was much more a controller of the ball, a measured, seemingly effortless swing being a model for others to copy. Consistent impact is the key and never more so than in bad weather, which was the case at Hoylake that year. Thomson was in a class of his own in winning by three strokes from Flory Van Donck. He was second a year later, won again in 1958 and again in 1965. Such a record is unsurpassed in modern times.

Roberto de Vicenzo, whose Open championship victory at Hoylake in 1967 was one of the most popular by an overseas player.

Opposite top: *Peter Thomson won the second of his five Open titles at Hoylake in 1956.*

Opposite bottom: *Every golfer goes through a practice routine before venturing on to the course. Here Peter Thomson launches himself into a fairway wood.*

Duncan's Recovery

George Duncan's victory at Royal Cinque Ports, Deal, in 1920 was remarkable in that he had to all intents and purposes put himself out of the championship with first and second rounds each time of 80, but the 1920 championship is of interest also as it represents the revival of the Open after the First World War.

Such was the fairly haphazard organization in those days that the play-off scores came from a concurrent tournament on the Eden course and already there were moves afoot to improve the running of the Open which, until then, had been in the hands of the club whose turn it was to host the championship.

The 1920 championship at Deal – their second and also their last – was therefore managed for the first time by the R & A, and they have managed subsequent Opens with increasing success ever since. Prize money, it is worth recalling, was £225 in 1920, with £75 going to the winner.

By now the days of Vardon, Braid and Taylor were over and the public was looking to a new generation to stimulate their appetites. Prominent among these were Duncan and Mitchell, whose close friendship with Samuel Ryder was in due course to lead to the founding of the Ryder Cup. Mitchell, however, to his mentor's intense disappointment never won the Open, though he deserved to have done.

It was Duncan who created the golfing philosophy that, 'if you are going to miss 'em, miss 'em quick' for he was an extremely fast player. He was a natural games player and at one time was tempted to become a professional footballer, being similarly fleet of foot.

While Duncan was a dashing man about the links, Mitchell, a former gardener, was much more methodical, relying very much on the strength of his hands, wrists and forearms. They were close friends and indeed had an agreement whereby they shared prize-money.

After 36 holes Mitchell (74,75) had a three-stroke lead at Deal and in his own interest as much as anything, Duncan advised him not to get to the course too early on the day of the last two rounds.

But Mitchell was a natural worrier. He could not rest and when he arrived at the course news soon reached him that Duncan, whom everyone had dismissed as out of it, was going great guns. Indeed he had finished a 71 third round just as Mitchell was setting out, by now so full of jitters that when he faced an 18 in (46 cm) putt on the first green, he left the ball a foot (30 cm) short!

Mitchell took a disastrous 84 in that third round and in one fell swoop his 13-stroke lead over Duncan was gone. There was now no stopping Duncan and with a last round of 72 he swept past his one remaining obstacle, Sandy Herd, to win by three strokes. Mitchell was meanwhile totally drained and, some said, never quite the same player again.

Deal's only other Open had been in 1909, this being at the height of the reign of the Triumvirate and J.H. Taylor's four-stroke win from James Braid tied the two of them, together with Harry Vardon, at four wins each. No doubt it was a measure of their golf that Taylor's total of 295 was eight strokes better than that of Duncan on the same course 11 years on.

Eyes right as spectators follow the flight of a George Duncan drive at Hoylake in 1930.

Sarazen Returns

Gene Sarazen's promise that he would keep coming back until he won the Open, swimming the Atlantic if necessary, was more ironic than he realized at the time. A depressed American economy in 1932 almost led to his cancelling his voyage until his wife, Mary, went out and borrowed the money to help meet his expenses for the sea voyage.

However, he had a special interest in playing this year because all winter he had been experimenting with what he called his 'secret weapon' – the sand wedge. Until then there had not been an effective club for getting out of bunkers and the broader and flatter club head which Sarazen designed prompted the club to bounce off the sand rather than dig in, which the sharper-bladed clubs tended to do.

There was another important factor in Sarazen's victory. Some years before, Walter Hagen had loaned him a caddie by the name of Skip Daniels when the Open was played in 1928 at Royal St. George's. It was a happy partnership. But by 1932 Daniels was in failing health and Sarazen found another caddie en route to Prince's. They were not, however, the same team at all and when Sarazen heard how despondent Daniels was, he promptly re-engaged him. Through the six rounds of the Open – everybody in those days had to go through two qualifying rounds – Daniels's word on club selection was law and when his life came to an end a few months later, he died a happy man.

The year before, Sarazen had finished in a tie for third place behind Tommy Armour at Carnoustie and in preparation for his assault at Prince's he went on a special diet as well as making a point of practising at home in the cold weather. He knew all about the bleakness of Kent.

Sarazen qualified comfortably with a 73 at Prince's and then a 76 at Royal St. George's. Having negotiated that minor hurdle, he led throughout the championship proper. A 70 late on the first day eased him ahead of Macdonald Smith, Percy Alliss, Charles Whitcombe and W.H. Davies, and though Alliss followed with another 71 on the second day amid the mournful booming of foghorns out in the Channel, Sarazen was inspired.

Great recovery play early on, some of it with his sand wedge, steadied him and he was out in 35. Coming to the 18th Sarazen needed a four for a 68 but pulled his second shot and then missed a quite short putt. Even so he was now three strokes clear.

The third and fourth rounds were then played on one day and Sarazen got something of a fright when Arthur Havers, the last Briton to have won the championship, at Troon in 1923, came in with a third round of 68. It narrowed the gap between them to four strokes but Sarazen's 70 showed no signs of weakness. He tired a little in the afternoon with a 74 but Havers took 76 and it was Macdonald Smith who finished runner up, five strokes behind.

The following day Bernard Darwin wrote of Sarazen: 'There could be no more popular winner, as there could be no more deserving one. He is a truly great golfer in every possible sense of the word and long may we see the delightful grin that spreads across his cheerful olive face as a doubtful putt drops in.'

Gene Sarazen battles his way through heavy rain during one round of the 1927 Open at St. Andrews.

Jacklin's Hour of Glory

Tony Jacklin at Royal Lytham in 1969 when, with a last round of 72, he brought the Open championship trophy home after 18 years without a British winner.

The note pinned to the door of Tony Jacklin's locker at Royal Lytham during the Open championship of 1969 consisted of only one word: 'Tempo'. He found it on the morning of the final day, left there by his good friend, Tom Weiskopf, who was already out on the course.

Weiskopf knew how important an afternoon it was going to be, not only for Jacklin but also for British golf and its supporters. For 18 years, since Max Faulkner won at Royal Portrush, they had been unable to acclaim a British winner, but now Jacklin was two strokes ahead of Bob Charles, with just 18 holes to play.

Already, Jacklin had made his mark. He had had the vision and bravery to test himself during a prolonged spell in America, and winning there had given him the proof that he had 'the game' to succeed in the highest company.

For two days he had dogged the footsteps of Charles, the only left-hander ever to have won the championship, or indeed any of the four major championships. Jacklin had a 68 to the New Zealander's 66 in the first round, a 70 to a 69 in the second. But on the third, the chief memory of which remains a succession of beautifully played, delicate bunker shots, he somehow kept his score down to 70 while Charles took 75. The boot at last was on the other foot.

Jacklin realized full well the importance of 'tempo' and when he went to the practice ground he used only one club, the seven iron. It was the one with which he felt most confident, and it was the one with which he played his last shot, apart from his putter.

Of course there were some missed heart-beats along the way but at length he came to the last still two ahead, his only remaining hurdle those angled bunkers far down the 18th fairway. Never was a good drive more important and seldom in such circumstances has one been hit so straight and true with such balance, precision or such tempo.

With his seven iron Jacklin found the middle of the green and then promptly disappeared amid the converging, stampeding hoards of spectators. He lost his shoe, found it again and with two putts, the second so short that he could have almost blown the ball into the hole, he was champion.

Ten years on, another favourite son, Severiano Ballesteros, won an equally celebrated victory at Lytham. When in 1976 Ballesteros had led for three rounds at Royal Birkdale before being overtaken by Johnny Miller, it was said that this was probably the best thing because the Spaniard was still very young, only 19. It could have been too much, too soon.

Now at Lytham he was 22 but that youthful abandon that sent his golf ball careering in some unlikely directions was still very much a part of his game. Scores through the first three rounds of 73,65,75 reflected the erratic quality of his golf, and it seemed likely that the greater experience and steadiness of Hale Irwin, who led by a stroke going into the last round, would prevail.

Instead, Irwin was totally destroyed by some golf that he could hardly believe. In 18 holes Ballesteros found only one fairway with his driver and he missed every one of the last six, which is supposed to be the hardest part of the golf course. No wonder Irwin, on arriving at the last green, pulled from his pocket a white handkerchief which he waved in surrender.

'I cannot believe anyone can drive as badly as that and still win an Open,' said Irwin later, more in amazement than criticism. In four rounds Ballesteros was in 15 greenside bunkers and only twice failed to get up and down in two.

A little harshly, he became known as the 'car park champion' because at the 16th in the last round he drove so far right that his ball finished under the wheels of a parked car. Yet he still got a birdie for the exquisiteness of his pitching and putting showed a touch given to very few.

The first time the Open was played at Lytham was in 1926 when it was won by Bobby Jones, though he only entered at the last minute. He had come over with the American Walker Cup team and was due to return with them on the *Aquitania*. He cancelled his reservation because he felt he owed the Open something, after having torn up his card in the third round at St. Andrews in 1921.

There was that year a regional qualifying round and the 66 Jones returned at Sunningdale has gone down as one of the most technically perfect ever played – 33 shots and 33 putts. At Lytham it was just one shot that turned imminent defeat into victory.

Despite some abysmal putting, Jones was level with Al Watrous with two holes to play but whereas Watrous found the middle of the 17th fairway, Jones hooked into a bunker and had no sight of the green 175 yards (160 m) away beyond clumps of intervening gorse. But with a minimum of preparation, he picked the

Bob Charles, the only left hander ever to win a major championship. He triumphed at Royal Lytham in 1963.

shot clean with his mashie iron, found the green and perhaps so surprised his opponent that Watrous three-putted.

This proved to be the decisive stroke by a man who in his time was just as popular with the British public as Arnold Palmer and Jack Nicklaus were to become years later. Jones also had humility. During the luncheon interval between the third and fourth rounds, Jones left the course with his chronicler, O.B. Keeler, for some ham sandwiches and tea in his nearby hotel. When he returned he realized that he had left behind his player's badge and was refused entry. Rather than make a fuss, Jones simply paid up just as if he were a spectator.

There has not been a tie in the championship since 1975 but there have been two at Lytham, both over 36 holes which was then the style – no sudden deaths in those days! In 1958 Peter Thomson defeated David Thomas, a big amiable Welshman who would have had much more success had he been able to pitch, while Bob Charles got the better of Phil Rodgers, a bubbling American, in 1963.

Any number of players might have won in 1958 for Eric Brown, who had had a 65 in the third round, looked a winner all the way when he needed a four at the last for a 69 and a total of 277. Instead he took six and eventually tied third.

Thomson and Thomas came next, dead level and needing fours to overtake Brown, which they both got. But that was not the end of it for behind them emerged that great Irishman, Christy O'Connor, and the Argentine, Leopoldo Ruiz, both with fours to tie, threes to win.

The scoring system was nothing like as informative as it is today and when both holed out it transpired that O'Connor had taken five via a bunker and Ruiz a seven after three attempts to get the ball out of another bunker. O'Connor therefore tied third with Brown, and Ruiz fifth with Flory Van Donck, of Belgium.

Hale Irwin congratulates Severiano Ballesteros on his Open championship victory at Royal Lytham in 1969, though afterwards he did say that he did not believe that anybody could drive as badly as that and still win.

Palmer's Honesty

Arnold Palmer had already that year won the Masters and the US Open when he first challenged for the centenary Open championship at St. Andrews in 1960. The third leg of the quadrilateral eluded him as he finished second to Kel Nagle but he determined to return and he was successful on each of his next two visits, at Royal Birkdale in 1961 and then at Troon in 1962.

The resurrection of the Open to, and ultimately beyond, its former status hinged very much on Palmer's presence. As the greatest and most identifiable golfer in the world at that time, he was a sort of Pied Piper to other Americans and the lead he gave to the game cannot be over-emphasized.

In thumbing through the files it is not often that one can select a round as apparently commonplace as a 73 as being of special significance, but anyone who was at Birkdale on that turbulent Thursday of the second round of the 1961 Open would place Palmer's very high on the list. Closer examination reveals that only one player, Peter Thomson, beat it with a 72 but the average score for the day was more like 76, many failing even to break 80.

I can remember at least two other occasions, one at a PGA championship at Royal St. George's and the other at a Spanish Open in La Manga, when Palmer set himself against the elements and it is therefore not difficult to imagine him, swathed in sweaters and waterproofs, jaw set firm and vast hands veritably glued to the grips of his clubs, relishing the challenge of it all.

His golf that day, for a spell at least, he still rates as just about the best of his life, for with the gale at its height, he played the first six holes in what was then five under par. He was out in 34 and only three other players scored less than 40.

Some idea of the strength of the wind that day can be judged by the fact that Palmer could not get near the second green in two, then a par five, and nowhere near the sixth either, also a par five. The short fourth was a one iron and the artful sixth a drive and six iron. Only at the fourth did he not get a birdie.

Par for the course was then 74 and when Palmer came in with 73 on his card, there was not one witness to the round who would have not sworn it should have been a 72. At the 16th, now the 17th, he was bunkered beside the green, he slightly thinned his recovery and took an apparent six. But as Palmer played that recovery, his ball had moved a fraction. Only he knew it but he called the shot on himself without hesitation and the six went down as a seven.

It might have had a crucial bearing on the championship but happily it did not, Palmer finishing with rounds of 69 and 72 to beat Dai Rees by a stroke.

Not even the best player plays every shot as he intended. Arnold Palmer can hardly believe where this one has finished.

Thomson's Success

By a coincidence Peter Thomson had also won his first Open at Birkdale, six years earlier, and by a further coincidence it was another bunker on the same hole that had played a crucial role. Rees, Bobby Locke and Sid Scott had already set a target of 284 and Thomson needed to play the last three holes in 4,3,4, par as the course was then, to win.

The 16th, now the 17th, was then a long par four and Thomson slightly pulled his second with a wood into the bunker furthest from the green. It left him with a blind shot of some 25 yards (23 m) over the shoulder of a dune and it had to be both judged and executed with absolute precision if he was to save his par.

Thomson did just that, pitching to 2 feet (0.6 m) but later, the first of his five championships under his belt, he almost dismissed the shot, saying modestly how perfect the lie had been, firm sand and a slight upslope. This was typical of the Australian, a man of intellect to whom golf was a means to an end rather than an end in itself. In the next four years of the championship he was first, first, second and first again and the rhythm and balance of his model swing helped to make golf in the fifties more golden than they would otherwise have been.

It is no doubt a measure of Birkdale as a golf course that all its Opens seem to have been good ones. Thomson came back again in 1965 to win his fifth title and vivid still too are the memories of Lee Trevino's first win in 1971. A month or so earlier he had beaten Jack Nicklaus in a play-off for the US Open at Merion, and had picked up the Canadian Open en route to Birkdale, where he arrived with little time for proper preparation but still talking nineteen to the dozen.

Tony Jacklin was very much a force in the game at this time but it was not Jacklin who gave Trevino his biggest fright but Lu Liang Huan, of Taiwan, who became better known as 'Mr. Lu' since he politely kept raising his little blue pork pie hat to the cheers of the crowd. A seven at the 17th in the last round might have unseated Trevino but he kept his head just as Mr. Lu did when he felled a woman spectator with an errant shot down the last but still took second place on his own.

Peter Thomson was a master of every type of shot, even this one from an awkward downhill lie.

Miller and Watson

Johnny Miller's sporadic brilliance had manifested itself in the United States Open of 1973 and three years later he had his reward as well in the 1976 Open at Royal Birkdale with a commanding victory. He won in the end by six strokes, though, as it happens, the championship will probably be remembered as much for the emergence of the then 19-year-old Spaniard, Severiano Ballesteros.

So limited was the English of Ballesteros that he had to have an interpreter accompany him each day to the Press tent as he either shared the lead or led on his own through the first three rounds. Yet it was not so much the fact that the young Spaniard set the pace as the manner in which he set it that captured the hearts of the nation.

In a way it was like watching a young Palmer all over again, raw aggression sending Ballesteros ploughing into the rough again and again in search of his ball amid the dunes but then, amid flying grass and sand, repeatedly finding the green from where, as often as not, he would hole the putt.

In the end the gas finally ran out, particularly when, under the fierce spotlight of the final round, Miller was able to summon experience as well as great skill to produce a 66, the second lowest concluding round by a champion.

The lowest score is Tom Watson's 65 at Turnberry the following year, four of his five championships being won in Scotland. The other was gained at Royal Birkdale in 1983 and beautifully he played too with rounds of 67,68,70,70, though it was only good enough to win by a stroke from Andy Bean and Hale Irwin who, at the 14th, went to tap in a minute putt one handed and missed the ball altogether. No one can exactly say 'but for that'. Even so, he will always wonder.

A supreme test for the champion is to find himself standing on the 18th tee needing a four to win particularly when the hole is playing quite long, as it was that year at 473 yards (432 m). Watson needed, therefore, a two iron to get home with his second shot. It is just about the most difficult club in the bag but Watson hit the most perfect shot with it at precisely the right time.

Left: *Johnny Miller holes another putt in his Open championship victory at Royal Birkdale in 1976. He had a last round of 66.*

Below: *All Tom Watson could hope to do was get the ball out of one of Royal Birkdale's more difficult bunkers. But he still won the title in 1983.*

Weiskopf Conquers Troon

There was a certain majesty about Tom Weiskopf, both in his always erect bearing and in the manner of his golf. At 6 ft 3 in (190 cm) he was above what is supposed to be the ideal height for a golfer but he had a swing that came right out of the text book. Jack Nicklaus, with whom his career ran parallel for a time, more than once suggested that if Weiskopf ever realized just how good he was, nobody would touch him.

The tall, courteous Arthur Havers, winner of the 1923 Open at Troon.

Certainly there was no more thrilling sight than Weiskopf at full bore, his drives and long irons whistling straight and far down the fairway, delivered there by a balance and timing that seemed to require little physical effort, just an easy 'lean' into the ball.

But there is more to golf than just hitting the ball and the one flaw in Weiskopf was that he had a temper. He could become a very angry man on the golf course and for some reason angry men are also unlucky. Four times Weiskopf was runner-up in the Masters, once second in the US Open, in which he was also third twice, and once third in the PGA. There was therefore justice that one of golf's most prized crowns, the Open championship, did not elude him.

Weiskopf won at Troon in 1973 and his victory had two distinctions. He was the first man since Henry Cotton in 1934 to lead from first to last, and his aggregate of 276 equalled the then championship record set by Arnold Palmer, also at Troon, in 1962.

This was fine play though it was not in fact a championship that entirely captured the imagination, largely, I think, because the weather was so bad. It rained a good deal and that is always dispiriting.

Already that year Weiskopf had won three American tournaments, as well as being second on three other occasions, and he led by a stroke after the first round with a 68, by three after a second round of 67 and by one again after a third round 71.

There was nevertheless anticipation going into the final round for the man breathing down Weiskopf's neck was Johnny Miller, who earlier that summer had snatched a thrilling US Open victory at Oakmont with a closing 63. This time there was no such spark for Miller made a mistake early in the last round. Weiskopf punished it with a birdie and he sailed home a deserved if somewhat soaked champion.

No one can ever tell how often opportunity will knock. For some of course it comes many times but for others very occasionally, perhaps only once. If it is then spurned, it may never come again and the 1982 Open at Troon will always go down as the one a young South African, Nick Price, lost.

This may appear disrespectful to Tom Watson, who became only the fifth man to win the Open and US Open in the same year, it also being his fourth 'British'. Watson did after all have a pretty sterling last round of 70 but even so it was Price's errors over the final stretch of Troon that let the American in, a lead of three strokes with six to play being lost.

Price was nevertheless not the only player to let opportunity slip, for the first two rounds were dominated by the young American,

Bobby Clampett, 67 and then 66 giving him a five-stroke lead with the second-best 36-hole aggregate (133) ever recorded.

But Clampett was to blow up, which left Price in the driving seat, particularly so when in the last round he turned for home with three successive birdies at the 10th, 11th and 12th. Watson was playing several holes ahead of the South African and when he dropped a shot at the 15th, he thought his chance had gone. He spent nearly an hour in the clubhouse, unable to do anything but watch the scoreboard.

It was an agonizing wait as first Price lost a stroke at the 13th after a pulled drive and then two at the 15th where he took six after another hook and then a mis-hit recovery into a bunker. Now it was three pars just to tie and when Price came up short at the 17th to drop yet another stroke, a dream was just a dream.

The Open was first played at Troon in 1923, though only because some course changes were being made at Muirfield. The opportunity was eagerly taken and history also made by the clubhouse being opened to competing professionals.

There was also controversy beforehand when the R & A outlawed some 'punched face' clubs that had become popular with the best players because they enabled more 'bite' on the approach shots. The Troon professional, Duncan McCulloch, had to work through the night filing them all down.

The championship was also notable for the victory of Arthur Havers. A tall, courteous man noted for his iron play, Havers had survived some tempestuous weather in which one competitor, Aubrey Boomer, in playing out of a bunker, hit his ball into his jacket pocket.

This was the year that Gene Sarazen, the US Open champion, made his first appearance and failed to qualify and it was therefore Walter Hagen, the defending champion, who became the chief threat to Havers. Afterwards Havers said that he had little idea that he was in contention until the last three holes and then played them in one under par, holing for a three from a bunker at the last.

As fate would have it Hagen, needing a birdie as well to tie at the last, was in the same bunker. In his autobiography he said that it was not a difficult shot and having sized it up from all sides, got exactly the right line but left his ball just 18 inches (46 cm) short.

It was not until 1950 that the Open returned to Troon, Bobby Locke making a successful defence of the championship. The story goes that beforehand Norman Von Nida enquired of the championship committee whether it was their intention to continue watering the already perfect greens. When informed that they would, Von Nida declared the championship to be Locke's and backed him with the bookmakers. The South African won by two strokes from Roberto de Vicenzo.

Tom Weiskopf lines up a putt on Troon's 5th green during the 1973 Open, which he won by three strokes from Neil Coles and Johnny Miller.

Arnold Palmer's win at Troon in 1962 was a runaway affair. He was then at the height of his career, had taken the trophy in some rough weather at Royal Birkdale 12 months earlier and now destroyed both the course and the field. Once he had overtaken the first round leader, Peter Thomson, there was no holding him and with 71,69,67,69, he had six holes to spare from Kel Nagle and 13 from Brian Huggett and Phil Rodgers. It was hardly a contest.

Hogan's Progression at Carnoustie

They called Ben Hogan the 'wee ice mon' when he won the Open at Carnoustie in 1953. His every shot and round was carefully planned after many hours of practice.

A recent feature of the Open championship has been the arrival of the leading Americans by Concorde on the Monday evening – often making a low sweep of the course – which leaves them only two clear days for practice. Compare this with the time Ben Hogan gave himself at Carnoustie in 1953.

It was his one assault on this particular golfing Everest, a decision not taken lightly, for Hogan was still a victim of the fearful injuries he had suffered in a car crash a few years earlier and had to plan his programme with care.

He crossed the Atlantic by boat and moved into the old Bruce Hotel, which overlooked the course, two weeks before the championship was due to begin. It became in a sense his Operations Room, where he plotted his strategy to become the only man in the game's history to win the Open, US Open and Masters all in the same year. No one else has come so close to the Grand Slam.

After his arrival, Hogan first walked the course, studying its features, perhaps even pacing it for the yardage chart was not then a part of the professional golfer's armoury. Then he started playing it. His routine would be practice in the morning, lunch and then 18 holes with two or three balls on every hole.

It was the first time Hogan had played the smaller 1.62 in (4.1 cm) ball which was in common usage in Britain at that time and this was a challenge in itself because he had heard it said the small ball would never suit his deep faced clubs. How emphatically he proved otherwise.

By such long preparation Hogan obviously hoped to play the course in all its moods and winds. Yet when it came to the day itself he had to hit a drive and two iron to the first green whereas on every other occasion that he had played the hole, it had been nothing more than a light eight iron second shot.

Hogan's putt for a birdie finished short and this at once reflected the one flaw in his overall performance; he never quite adjusted to greens very much slower than they are in America. Even so, his progression through the field after an opening round of 73, three strokes behind the amateur, Frank Stranahan, was remorseless.

In sequence his rounds were 73,71,70,68, Stranahan with a 69 in the last round being the only other player to break 70 all week. It was not until the end of the third round that Hogan jointly led the field with Roberto de Vicenzo but from past experience he knew that the adrenalin would be in full flood for the

afternoon's last round and he then hit the ball so much further that he eased a club down for all his second shots.

His ultimate triumph was by then inevitable and nothing has been passed down into history more than Hogan's play of the par five sixth. In each round he took the bold line between the out of bounds fence on the left and the bunker, and eye witnesses still swear that every time he aimed his drive over the fence and let the wind drift it back into play. Such was the extreme confidence of the supreme golfer in the world at that time. He won by four strokes from Stranahan, Dai Rees, Peter Thomson and Tony Cerda.

If the most celebrated of Henry Cotton's three Open championship victories was that at Royal St. George's in 1934, Cotton himself just rates that at Carnoustie in 1937 as the better performance. The reason was that the Ryder Cup had been played at Southport and Ainsdale shortly before, the Americans had won quite comfortably and the whole of that victorious team made their way north to Scotland.

And quite a force it was, too, with Horton Smith, Sam Snead, Byron Nelson, Densmore Shute, Ralph Guldahl, Gene Sarazen and even Walter Hagen all competing. Yet another member of that team, Ed Dudley, led at the end of the first round with a 70.

Cotton began with a 74 and followed with a 72 which kept him in touch with the new leader, Reg Whitcombe, who was on 142, two ahead of his brother, Charles, while Shute and Alf Padgham were bracketed with Cotton on 146. Horton, Hagen, Dai Rees and the young Bobby Locke were also very much in the thick of things.

The final day was one of the worst in the championship's history and but for the cutting of new holes at lunch to combat the mounting tide of rain, it probably would never have been finished. Reg Whitcombe still led with 18 holes to play but Cotton had narrowed the gap and was now scenting victory.

His golf in the last round showed tremendous resolution for despite being soaked to the skin, every item of equipment saturated, he went through the turn in 35, which was tremendous golf. Huge crowds, quite undeterred by the increasing downpour, simply willed Cotton to win and though he faltered by dropping a stroke at the 15th, he played the last three without a tremor, his 71 leaving him with two strokes to spare from Reg Whitcombe.

No doubt dearer to Scottish hearts was the victory by Tommy Armour in 1931. One of the great teachers of the game, he had been born in Edinburgh but emigrated to America where he made his fortune. Already he was a former American Open and PGA champion and now, as the local boy who made good, he came home to triumph on his native soil.

The 1938 Open at Royal St. George's suffered some of the worst gales. Not even Henry Cotton could keep the ball straight all the time and he finished third behind Reg Whitcombe.

It was not easily gained as his scores progressed 73,75,77 but a 71 in the last turned the tables as Jose Jurado of Argentina, needing a 75 to win, found the pressure too much over the last nine holes and finished second by a stroke.

It was at Carnoustie in 1968 that Gary Player won the second of his three Opens as he held off Jack Nicklaus and Bob Charles though the best chance had probably been in the hands of Billy Casper until he drove out of bounds at the 14th, where Player had an eagle three.

But already there were question marks as to Carnoustie's suitability as an Open championship venue and, to date, the 1975 championship has been their last. It has also been the last in which a play-off has been necessary, Tom Watson beating the Australian, Jack Newton, over 18 holes (71 against 72) after they had tied on 279.

Watson, like Tony Lema a few years before, was a winner at the first attempt but it was far from being his last. Newton was less fortunate. Some years later he was to lose an arm and an eye in an accident involving the propeller of an aeroplane.

Watson's Finest Hour

It was not until 1977 that the Open championship was first played at Turnberry and, in the opinion of Gary Player, it will never be surpassed. Since Player was on this occasion no more than a member of the supporting cast, this is praise indeed. Still, few would take issue with him.

Earlier that year Tom Watson and Jack Nicklaus had had a dramatic confrontation in the Masters at Augusta, Watson winning by two strokes with a final round of 67 despite a last desperate thrust by Nicklaus, who had a superb 66.

Yet even that paled by comparison with the titanic duel they had in the blazing sunshine – admittedly interrupted on one occasion by a summer storm – at Turnberry when, from first to last, Watson and Nicklaus were locked together so closely and ultimately so far ahead of the field that the arena seemed to be theirs and theirs alone.

Again it was Watson, the new heir to the throne of world golfing supremacy, who won but the old king did not abdicate without a fight and what a fight! Records tumbled in all directions and it was only by a single stroke that Nicklaus lost. Hubert Green was third another 10 strokes behind and he later described himself with a wry smile as 'the winner of the other tournament'.

Never, before nor since, has there been golf like it as Watson and Nicklaus matched one another shot for shot in the third round with 65s apiece before Watson got home by a short head with another 65 in the fourth against Nicklaus's 66.

The pace had been hot from the first day when John Schroeder, son of Ted Schroeder, the former Wimbledon singles champion, stole the lead amid lengthening evening shadows with an opening 66. Watson and Nicklaus both had 68s for a share of third place and with

Jack Nicklaus gives his drive one last look before stooping to remove his tee peg in his classic confrontation with Tom Watson at Turnberry in 1977.

Though Tom Watson beat Jack Nicklaus by a stroke in the 1977 Open at Turnberry, it was far from plain sailing.

second rounds of 70 had moved into a tie with Green and Lee Trevino a stroke behind another American, Roger Maltbie, after 36 holes.

Briefly it was Nicklaus who drew ahead in the third round with an outward half of 31 to 33 but Watson got the strokes back coming home in 32 against 34 and both were round in 65, five under par. They were three strokes clear and the eyes of the world were on them.

Within four holes on the last day Nicklaus had again slipped the noose, three strokes ahead with two birdies while Watson also dropped a shot at the second. But by the turn the margin was back to one, until Nicklaus eased himself two clear again at the 12th with a birdie.

Watson got the stroke back with a three at the 14th but it was the putt he holed from off the green at the short 15th for a two that stopped Nicklaus in his tracks. He very slightly underclubbed to the 17th, chipped well but failed with his putt and went behind to Watson's birdie four.

Suddenly, it seemed, the championship had been decided, particularly when Nicklaus, going for the big drive at the 18th, almost put his ball in the gorse on the far side of the dog-leg. It was an even more hopeless cause when Watson, having found the middle of the fairway, then hit a seven iron to within some 18 inches (46 cm) of the flag.

But Nicklaus, summoning himself for one last fling, hit a great recovery from long grass to the right-hand edge of the green and then, the embodiment still of concentration, holed the putt for a three and a round of 66. Only Watson seemed less than surprised. He had told himself that Nicklaus would hole it and was ready therefore for his short putt, a 65 and the championship.

Norman's Talent Fulfilled

For a time it appeared as if Greg Norman's talent might never be fulfilled. Tall, blond and handsome, the popular Australian had threatened many times in the majors, notably in the 1984 US Open when he lost a play-off to Fuzzy Zoeller and then in the 1986 Masters when only a mis-hit four iron to the last hole denied him a tie with Nicklaus.

There was consequently some question as to whether Norman had the stomach for the big occasion and within a few months of the Masters he was to lead again going into the last round of the US Open at Shinnecock Hills only to fade into obscurity. At Turnberry, however, in that wild and windy week of '86, Norman at last came into his own.

This was not the riveting Open it had been nine years earlier but more the celebration of one of the most gifted and strongest players of the modern generation. He won by five strokes and if ever one early round proved to be the decisive one, it was Norman's second round of 63 that did it.

It equalled the championship record, by Mark Hayes on the same course in 1977 and by Isao Aoki in the Muirfield Open of 1980, but

Greg Norman built his Open victory at Turnberry in 1986 on a second round of 63. It might have been less even than that for he three-putted the last.

A relieved Greg Norman after his Open victory. At midnight he could be found playing the bagpipes by the 18th green.

the circumstances were different. The weather, certainly until Norman reached the turn, was far from easy and the severity of the rough, given the conditions, was enough for the R & A to admit subsequently that they had rather overdone it in places.

Norman had also, because of his showing in the Masters and US Open, come into the championship among the favourites though this was hardly substantiated when he had an opening 74 as only Ian Woosnam succeeded in matching the par of 70. This second round was therefore a make-or-break one for Norman and it made him.

It began most promisingly: with three successive birdies from the second and with an eagle three at the seventh (which made up for the shots dropped at the fifth and eighth), he was out in 32. It was, however, his inward half of 31 that seemingly brought the whole golf course to a standstill for as he surveyed not the longest of putts on the 17th green, there were visions of his coming home in 28 for a 60.

Norman had started back with birdies at the 10th and 11th, made another superb one at the 14th where his second shot with a three iron bounced against the flag and followed that with a three at the 16th.

At the 17th Norman was home with a five iron second and had a putt for an eagle from about 15 feet (4.6 m). If he got that in and then birdied the 18th, it would indeed have been a score of 28 home. But the eagle putt slipped comfortably by and it was amid something of an anti-climax that he finished with three putts at the 18th.

His figures for the second round were: 433 253 354 (32) 324 433 345 (31) = 63 and Norman did not look back. Some really vile weather on the Saturday led him into a third round of 74 but he was still in front and with an accomplished 69 on the last day as the sun at last broke through, he was home and dry, the only man to match the par of 280.

British Open

Players from Great Britain unless otherwise stated
An asterisk (*) denotes an amateur
Prize money unchanged unless shown

1860 Prestwick
174 Willie Park 55,59,60
176 Tom Morris Snr. 58,59,59
180 Andrew Strath

1861 Prestwick
163 Tom Morris Snr. 54,56,53
167 Willie Park 54,54,59
171 William Dow 59,58,54

1862 Prestwick
163 Tom Morris Snr. 52,55,56
176 Willie Park 59,59,58
178 Charles Hunter 60,60,58

1863 Prestwick (£10)
168 Willie Park 56,54,58 (£6)
170 Tom Morris Snr. 56,58,56
172 David Park 55,63,54

1864 Prestwick
167 Tom Morris Snr. 54,58,55
169 Andrew Strath 56,57,56
175 Robert Andrew 57,58,60

1865 Prestwick
162 Andrew Strath 55,54,53
164 Willie Park 56,52,56
171 William Dow

1866 Prestwick
169 Willie Park 54,56,59
171 David Park 58,57,56
176 Robert Andrew 58,59,59

1867 Prestwick
170 Tom Morris Snr. 58,54,58
172 Willie Park 58,56,58
174 Andrew Strath 61,57,56

1868 Prestwick
157 Tom Morris Jnr. 50,55,52
159 Robert Andrew 53,54,52
162 Willie Park 58,50,54

1869 Prestwick
154 Tom Morris Jnr. 51,54,49
157 Tom Morris Snr. 54,50,53
165 S. Mure Fergusson* 57,54,54

1870 Prestwick
149 Tom Morris Jnr. 47,51,51
161 Bob Kirk 52,52,57
David Strath 54,49,58

1871 No competition

1872 Prestwick
166 Tom Morris Jnr. 57,56,53
169 David Strath 56,52,61
177 William Doleman* 63,60,54

1873 St. Andrews
179 Tom Kidd 91,88
180 Jamie Anderson 91,89
183 Tom Morris Jnr. 94,89
Bob Kirk 91,92

1874 Musselburgh
159 Mungo Park 75,84
161 Tom Morris Jnr. 83,78
162 George Paxton 80,82

1875 Prestwick
166 Willie Park 56,59,51
168 Bob Martin 56,58,54
171 Mungo Park 59,57,55

1876 St. Andrews
176 Bob Martin 86,90
David Strath 86,90
183 Willie Park
Martin declared winner when Strath refused to play off

1877 Musselburgh
160 Jamie Anderson 40,42,37,41
162 Bob Pringle 44,38,40,40
164 Bob Ferguson 40,40,40,44
William Cosgrove 41,39,44,40

1878 Prestwick
157 Jamie Anderson 53,53,51
159 Bob Kirk 53,55,51
161 J.O.F. Morris 50,56,55

1879 St. Andrews
169 Jamie Anderson 84,85
172 James Allen 88,84
Andrew Kirkaldy 86,86

1880 Musselburgh
162 Bob Ferguson 81,81 (£8)
167 Peter Paxton 81,86
168 Ned Cosgrove 82,86

1881 Prestwick
170 Bob Ferguson 53,60,57
173 Jamie Anderson 57,60,56
177 Ned Cosgrove 61,59,57

1882 St. Andrews
171 Bob Ferguson 83,88
174 Willie Fernie 88,86
175 Jamie Anderson 87,88
John Kirkaldy 86,89
Bob Martin 89,86
Fitz Boothby* 86,89

1883 Musselburgh
159 Willie Fernie 75,84
Bob Ferguson 79,80
160 W. Brown 83,77
Fernie won play-off 158 (81,77), Ferguson 159 (82,77)

1884 Prestwick
160 Jack Simpson 78,82
164 David Rollan 81,83
Willie Fernie 80,84

1885 St. Andrews
171 Bob Martin 84,87
172 Archie Simpson 83,89
173 David Ayton 89,84

1886 Musselburgh
157 David Brown 79,78
159 Willie Campbell 78,81
160 Ben Campbell 79,81

1887 Prestwick
161 Willie Park Jnr. 82,79
162 Bob Martin 81,81
164 Willie Campbell 77,87

1888 St. Andrews
171 Jack Burns 86,85
172 David Anderson Jnr. 86,86
Ben Sayers 85,87

1889 Musselburgh
155 Willie Park Jnr. 39,39,39,38
Andrew Kirkaldy 39,38,39,39
159 Bernard Sayers 39,40,41,39
Park won play-off 158 (82,76), Kirkaldy 163 (85,78)

1890 Prestwick
164 John Ball* 82,82
167 Willie Fernie 85,82
A. Simpson 85,82

1891 St. Andrews
166 Hugh Kirkaldy 83,83
168 Willie Fernie 84,84
Andrew Kirkaldy 84,84

1892 Muirfield
305 Harold Hilton* 78,81,72,74
308 John Ball* 75,80,74,79
James Kirkaldy 77,83,73,75
Alex Herd 77,78,77,76

1893 Prestwick (£100)
322 Willie Auchterlonie 78,81,81,82 (£30)
324 Johnny Laidlay* 80,83,80,81
325 Alex Herd 82,81,78,84

1894 Sandwich
326 J.H. Taylor 84,80,81,81
331 Douglas Rolland 86,79,84,82
332 Andrew Kirkaldy 86,79,83,84

1895 St. Andrews
322 J.H. Taylor 86,78,80,78
326 Alex Herd 82,77,82,85
332 Andrew Kirkaldy 81,83,84,84

British Open

1896 Muirfield
316 Harry Vardon 83,78,78,77
J.H. Taylor 77,78,81,80
319 Freddie Tait* 83,75,84,77
Vardon won play-off 157, Taylor 161

1897 Hoylake
314 Harold Hilton* 80,75,84,75
315 James Braid 80,74,82,79
317 Freddie Tait* 79,79,80,79
G. Pulford 80,79,79,79

1898 Prestwick
307 Harry Vardon 79,75,77,76
308 Willie Park Jnr. 76,75,78,79
309 Harold Hilton* 76,81,77,75

1899 Sandwich
310 Harry Vardon 76,76,81,77
315 Jack White 79,79,82,75
319 Andrew Kirkaldy 81,79,82,77

1900 St. Andrews (£115)
309 J.H. Taylor 79,77,78,75 (£50)
312 Harry Vardon 77,78,79,78
322 James Braid 82,81,80,79

1901 Muirfield
309 James Braid 79,76,74,80
312 Harry Vardon 77,78,79,78
313 J.H. Taylor 79,83,74,77

1902 Hoylake
307 Alex Herd 77,76,73,81
308 Harry Vardon 72,77,80,79
James Braid 78,76,80,74

1903 Prestwick
300 Harry Vardon 73,77,72,78
306 Tom Vardon 76,81,75,74
308 Jack White 77,78,74,79

1904 Sandwich
296 Jack White 80,75,72,69
297 James Braid 77,80,69,71
J.H. Taylor 77,78,74,68

1905 St. Andrews
318 James Braid 81,78,78,81
323 J.H. Taylor 80,85,78,80
R. Jones 81,77,87,78

1906 Muirfield
300 James Braid 77,76,74,73
304 J.H. Taylor 77,72,75,80
305 Harry Vardon 77,73,77,78

1907 Hoylake
312 Arnaud Massy (France) 76,81,78,77
314 J.H. Taylor 79,79,76,80
317 Tom Vardon 81,81,80,75
G. Pulford 81,78,80,78

1908 Prestwick
291 James Braid 70,72,77,72
299 Tom Ball 76,73,76,74
301 Ted Ray 79,71,75,76

1909 Deal
295 J.H. Taylor 74,73,74,74
301 James Braid 79,75,73,74
Tom Ball 74,75,76,76

1910 St. Andrews (£125)
299 James Braid 76,73,74,76 (£50)
303 Alex Herd 78,74,75,76
304 George Duncan 73,77,71,83

1911 Sandwich
303 Harry Vardon 74,74,75,80
Arnaud Massy (France) 75,78,74,76
304 Harold Hilton 76,74,78,76
Vardon won play-off; Massy conceded after 35th hole

1912 Muirfield
295 Ted Ray 71,73,76,75
299 Harry Vardon 75,72,81,71
303 James Braid 77,71,77,78

1913 Hoylake
304 J.H. Taylor 73,75,77,79
312 Ted Ray 73,74,81,84
313 Harry Vardon 79,75,79,80
Michael Moran (Ireland) 76,74,89,74

1914 Prestwick
306 Harry Vardon 73,77,78,78
309 J.H. Taylor 74,78,74,83
310 H.B. Simpson 77,80,78,75

1915–1919 No competition

1920 Deal (£225)
303 George Duncan 80,80,71,72 (£75)
305 Alex Herd 72,81,77,75
306 Ted Ray 72,83,78,73

1921 St. Andrews
296 Jock Hutchison (US) 72,75,79,70
Roger Wethered* 78,75,72,71
298 Tom Kerrigan (US) 74,80,72,72
Hutchison won play-off 150 (74,76), Wethered 159 (77,82)

1922 Sandwich
300 Walter Hagen (US) 76,73,79,72
301 George Duncan 76,75,81,69
Jim Barnes (US) 75,76,77,73

1923 Troon
295 Arthur Havers 73,73,73,76
296 Walter Hagen (US) 76,71,74,75
297 Macdonald Smith (US) 80,73,69,75

1924 Hoylake
301 Walter Hagen (US) 77,73,74,77
302 Ernest Whitcombe 77,70,77,78
304 Macdonald Smith (US) 76,74,77,77
Frank Ball 78,75,74,77

1925 Prestwick
300 Jim Barnes (US) 70,77,79,74
301 Archie Compston 76,75,75,75
Ted Ray 77,76,75,73

1926 Royal Lytham
291 Bobby Jones* (US) 72,72,73,74
293 Al Watrous (US) 71,75,69,78
295 Walter Hagen (US) 68,77,74,76
George Von Elm (US) 75,72,76,72

1927 St. Andrews (£275)
285 Bobby Jones* (US) 68,72,73,72 (£100)
291 Aubrey Boomer 76,70,73,72
Fred Robson 76,72,69,74

1928 Sandwich
292 Walter Hagen (US) 75,73,72,72
294 Gene Sarazen (US) 72,76,73,73
295 Archie Compston 75,74,73,73

1929 Muirfield
292 Walter Hagen (US) 75,67,75,75
298 John Farrell (US) 72,75,76,75
299 Leo Diegel (US) 71,69,82,77

1930 Hoylake (£400)
291 Bobby Jones* (US) 70,72,74,75
293 Leo Diegel (US) 74,73,71,75
Macdonald Smith (US) 70,77,75,71

1931 Carnoustie
296 Tommy Armour (US) 73,75,77,71
297 Jose Jurado (Argentina) 76,71,73, 77
298 Percy Alliss 74,78,73,73
Gene Sarazen (US) 74,76,75,73

1932 Prince's
283 Gene Sarazen (US) 70,69,70,74
288 Macdonald Smith (US) 71,76,71,70
289 Arthur Havers 74,71,68,76

1933 St. Andrews
292 Densmore Shute (US) 73,73,73,73
Craig Wood (US) 77,72,68,75
293 Sid Easterbrook 73,72,71,77
Gene Sarazen (US) 72,73,73,75
Leo Diegel (US) 75,70,71,77
Shute won play-off 149 (75,74), Wood 154 (78,76)

1934 Sandwich
283 Henry Cotton 67,65,72,79
288 Sid Brews 76,71,70,71
290 Alf Padgham 71,70,75,74

British Open

1935 Muirfield
283 Alf Perry 69,75,67,72
287 Alf Padgham 70,72,74,71
288 Charles Whitcombe 71,68,73,76

1936 Hoylake
287 Alf Padgham 73,72,71,71
288 Jimmy Adams 71,73,71,73
289 Henry Cotton 73,72,70,74
Marcel Dallemagne (France) 73,72, 75,69

1937 Carnoustie
290 Henry Cotton 74,72,73,71
292 Reg Whitcombe 72,70,74,76
293 Charles Lacey (US) 76,75,70,72

1938 Sandwich
295 Reg Whitcombe 71,71,75,78
297 Jimmy Adams 70,71,78,78
298 Henry Cotton 74,73,77,74

1939 St. Andrews (£500)
290 Dick Burton 70,72,77,71
292 Johnny Bulla (US) 77,71,71,73
294 Johnny Fallon 71,73,71,79
Sam King 74,72,75,73
Reg Whitcombe 71,75,74,74
Alf Perry 71,74,73,76
Bill Shankland (Australia) 72,73, 72,77

1940–1945 No competition

1946 St. Andrews (£1,000)
290 Sam Snead (US) 71,70,74,75 (£150)
294 Bobby Locke (S. Africa) 69,74,75,76
Johnny Bulla (US) 71,72,72,79

1947 Hoylake
293 Fred Daly 73,70,78,72
294 Reg Horne 77,74,72,71
Frank Stranahan* (US) 71,79,72,72

1948 Muirfield
284 Henry Cotton 71,66,75,72
289 Fred Daly 72,71,73,73
290 Norman Von Nida (Australia) 71, 72,76,71
Jack Hargreaves 76,68,73,73
Charlie Ward 69,72,75,74
Roberto de Vicenzo (Argentina) 70, 73,72,75

1949 Sandwich
283 Bobby Locke (S. Africa) 69,76,68,70
Harry Bradshaw (Eire) 68,77,68,70
285 Roberto de Vicenzo (Argentina) 68,75,73,69
Locke won play-off 135 (67,68), Bradshaw 147 (74,73)

1950 Troon (£1,700)
279 Bobby Locke (S. Africa) 69,72,70,68 (£300)
281 Roberto de Vicenzo (Argentina) 72,71,68,70
282 Fred Daly 75,72,69,66
Dai Rees 71,68,72,71

1951 Royal Portrush
285 Max Faulkner 71,70,70,74
287 Tony Cerda (Argentina) 74,72,71,70
290 Charlie Ward 75,73,74,68

1952 Royal Lytham
287 Bobby Locke (S. Africa) 69,71,74,73
288 Peter Thomson (Australia) 68,73,77, 70
289 Fred Daly 67,69,77,76

1953 Carnoustie
282 Ben Hogan (US) 73,71,70,68
286 Frank Stranahan* (US) 70,74,73,69
Dai Rees 72,70,73,71
Peter Thomson (Australia) 72,72,71, 71
Tony Cerda (Argentina) 75,71,69,71

1954 Royal Birkdale
283 Peter Thomson (Australia) 72,71,69, 71
284 Sid Scott 76,67,69,72
Dai Rees 72,71,69,72
Bobby Locke (S. Africa) 74,71,69,70

1955 St. Andrews (£3,750)
281 Peter Thomson (Australia) 71,68, 70,72 (£1,000)
283 Johnny Fallon 73,67,73,70
284 Frank Jowle 70,71,69,74

1956 Hoylake
286 Peter Thomson (Australia) 70,70,72, 74
289 Flory van Donck (Belgium) 71,74, 70,74
290 Roberto de Vicenzo (Argentina) 71, 70,79,70

1957 St. Andrews
279 Bobby Locke (S. Africa) 69,72,68,70
282 Peter Thomson (Australia) 73,69,70, 70
283 Eric Brown 67,72,73,71

1958 Royal Lytham
278 Peter Thomson (Australia) 66,72, 67,75
David Thomas 70,68,69,71
279 Eric Brown 73,70,65,71
Christy O'Connor (Eire) 87,68,73,71
Thomson won play-off 139 (68,71), Thomas 143 (69,74)

1959 Muirfield
284 Gary Player (S. Africa) 75,71,70,68
286 Flory van Donck (Belgium) 70,70, 73,73
Fred Bullock 68,70,74,74

1960 St. Andrews (£7,000)
278 Kel Nagle (Australia) 69,67,71,71 (£1,250)
279 Arnold Palmer (US) 70,71,70,68
282 Bernard Hunt 72,73,71,66
Harold Henning (S. Africa) 72,72, 69,69
Roberto de Vicenzo (Argentina) 67,67,75,73

1961 Royal Birkdale
284 Arnold Palmer (US) 70,73,69,72
285 Dai Rees 69,74,71,71
288 Christy O'Connor (Eire) 71,77,67, 73
Neil Coles 70,77,69,72

1962 Troon
276 Arnold Palmer (US) 71,69,67,69
282 Kel Nagle (Australia) 71,71,70,70
289 Brian Huggett 75,71,74,69
Phil Rodgers (US) 75,70,72,72

1963 Royal Lytham
277 Bob Charles (NZ) 68,72,66,71
Phil Rodgers (US) 67,68,73,69
278 Jack Nicklaus (US) 71,67,70,70
Charles won play-off 140 (69,71), Rodgers 148 (72,76)

1964 St. Andrews (£6,500)
279 Tony Lema (US) 73,68,68,70 (£1,500)
284 Jack Nicklaus (US) 76,74,66,68
285 Roberto de Vicenzo (Argentina) 76,72,70,67

1965 Royal Birkdale (£10,000)
285 Peter Thomson (Australia) 74,68, 72,71
287 Christy O'Connor (Eire) 69,73,74, 71
Brian Huggett 73,68,76,70

1966 Muirfield
282 Jack Nicklaus (US) 70,67,75,70
283 David Thomas 72,73,69,69
Doug Sanders (US) 71,70,72,70

1967 Hoylake (£15,000)
278 Roberto de Vicenzo (Argentina) 70,71,67,70 (£2,100)
280 Jack Nicklaus (US) 71,69,71,69
284 Clive Clark 70,73,69,72
Gary Player (S. Africa) 72,71,67, 74

British Open

1968 Carnoustie
289 Gary Player (S. Africa) 74,71,71,73
291 Jack Nicklaus (US) 76,69,73,73
Bob Charles (NZ) 72,72,71,76

1969 Royal Lytham
280 Tony Jacklin 68,70,70,72
282 Bob Charles (NZ) 66,69,75,72
283 Peter Thomson (Australia) 71,70,70, 72
Roberto de Vicenzo (Argentina) 72,73,66, 72

1970 St. Andrews (£40,000)
283 Jack Nicklaus (US) 68,69,73,73 (£5,250)
Doug Sanders (US) 68,71,71,73
285 Harold Henning (S. Africa) 67,72,73, 73
Lee Trevino (US) 68,68,72,77
Nicklaus won play-off 72, Sanders 73

1971 Royal Birkdale
278 Lee Trevino (US) 69,70,69,70
279 Lu Liang Huan (Formosa) 70,70,69, 70
280 Tony Jacklin 69,70,70,71

1972 Muirfield
278 Lee Trevino (US) 71,70,66,71
279 Jack Nicklaus (US) 70,72,71,66
280 Tony Jacklin 69,72,67,72

1973 Troon (£50,000)
276 Tom Weiskopf (US) 68,67,71,70 (£5,500)
279 Neil Coles 71,72,70,66
Johnny Miller (US) 70,68,69,72

1974 Royal Lytham
282 Gary Player (S. Africa) 69,68,75,70
286 Peter Oosterhuis 71,71,73,71
287 Jack Nicklaus (US) 74,72,70,71

1975 Carnoustie (£75,000)
279 Tom Watson (US) 71,67,69,72 (£7,500)
Jack Newton (Australia) 69,71,65,74
280 Bobby Cole (S. Africa) 72,66,66,76
Jack Nicklaus (US) 69,71,68,72
Johnny Miller (US) 71,69,66,74
Watson won play-off 71, Newton 72

1976 Royal Birkdale
279 Johnny Miller (US) 72,68,73,66
285 Jack Nicklaus (US) 74,70,72,69
Severiano Ballesteros (Spain) 69,69, 73,74

1977 Turnberry (£100,000)
268 Tom Watson (US) 68,70,65,65 (£10,000)
269 Jack Nicklaus (US) 68,70,65,66
279 Hubert Green (US) 72,66,74,67

1978 St. Andrews (£125,000)
281 Jack Nicklaus (US) 71,72,69,69 (£12,500)
283 Simon Owen (NZ) 70,75,67,71
Ben Crenshaw (US) 70,69,73,71
Tom Kite (US) 72,69,72,70
Ray Floyd (US) 69,75,71,68

1979 Royal Lytham (£155,000)
283 Severiano Ballesteros (Spain) 73,65, 75,70 (£15,000)
286 Jack Nicklaus (US) 72,69,73,72
Ben Crenshaw (US) 72,71,72,71

1980 Muirfield (£200,000)
271 Tom Watson (US) 68,70,64,69 (£25,000)
275 Lee Trevino (US) 68,67,71,69
277 Ben Crenshaw (US) 70,70,68,69

1981 Sandwich
276 Bill Rogers (US) 72,66,67,71
280 Bernhard Langer (W. Germany) 73, 67,70,70
283 Mark James 72,70,68,73
Ray Floyd (US) 74,70,69,70

1982 Royal Troon (£250,000)
284 Tom Watson (US) 69,71,74,70 (£32,000)
285 Peter Oosterhuis 74,67,74,70
Nick Price (S. Africa) 69,69,74,73

1983 Royal Birkdale (£310,000)
275 Tom Watson (US) 67,68,70,70 (£40,000)
276 Hale Irwin (US) 69,68,72,67
Andy Bean (US) 70,69,70,67

1984 St. Andrews (£451,000)
276 Severiano Ballesteros (Spain) 69,68,70,69 (£55,000)
278 Bernhard Langer (W. Germany) 71,68,68,71
Tom Watson (US) 71,68,66,73

1985 Royal St. George's (£520,000)
282 Sandy Lyle 68,71,73,70 (£65,000)
283 Payne Stewart (US) 70,75,70,68
284 Jose Rivero (Spain) 74,72,70,68
Christy O'Connor Jnr. 64,76,72,72
Mark O'Meara (US) 70,72,70,72
Bernhard Langer (W. Germany) 72,69,68,75
David Graham (Australia) 68,71, 70,75

1986 Turnberry (£601,550)
280 Greg Norman (Australia) 74,63,74, 69 (£70,000)
285 Gordon J. Brand 71,68,75,71
286 Bernhard Langer (W. Germany) 72,70,76,68
Ian Woosnam 70,74,70,72

1987 Muirfield (£651,050)
279 Nick Faldo 68,69,71,71 (£75,000)
280 Paul Azinger (US) 68,68,71,73
Rodger Davis (Australia) 64,73,74,69

Rough held no fear for Arnold Palmer. He had six strokes to spare when he won his second Open at Troon in 1962.

US PGA CHAMPIONSHIP

In the beginning the American PGA championship was played by match-play. It remained so from 1916 until 1957. But by then the card and pencil were becoming sacrosanct among the professionals. They felt a moral indignation that one of them might go round in 68 and lose by one hole when another might be heading for a 73 and still win.

That however *is* match-play, for in this form of golf it is not man against the course but one player against another. It is not always necessary to play well, only to play better than your opponent. It is much more a game of strategy, to weigh up what your opponent has done or might do with his shot and then to decide what you should do with yours.

So far as the spectators are concerned, it is hugely popular. Every game is a game in itself, with a definite result and in Britain still there is talk of the time when in the World Matchplay championship, Gary Player came from seven down and 17 to play against Tony Lema and still won. And that was only in the semifinals. Such drama in medal-play comes only in the final round.

Consequently, there are still those who very much regret the PGA bowing to their professionals' demands and in 1958 introducing stroke-play. Something almost certainly went out of the championship that year for with the British Open, US Open and Masters traditionally medal-play events, it merely conformed.

Golf's Grand Slam, at least the modern version of it, is still an unattained goal. It should represent the complete golfer, as it did in the days of Bobby Jones, when the British and American Open championships were by stroke-play and the two amateur championships, match-play. Jones proved then that he was master at both games.

For all that, the PGA does now complete the quadrilateral, the last of the year's four majors. It is, however, the least glamorous of the four, tenuously secure only because of its slot towards the end of the American season.

Of recent years the PGA has tried to improve its image by staging its championship at the classical venues chosen by the USGA for the Open; Inverness, Cherry Hills, Atlanta Athletic Club, Oak Hill, Oakland Hills, Oakmont, Pebble Beach and Congressional have all been visited in the last dozen years. Before that many of the venues were obscure.

Even so, the PGA has had its dominant personalities both when it was played by match-play and also since it went over to stroke-play. Walter Hagen won it five times and Jack Nicklaus has won it five times.

Left: *Larry Nelson has won the American PGA twice, in 1981 at Atlanta and in 1987 at PGA National.*

Right: *Larry Nelson holds aloft the PGA Cup, which is certainly in weight the biggest of the four major championship prizes.*

Pebble Beach

Pebble Beach, on the shores of Carmel Bay along which roll the majestic breakers of the Pacific, is without question the finest championship course in the whole of the western United States. The specification 'championship' is, however, deliberate, for the average golfer might very well prefer to play more of his golf at Cypress Point, which is only minutes away by car and in a class by itself.

For there to be two such gems, lying so close together, is almost a freak of nature. Yet it is only comparatively recently that Pebble Beach has got the recognition it deserves. It has only staged two US Open championships, in 1972 and 1982, and only three American Amateur championships, the first of which, in 1929, appears in the records as being held at the Del Monte Country Club.

The clue to all this was that the whole area was designed as a playground for the rich, the exclusive Del Monte Lodge hotel being its focal point amid the pine forests of the Monterey Peninsula. However, the course, which was laid out by Jack Neville soon after the First World War, rapidly became an attraction in itself; marvellous scenery and a first-class test at some 6,800 yards (6,218 m). That the Open was not held here until 1972 was principally due to difficulties of accommodation but happily these have now been resolved.

Pebble Beach is also a public course and much more heavily played than its very private and exclusive little brother, Cypress Point. Together with Spyglass Hill they form a trinity of courses which annually staged the old Bing Crosby tournament, now the AT&T pro–am. Pebble Beach also hosted the 1977 PGA championship in which Lanny Wadkins beat Gene Littler in a play-off.

It is of course the sea holes that are the making of Pebble Beach. These begin at the fourth, a pleasing short par four, and then, after a short hole turning inland, blossom in all their glory from the sixth through to the 10th. The view from the fairway of the long sixth, with the rocky coastline stretching away on either side, is one of the finest in the world while the short seventh, a tiny hole of only 110 yards (100 m) to a green perched below among the rocks and spray, is totally captivating.

At once one comes to a breathtaking par four, the second shot having to be played over a great chasm in the cliffs to a small, perilously placed green at the foot of a tumbling bank on one side and a drop to the beach on the other.

The ninth and 10th holes follow the line of

There is no more glorious sweep of cliff-top golf than that at Pebble Beach. The second shot to the eighth green is particularly demanding.

the cliffs on the right to greens dangerously close to the edge. Both fall slightly downhill with something of a tilt towards the sea and are as wonderfully exhilarating as they are dangerous. After that the course turns inland before emerging again by the sea for two demanding finishing holes. The tee shot at the short 17th, more than 200 yards (183 m), is aimed directly at the Pacific and once Arnold Palmer took a nine here, going too far and landing on the rocks. This was the clinching hole for both Jack Nicklaus's Open in 1972 and Tom Watson's in 1982. Both had twos, Nicklaus hitting the stick from the tee and Watson chipping in.

Many would rate the 18th the best finishing hole in the world: a par five bending left all the way round the curve of the beach and threatening both the drive and the second shot. A strong nerve is needed for a birdie.

Pebble Beach

Hole	Yards	Par	Hole	Yards	Par
1	379	4	10	424	4
2	506	5	11	382	4
3	395	4	12	204	3
4	327	4	13	393	4
5	170	3	14	565	5
6	516	5	15	395	4
7	110	3	16	403	4
8	433	4	17	209	3
9	467	4	18	548	5

Yards 6,826 Par 72

The 18th green at Pebble Beach and beyond the Pacific Ocean.

Pinehurst No. 2

It is one of golf's tragedies that Pinehurst No. 2 – the numerical identification is necessary because there are now seven courses in this golfing spa – has never staged a US Open and only one PGA, which was as long ago as 1936 when Densmore Shute defeated Jimmy Thomson by three and two in a championship then being conducted by match-play. It is, to my mind, one of the very best in the whole of America.

The little town itself is almost unreal in its quaintness and there is not even a petrol station at which to top up the petrol tank. It can be compared to Carmel in California or a set straight out of Peyton Place. It was a Boston pharmacist, J.W. Tufts, who conceived the idea of this golfing resort in North Carolina and quite apart from the seven Pinehurst courses there are a host of others within easy reach, the Country Club of North Carolina being perhaps the best known.

There is no finer inland course in the United States than Pinehurst No. 2. It will remind the British visitor of Sunningdale or Woodhall Spa.

Pinehurst No. 2 is nevertheless the jewel in the crown and to the British visitor it will remind him at once of Sunningdale in England or perhaps Blairgowrie in Scotland. Donald Ross, its architect, has never produced a better work and the testimony to its charm is that even after a brief visit, the holes can be recalled long afterwards. So many American courses tend to blur into one another.

With its pine-fringed fairways, each hole is somehow in a world of its own and the player is conscious only of himself and his golf. Mercifully, too, there is no water, or at least just one small pond which marginally threatens the drive at the long 16th.

Against that, the bunkering is splendidly traditional, deep, seemingly natural traps amid sandy soil that is more typical of a links than the heart of a mainland. They gather even the marginally mis-hit stroke but are clearly defined even from a distance while clumps of course grass in the rough are an

additional hazard, much as they are on the seaside courses of the United Kingdom.

There is a wonderful variation to all the holes, no two of which are alike, but if one had to be singled out, it would probably be the fifth, a par four played to a gently rising fairway before a second shot across a shallow valley to an angled, tightly bunkered green.

Only on rare occasions has the American Tour stopped off at Pinehurst but it has staged the world amateur team championship for the Eisenhower Trophy in 1980 and also the Ryder Cup in 1951. It is safe to say that none of the players engaged on those occasions will ever forget it.

Pinehurst No. 2

Hole	Yards	Par	Hole	Yards	Par
1	414	4	10	596	5
2	454	4	11	434	4
3	345	4	12	423	4
4	532	5	13	378	4
5	438	4	14	444	4
6	216	3	15	206	3
7	398	4	16	504	5
8	464	4	17	187	3
9	162	3	18	433	4

Yards 7,028 Par 71

The sixth green at Pinehurst No. 2, a short hole. There are now seven courses at this American golfing haven.

Southern Hills

Few golf courses are less appropriately named than Southern Hills, in Tulsa, Oklahoma. Broadly speaking, the course is as flat as you might expect in a state where the corn is traditionally as high as an elephant's eye, and the only rise in the ground is on the ninth and 18th holes, which climb back to a clubhouse atop something of a hill.

The course was built during the depths of the American depression in the thirties at the whim of a handful of millionaires who had made their money in oil. By today's prices the course and clubhouse cost little more than the refurbishment of a modern locker room.

Perry Maxwell was the course architect and his demands were centred very much on driving. It is totally crucial at Southern Hills for no one has ever won anything of note here without hitting the ball from the tee both long and straight. Such a virtue comes into its own at every turn, for all but two of the par fours as well as the two par fives bend left or right and require absolute placement of the ball.

Because of the summer heat, the course is entirely sown with Bermuda grass, which is the most resilient to high temperatures, but in the rough, which stands ankle high, it is the very devil from which to escape. It has all the characteristics of steel wool and in the 1958 US Open Hogan had to withdraw because he had injured his wrist in playing a recovery shot.

In a matter of minutes a player's shirt can be soaked with sweat and in the long periods without rain it is not uncommon for 400,000 gallons (1.8 million litres) of water to be poured on the course in 24 hours. When Raymond Floyd won the PGA championship here in 1982, the hoses were spraying the greens every time one group of players departed and before the next group arrived.

Floyd built his victory that year on a staggering opening round of 63, followed it with 68,69 and 72, and won by three strokes from Lanny Wadkins. Dave Stockton was the other PGA winner here in 1970 but Southern Hills will always be remembered for Hubert Green's US Open victory in 1977.

Green had already embarked on his final round when the United States Golf Association received a telephone call saying that three men were on their way to assassinate him. Unwilling to take the threat as a hoax, Sandy Tatum, then president of the USGA, took it upon himself to inform Green that he could be in danger as he left the 14th green.

Green's response was wholly admirable. Though flanked now by armed guards, he rifled his next drive straight down the middle, holed a nasty second putt to save his par and, even more courageously, sank another of 4 feet (1.2 m) on the last hole to beat Lou Graham by a stroke.

One other point should be made about Southern Hills. It has some of the most difficult bunkers, not because of any great depth but because they are filled with a particularly fine sand from the nearby Arkansas River known as 'Number Six Wash'. It is not unlike talcum powder and the pros, not to put too fine a point on it, hate it.

Above: *Trees flanked the fairway of the 18th hole at Southern Hills. An armed guard also flanked Hubert Green here when he won the 1977 US Open after an anonymous telephone caller had threatened his life.*

Southern Hills

Hole	Yards	Par	Hole	Yards	Par
1	447	4	10	375	4
2	459	4	11	165	3
3	406	4	12	444	4
4	366	4	13	465	4
5	614	5	14	207	3
6	175	3	15	407	4
7	383	4	16	569	5
8	215	3	17	354	4
9	373	4	18	449	4

Yards 6,873 Par 70

Opposite: *A view back down the 13th fairway at Southern Hills, the site in 1982 of the American PGA where, in intense heat, Raymond Floyd won the title.*

Firestone

Firestone, in Akron, Ohio, is what might be termed the golf course of the future. It is long, very long – the longest on the American tour – measuring just short of 7,200 yards (6,538 m). Only two of its par fours are of less than 400 yards (366 m) and five are a minimum of 460 yards (420 m). Only one of its par threes is shorter than 200 yards (183 m), the other three being at least 225 yards (205 m). There are only two par fives, one of them 500 yards (457 m) and the other 625 yards (571 m).

But in these times when players are both fitter and stronger, the golf shaft more powerful and the ball technically close to perfection, it is length that, in some quarters, is looked upon as the best test of a modern course.

It was with championship golf very much in mind that Trent Jones was called in to doctor Firestone in time for the 1960 PGA championship. His surgery was far from cosmetic. Indeed the whole character of the place was changed from the original 18 holes Harvey Firestone, a multi-millionaire industrialist, presented to his work-force for their enjoyment during their days off. Jones added 50 bunkers, dug up two greens and enlarged the other 16 to two and three times their previous size. New tees were also positioned.

The result was that the professionals, who spend much of their lives playing eight and nine irons, or even wedges to the greens for their second shots, here at least have to reach more often for their long irons and even woods. That 1960 PGA was only the third to be decided by stroke-play and Jay Hebert won

There are few dog-legs at Firestone, traditional home of the World Series and in 1975 the site of one of Jack Nicklaus's five PGA victories. This is the 10th hole.

The longest hole at Firestone is the 625-yard (575-m) 16th. It cost Jack Nicklaus dear in the 1975 PGA for he had not realized that the tee had been moved forward, told his caddie to walk down the fairway, and got into trouble with his driver when only a three-wood was needed.

with a one over par total of 281. In 1966 Al Geiberger went one better but in 1975 Jack Nicklaus (who else?) brought it down to 276.

Since 1976 Firestone has become the permanent home of the World Series, which is recognized as the last of the bigger tournaments of the year in America. Scoring in this has been consistently lower and Lanny Wadkins holds the record with 267 in 1977. Not even those 7,200 yards has therefore proved much of an obstacle.

This televised tournament has made Firestone as well known to American viewers as Augusta and it is highly rated not only by the long hitters but also by those with rather less muscle. Its critics would claim that it is a rather boring course, not only because of its unremitting length but because of its eternally parallel fairways. There is little variation in direction, other than total reverse.

Bobby Nichols, as head professional, has given Firestone distinction. A promising young amateur, he was at 16 gravely injured in a car crash and told by doctors that he would never walk again. However, encouraged by Ben Hogan, Nichols not only did walk again but resumed his successful career. Twelve years after the accident he won the PGA at Columbus, Ohio, in 1964.

Firestone

Hole	Yards	Par	Hole	Yards	Par
1	400	4	10	405	4
2	500	5	11	365	4
3	450	4	12	180	3
4	465	4	13	460	4
5	230	3	14	410	4
6	465	4	15	230	3
7	225	3	16	625	5
8	450	4	17	390	4
9	465	4	18	465	4

Yards 7,180 Par 70

Oak Hill

Oak Hill, in Rochester, New York, is so named because of the many oak trees that were planted during its construction and in the early years of the course in the 1920s. It shows the distinctive architectural hand of Donald Ross, though the chairman of the landscaping committee was a Dr. John R. Williams, who was responsible for most of the tree planting.

There are two courses, the East and the West, but it is the East which is the big one at just short of 7,000 yards (6,400 m). The landscape is relatively flat but a winding brook comes into play on eight holes and must be negotiated as carefully as the bordering trees – tulip, Chinese rain, Lemoine crab apple as well as oak – which particularly come into play at the subtly designed dog-legs.

In the days leading up to the 1956 US Open, Ben Hogan made it known that the East was not a strong enough course on which to stage the championship. It was an opinion he later revised, though not entirely because he lost by a stroke to Cary Middlecoff after missing a putt of less than a yard on the 71st green. Hogan had grown to appreciate the values the course put on shot placement and went so far as to say that the first was the toughest opening hole in his experience. While the fairway is generous, the approach to a small green pinched by bunkers, trees and the famous creek demands absolute precision.

Local opinion has it that the sixth is the best hole, a dog-leg right of 440 yards (402 m). The drive has to be hit with some care to avoid running out of fairway or, alternately, not far enough to clear the impeding trees overhanging the near side of the fairway. Beneath them winds the creek which then turns menacingly and diagonally across the front of a sloping and tightly bunkered green.

Oak Hill was first recognized by the USGA

Oak Hill's seventh hole. It is a course Ben Hogan came to rate highly after initially doubting its quality.

for the American Amateur championship of 1949 when Charles Coe demolished Rufus King by the almost indecent margin of 11 and 10 in the 36-hole final. It is also a golf course that will for ever be a great favourite with Lee Trevino.

It was here in 1968 that he became the first and still the only man to win the US Open with his every round in the sixties. His scores were 69,68,69,69 and he beat Jack Nicklaus by four strokes. Trevino was something of an unknown quantity until that week, dismissed by the purists as having too unconventional a method for it to stand up to the stress of major championships. He proved them wrong not only that week but subsequently, too, with a second US Open in 1971 (this time beating Nicklaus in a play-off), two PGA championships and two British Opens. That places him 11th in the major championship league table while for public popularity he would almost certainly be placed higher than that.

An aerial view of the 18th at Oak Hill. The back-and-forth nature of some of the holes is evident.

Oak Hill

Hole	Yards	Par	Hole	Yards	Par
1	445	4	10	420	4
2	390	4	11	192	3
3	208	3	12	380	4
4	571	5	13	602	5
5	180	3	14	327	4
6	440	4	15	163	3
7	443	4	16	441	4
8	432	4	17	463	4
9	416	4	18	449	4

Yards 6,962 Par 70

Cherry Hills

The 13th at Cherry Hills and in the distance the Rockies. There are a number of fine courses in the Denver area.

Cherry Hills is probably the best known of a number of fine courses around Denver, that mile-high city in the mid-west. Another is the more recently built Castle Pines, the home of the annual International tournament, which is played by a variation to the Stableford scoring system. Closer to the city itself is the Denver Country Club where in 1982 Great Britain and Ireland suffered one of their multiple Curtis Cup defeats. Both Cherry Hills and Castle Pines afford marvellous views of the snow-capped peaks of the Rockies.

It was at Cherry Hills that Arnold Palmer won his celebrated US Open in 1960 with a last round of 65. It was also here that Andy North won the first of his two US Opens, in 1978. Peculiarly, his golfing career has included only one other tournament victory, in the 1977 Westchester Classic. North is a big man at 6 ft 4 in (193 cm) and he also displayed that he has a big heart. In the final round he came to the last hole, a par four which skirts a lake and plays shorter than its 480 yards (439 m) because of the altitude, needing only a five to win.

Playing cautiously with a three iron from the tee, he still put his ball in the rough. Then he hit into the rough on the other side of the fairway and knocked his third into a bunker. When he came out to within some 5 feet (1.5 m) of the hole, he twice had to back away because of a buffeting wind. But he still holed the putt for his bogey five and victory.

Hubert Green, who had preceded North as American Open champion, won his PGA championship at Cherry Hills in 1985. He was then 38 and beat into second place Lee Trevino, who 12 months earlier had become the PGA's second oldest winner at 44. Julius Boros was 48 when he won in 1968.

Cherry Hills was opened in 1922 and designed by William S. Flynn. Not its least merit is that there are no parallel fairways, the course falling away from the clubhouse, which commands the best outlook on the Rockies.

The greens are generally small by American standards and the finish is particularly good. Ben Hogan rates the 14th one of the toughest par fours he knows. Though measuring 486 yards (444 m) in the 1978 US Open, it still rated a par four. The fairway climbs away from the tee; out of bounds is on the right and a rough bank on the left tumbles down to a creek. The fairway then swings sharply left to a tight green with a big bunker on one side and the creek on the other.

Though more than 200 yards (183 m), the 15th green is tightly encircled by trees and bunkers. The 16th asks an equally exacting second shot while the 17th is a very long par five. The threat of the lake is the chief feature of the finishing hole and anyone who comes through those last five holes in par or better can take great satisfaction.

Cherry Hills

Hole	Yards	Par	Hole	Yards	Par
1	399	4	10	437	4
2	419	4	11	594	5
3	323	4	12	203	3
4	429	4	13	382	4
5	543	5	14	486	4
6	166	3	15	208	3
7	384	4	16	419	4
8	229	3	17	550	5
9	432	4	18	480	4

Yards 7,083 Par 71

There are not so much bunkers as sand traps in America. They hold little fear to the good player.

Hagen the Supreme Match-player

Match-play golf was made for Walter Hagen. His extrovert personality, total confidence in his own ability to bring off the impossible shot and knack of being able to share a joke one second and bring 100 per cent concentration to his next shot unnerved many an opponent. Though he won the British Open twice and the American Open twice, the PGA was his metier. He won it first in 1921 and four times in a row between 1924 and 1927.

Bernard Darwin once wrote: 'Hagen's demeanour towards his opponents, though entirely correct, had yet a certain suppressed truculence; he exhibited so supreme a confidence that they could not get it out of their minds and could not live against it.'

Hagen is credited as the originator of a number of golf's most famous quotes. One came in the PGA championship at Olympia Fields, Illinois, in 1925 when he was defending the title. The style of his arrival was typical of Hagen, chauffeur-driven car, accompanying secretary and locker room attendant ready to carry the bags. As Hagen swept into the locker room, his courtiers in his wake, such players as Al Watrous, Leo Diegel, Harry Cooper, Tommy Armour and 'Wild Bill' Mehlhorn were sitting around having a beer or two. They pretended not to notice Hagen, but Diegel said in a loud voice: 'I'll take Walter this year.'

'No you won't,' piped up Watrous. 'This is my year', which was at once contested by Mehlhorn. It was all said in good part and it was then that Hagen stopped in his tracks and said very deliberately: 'I wonder which of you fellows is going to be second this year?' It turned out to be Mehlhorn.

As it happened, Hagen also beat Watrous in the first round but his toughest match was against Diegel in the third and within it there were two instances of Hagen's flair for match-play, allied to an ability also to unsettle an opponent.

He had been trailing Diegel all day and at two down and two to play stared defeat in the face. Not that Hagen ever thought in such terms and when Diegel put his second shot into a ditch short of the green, there was every possibility that he would get one hole back. Instead, Diegel somehow got the ball out of the ditch and then holed a huge putt for a four. Most golfers would at such a moment just accept that it was not to be their day. Not Hagen. He hardly seemed to notice and promptly holed an almost equally long, swinging putt for a birdie to keep the match alive.

When the match went into extra holes, both got themselves into difficulties at the 39th, each leaving themselves awkward second putts. Hagen's was slightly the longer and when he holed it, he staggered everyone by picking up Diegel's ball and conceding the half. It was the art of fair gamesmanship at its best. Diegel was wrong-footed, still pondering the matter as he arrived on the next tee to find that Hagen had already driven. Hurrying his drive, Diegel topped and went out at the 40th.

Hagen beat Jim Barnes in two of his finals, Mehlhorn, Diegel and Joe Turnesa in the others. The only final he lost was to Gene Sarazen and in many ways he was the making of the PGA.

When the PGA began, it was held as a match-play tournament, reverting to stroke-play as recently as 1958. Walter Hagen was a master at the original format and won the title five times, since equalled by Jack Nicklaus at stroke-play.

Sarazen's Absentmindedness

In these days of carefully prepared schedules, it is hard to imagine the somewhat haphazard manner in which professional golfers went about their business more than half a century ago. Behind Gene Sarazen's PGA victory at Oakmont in 1922, the first of his three, lies an amusing story to illustrate this.

Sarazen, though only 20, had already that year won the US Open at Skokie and in the succeeding weeks remained in something of a daze at all the fuss that was being made of him. He was in repeated demand for exhibition matches and one of them took him to Dayton, Ohio.

It was afterwards, over dinner, that someone quite casually asked Sarazen whether he was playing in the PGA the following day. He went pale; he had forgotten all about it! Hasty arrangements had to be made for him to catch a late train via Columbus with a connecting train on to Pittsburgh. It was late and at the appointed hour when Sarazen was due to drive off against Tom Mahan, there was no sign of him at all.

These days such absence would result in instant disqualification but this was those days. Sarazen was, after all, Open champion and special dispensation was made for him to change his starting time. Without so much as a practice shot, Sarazen raced straight for the tee, played nine holes in 35, beat Mahan by three and two, won again in the afternoon and thereby took two rather hectic strides towards further inclusion in the history books. He could always be thankful for the more lenient rules of that time.

Sarazen roomed that week with Emmet French in the Oakmont clubhouse but when they came through to meet one another in the final, they decided it was better to split up. Sarazen won by four and three over the 36 holes to prove himself the master of match-play as well as stroke-play, even if Walter Hagen was absent. Hagen was busy making money in exhibition matches.

Hagen and Sarazen were nevertheless the two big names in American professional golf and a year later they were seeded to meet in the final of the PGA at Pelham, New York. It was the first time the system had been tried and it worked perfectly. First, however, Sarazen had another score to settle, against Jim Barnes, PGA champion in 1919, US Open champion in 1921 and subsequently British Open champion in 1925.

When practising for the 1922 US Open, Sarazen had approached Francis Ouimet asking if he might make up the four, of whom Barnes was already one. Ouimet was only too pleased but Barnes was indignant, saying that he did not want a 'fresh kid' in his foursome. However, the 'fresh kid' won the championship.

Now, in the quarter-finals of the PGA, they met head-to-head and Sarazen gained further revenge when he won by one hole despite a late rally from Barnes, who had three birdies and an eagle in the last seven holes.

This further paved the way for the perfect final against Hagen. It was an appropriately close match, Sarazen one up at lunch, three up at the turn in the afternoon and two up and three to play. But Hagen never knew when to lie down and sure enough they had to go into extra holes. It was Sarazen who won at the 38th, playing a thrilling recovery out of thick rough close to the hole for a birdie. It was the sort of shot Hagen often played to demoralize opponents; but this time it was Hagen who was demoralized.

As with the 10-year interval between Sarazen's two US Open victories, it was another 10 years before he took the PGA again, at Blue Mound, Wisconsin, in 1933, but by then there was no doubting his standing in the game.

Gene Sarazen with two of his prizes, including the British Open's claret jug.

Verb to 'Diegel'

Walter Hagen's fine run of four successive PGA championships was finally brought to an end in 1928 at Five Farms, Baltimore. He was beaten in the quarter-finals by Leo Diegel who, just to prove it was no fluke, then walked all over Gene Sarazen in the semi-finals, beating him by nine and eight over 36 holes.

Showing a consistency that was not exactly in character since his temperament was said to be suspect, Diegel then beat Al Espinosa in the final by six and five, his golf in those three matches being the best of his career. Furthermore Diegel successfully defended the title at Hill Crest, Los Angeles, in 1929. These were his two major championships though his most lasting contribution to the game was that his surname became a verb.

Olin Dutra won the American PGA at Keller, Minnesota, in 1932.

Suspect on the greens, Diegel adopted a putting method in which, instead of having his elbows by his side, he moved them out at right angles so that his forearms formed virtually a straight line. Others tried it in attempts to overcome 'the twitch' and it became known as 'Diegling'.

The only other back-to-back winner before the Second World War was Densmore Shute in 1936–37, though Paul Runyan split his two victories between 1934 and 1938, the latter at Shawnee, Pennsylvania, causing a certain amount of shock waves not so much because he beat Sam Snead but because he beat Snead by eight and seven. Runyan was nevertheless 24 under par for the 196 holes he played during that week.

Snead lost another final, to the great Byron Nelson at Hershey, Pennsylvania, in 1940, before he came into his own with three victories, the first in 1942 at Seaview, New Jersey, then in 1949 at Hermitage, Virginia, and in 1951 at Oakmont, Pennsylvania.

Like Snead, Nelson was beaten in two finals as well as winning two, and after the war came as well the turn of Ben Hogan. He beat Porky Oliver at Portland, Oregon, in 1946 and then Mike Turnesa, one of a prolific golfing family, at Norwood, Missouri, in 1948. But for his near fatal car accident in 1949, Hogan might well have accumulated more. So weak were his legs, however, that he could no longer endure 36 holes in a day and consequently he had to pass up the PGA.

By now of course a modern generation with different ideas was springing up and when Lionel Hebert beat Dow Finsterwald at Miami Valley in 1957, the curtain was brought down on match-play golf.

Leo Diegel had an unusual style on the greens and sometimes even on the tee. Here he is seen in action in the 1929 Ryder Cup match at Moortown, England.

Another First for Player

In 1961 Gary Player became the first overseas golfer to win the Masters. Since, in 1959, he had also taken the British Open, the little South African could be said to be well and truly on his way. Yet, in the weeks leading up to his breaking further new ground in the PGA at Aronimink, Pennsylvania, in 1962, he seriously considered giving the game up.

Immediately beforehand, he had failed to qualify for the last rounds of the British Open at Troon; so irritated was he by some freak bounces on hard, sun-baked fairways that he did not even try over the last few holes of the second round. It seemed to be the last straw at a time of increasing disappointment that had begun a few months earlier when he had lost a play-off for the Masters to Arnold Palmer.

In a thoroughly depressed state by the time he arrived back in America for the PGA, Player telephoned his manager, Mark McCormack, saying that he did not think he could go on with 'this ridiculous life . . . chasing round the world like an idiot . . . living out of suitcases . . . changing equipment everywhere I go . . .' All he wanted to do was go home to South Africa and stay there.

A remarkable change nevertheless came over him when he turned up for his first practice round at Aronimink. The fairways were green and lush, the greens holding and even the dazzling white bunkers aesthetically pleasing. It was a different world to Troon and Player felt a new man. He also began to play like one.

His strategy was still somewhat defensive, often using a four-wood from the tee. However, it kept him out of trouble and by the end of the third round, Player was in front. His last round was mainly a tussle with Bob Goalby but every time Goalby holed a birdie putt, Player would follow him in and with 72,67,69,70, he got home by a stroke.

Player's other PGA victory was in 1972 at Oakland Hills. It will be remembered for just one shot. The 16th hole is a par four of a little over 400 yards (366 m) and dog-legs sharply right so that the second shot was to be played over a lake. Player was tieing the lead when he came to it in the final round but cut his drive into the rough.

He was some 150 yards (137 m) from the green but now, as well as the lake, he had some tall trees between himself and the flag. At any time it would have been a most demanding shot, almost indeed impossible. But Player was in no position to play safe. He had to go for it with a nine iron in order to clear the trees; but was a nine iron enough club also to clear the water? It was. Player landed his recovery 4 feet (1.2 m) from the flag, holed for a birdie and beat Tommy Aaron and Jim Jamieson by two strokes.

It was a moment of sheer genius, though one of Player's most heroic years – for very different reasons – was in the 1969 PGA when he finished runner-up by a stroke to Raymond Floyd at Dayton, Ohio. It was at a time when anti-apartheid feelings in America were running very high and, as a South African, Player came in for some unprecedented abuse.

There were shouts of 'miss it, miss it' when he putted, empty beer cans were thrown at

Gary Player felt like giving the game up immediately before the 1962 PGA at Aronimink, so disheartened had he become over his play in the British Open at Troon. But, driving often with a four wood, he regained his appetite and won the championship.

him as he passed and once, when about to drive, he was hit in the small of the back when a spectator threw a telephone directory at him. An armed guard was called up to protect him and, despite everything, his concentration never wavered. Afterwards, at the prize giving, he made the customary thank you's, paused and looked round at the crowd, some of whom had done their best to distract him. 'And I love you all,' he said. At that moment Gary Player became an ambassador as well as a golfer.

Gary Player keeps his head down during the 1985 PGA at Cherry Hills.

Dave Marr: Mind of a Champion

It takes multiple qualities to win a major championship. A good many players seemingly have the game; one only has to stand for half an hour or so by any major club's practice ground to see that, as a succession of often unidentifiable golfers pump shot after perfect shot into the distance. But, as the late Sir Henry Cotton often remarked: 'There is more to playing golf than hitting the ball.'

Dave Marr was considered 'too intelligent' to win a major; he had too much imagination, too much awareness of its importance, too much sensitivity. Yet Marr did win and the manner of his PGA victory at Laurel Valley in 1965 when, over the last five holes he weathered a succession of crises, revealed an intriguing insight into the mind of a champion.

Marr, now a television commentator, had been two strokes ahead of Billy Casper and Jack Nicklaus going into the last round and for another 13 holes he continued to play with total conviction, neither losing nor gaining ground.

But at the 14th, a short hole, he missed the green. It was his first bad shot and he dropped a stroke. The approach to the 15th required absolute precision for the green was small and there were bunkers front and back. Marr played a soft four iron and holed the putt for a birdie. Again he was two strokes clear.

The 16th was a longer par four and Marr was left with a three iron second shot. The place not to go was right. Marr went left into a bunker but then played a marvellous bunker shot to 18 inches (46 cm). He missed the putt. Once more his lead was back to a single stroke.

At the 17th, a long short hole, Marr found the green with a four wood but the putt was fast and he left it 8 feet (2.4 m) beyond the hole. It was a critical moment but, hardly giving the ball a second glance, he knocked it in. But Marr was not yet through the wood.

At the 18th he bunkered his drive and had no chance of getting up in two. However, he picked a seven iron off the top of the sand, hit a full blooded nine iron to within a yard of the flag and holed the putt. He was round in 71 and beat Casper and Nicklaus by the same two strokes with which he had led at the beginning.

Some weeks later Marr described all the things that were going through his mind over those last holes. At the 14th, where he dropped a shot, he had begun to rehearse his winning speech and then told himself to forget it.

At the 15th, where he got a birdie, he began to think how much his victory would mean to his family, his friends and his coach. At the 16th, where he missed that tiny putt, he had told himself to be careful.

At the 17th, where he holed that quite long second putt, he was still seething at the possibility of throwing the championship away: 'I just wanted to do something decisive.' At the 18th he knew a nine iron was the right club because he had seen Bob Goalby hit a nine from the same spot. And then he thought of Claude Harman, his coach. 'Claude used to say, "trust your swing, trust your swing".' Marr did trust it and that trust was justified.

Dave Marr, PGA champion in 1965, played the same year in the Ryder Cup match at Royal Birkdale. He went on to captain the American team at Walton Heath in 1981 and is now a highly respected television commentator.

Boros Withstands the Pressure

Julius Boros had a naturally easy swing that lasted. He was 48 when he won the PGA in 1968 and remains the oldest champion.

Julius Boros has been to American golf what Christy O'Connor (Senior that is) has been to Irish golf. Both are big men, strong in the arm and leg but with a wonderfully delicate touch in the hands; true golfing craftsmen. Once somewhat scorned by a young professional who had just knocked a seven iron onto a green during a practice round, whereas O'Connor had hit a five, the Irishman dropped 13 balls on the same spot and, with his 13 clubs, proceeded to manufacture 13 different shots, each of which he hit onto the green.

Boros, born in 1920 and therefore four years older than O'Connor, had that same mastery over the golf ball. He was, however, a better putter and it was this which undoubtedly helped him to win two US Opens, as far apart as 1952 and 1963, and also the PGA at Pecan Valley, Texas, in 1968. He was then 48 years and four months, the oldest man to have won any of the four major championships, a record which still holds.

Two of Boros's majors were in fact in the stifling heat of a Texas summer for his first US Open was gained at Northwood. In the PGA he even had to carry an umbrella as protection against the burning sun while Jack Nicklaus, who missed his first cut in the PGA, came away saying that it was 'just too hot'.

Like O'Connor, Boros was self-deprecating about his golf. 'I just throw some junk in the air and hope it stays out of rough and eventually gets to the green,' he explained as he went into the last round tied with Arnold Palmer, who found the PGA as elusive as, in another era, Sam Snead had found the US Open.

'It's too hot and there are too many hills for an old codger like me to win,' Boros had told some friends over dinner on the eve of the final round; but he was still tied at the turn, not only with Palmer but also now with Marty Fleckman and Bob Charles, the New Zealander.

But it was Boros who broke the deadlock, taking at one point a two-stroke lead that was then halved when he dropped a shot at the 17th. The 18th had been a controversial hole all week, nearly 460 yards (420 m) in length but with a 15 feet (4.6 m) wide creek crossing the fairway which stopped the players using their drivers. Half way through the championship, it was decided to move the tee back so that the drivers could come out. But it still left a mighty long second shot.

Palmer was up ahead of Boros, a stroke behind even though he had hardly been able to sink a putt. At so brutal a hole a birdie for Palmer might yet have done it and, from the rough, he hit one of the great shots of his career, a three wood that came to rest 8 feet (2.4 m) from the flag.

Ten years earlier Palmer would probably have holed the putt But 10 years is a long time in the life of a golfer and he never, as the saying goes, 'had a prayer'. Nevertheless, Boros still needed a four to win and he could not get up in two. It did not matter. With one of those lovely low wedge shots, all bite and touch, he got the ball to 4 feet (1.2 m) and knocked the putt in just as safely.

Nicklaus's Full House

The PGA has been Jack Nicklaus's second most rewarding stamping ground. Only in the Masters has he recorded more victories, six in all. In the PGA he has won five times and that equals the record of Walter Hagen: Nicklaus supreme at stroke-play, Hagen at match-play. No one else in the stroke-play era has won more than twice.

A further measure of the man is that in the PGA Nicklaus has also been second four times and third three times. On the basis of awarding three points for a win, two for second place and one for third, Nicklaus's tally would be 28 points from the Masters, 26 each from the PGA and British Open and 21 from the US Open.

No man has ever dominated golf so much as Nicklaus. Whether he is the best player that has ever been, no one can say. All any man can do is be the best player of his time and Nicklaus has certainly been that. He had the reputation in his early days of being a mighty

Jack Nicklaus has been the dominant player of the modern era, his five PGA victories equalling the record of Walter Hagen.

Right: *Lanny Wadkins gives a putt some 'body English'. An admirably quick player, he has threatened in many major championships but has won only one, the 1977 PGA at Pebble Beach.*

Below: *Not an easy chip for Jack Nicklaus but he always gave his every shot maximum concentration.*

hitter, but he has been much more than that.

He brought a ferocity of concentration reminiscent of Ben Hogan. But, unlike Bobby Jones, the finest golfer of his time and whose record of 13 major championships has long since been left far behind, competition has been food and drink to Nicklaus. To Jones, brilliant though he was at it, it was almost a poison, draining him until he became ill.

It was Nicklaus who popularized the yardage chart. He would pace off everything and work out every distance. No one has been more consistently accurate at predicting a winning score and pacing himself to that end. He thrived on 'clutch golf' over the closing holes and though he did not rate himself a great putter, he was the only person in the world who didn't. In that crouched, utterly still position he could maintain until one suspected he might never move again, he positively defied the ball not to go in.

Nicklaus won his first PGA at Dallas, Texas, in 1963. It was blazingly hot and, other

than to play golf, he hardly moved from his air-conditioned hotel bedroom. When the cup was due to be presented it was too hot to hold. Victory did not, however, immediately open the floodgates for it was another eight years before Nicklaus won again, this time at PGA National in Florida.

Victory number three came at Canterbury, Ohio, in 1973, and number four two years later at Firestone in Akron, one of his favourite courses. This contained what Nicklaus felt was one of his 'dumbest' moments. At the 16th, victory now approaching, he had assumed the tee would be at the back, took his driver and sent his caddie forward down the fairway of a hole that measures more than 600 yards.

However the tee had been moved forward 30 yards (27 m) and Nicklaus now had the wrong club. Rather than call up his caddie, he tried to ease up on the shot and hit it into a water hazard. Dropping out under penalty, Nicklaus then put his third behind a tree and the shot looked impossible. Somehow, however, he managed to cut a nine iron 30 feet (9 m) from the hole and sank the putt for his par five! It could, as Nicklaus knew only too well, have been anything.

Nicklaus's last PGA victory was also his most convincing. At Oak Hill, New York, in 1980, he beat Andy Bean by no less than seven strokes. There was no more answer to him then than there has been on so many other occasions.

Mahaffey's Dream, Watson's Nightmare

In 1975 John Mahaffey suffered one of golf's hardest disappointments. He tied for the US Open at Medinah but then lost the play-off to Lou Graham. It was nothing, however, to the pain he was to endure over the next two years. In the 1976 PGA championship he began to suffer some twinges in his left elbow. It was diagnosed as hypertendonitis. Mahaffey was hardly able to play at all in 1977 and then, just as he began to recover, he fell off a ladder and broke a finger.

These were in fact only the beginnings of Mahaffey's troubles, for later he was to be put out of the game again with more tendon trouble, this time in the hand, his marriage broke up and he found consolation only in drink. However, in 1978 a rare shaft of sunlight broke through when, in unusual circumstances, he won the PGA championship at Oakmont, Pennsylvania.

The circumstances were unusual because Tom Watson, who was at that time golf's

John Mahaffey lost a play-off for the US Open at Medinah in 1975. He was more successful in a play-off for the PGA at Oakmont three years later.

Hubert Green has an unusual style, hands very low at the address. But it was good enough to win him the US Open in 1977 and the PGA, aged 38, at Cherry Hills in 1985.

hottest property, seemingly had the championship locked away. A player of absolute pedigree, one who had three times in the last three years looked Jack Nicklaus straight in the eye and beaten him – in two Masters and one British Open – there seemed no way that Watson could lose.

On this, one of the toughest courses in the whole of the United States, Watson had played superlative golf for three rounds – 67,69,67 – and led the field by five strokes. Jerry Pate, US Open champion the year before and much later to become victim of a neck injury that cut him down in full stride, was nearest to Watson but Mahaffey was seven strokes back. If the conclusion seemed foregone, it was not to be.

Though Watson had some troubles early in his final round, he made an eagle three at the ninth and was still four clear. But everything began to change at the 10th, partly through bad luck, partly through bad play. He was unfortunate to drive into a divot, hit his second into a bunker, came out poorly and took three putts.

Yet another divot hole at the 11th further unsettled Watson and it was then that Mahaffey and Pate, his two playing partners, began to make up ground. Once the bleeding started, it was hard to stop it, and with Watson now trying to steer the ball and making a mess of the short holes, he found himself a scarcely believable stroke behind, with Mahaffey and Pate now tied.

Hope flickered again for Watson when he made a birdie at the 17th, but so did Pate, who further tightened the screw with two good shots to the 18th green. Neither Watson nor Mahaffey could summon the birdies they needed to tie and the crowd settled for the short putt Pate had for the championship. He missed it, which was about as much of a shock to the system as Tom Watson had already endured.

Destiny, it seemed, was on Mahaffey's side and sure enough he landed the title at the second extra hole of the PGA's first three-man play-off. Certainly no other PGA championship had contained quite so many unexpected twists.

Year of the Two Golden Oldies

When Lee Trevino won his first US Open in 1968, hardly anyone had ever heard of him. About the best anyone could come up with was that he was the son of a Mexican gravedigger. By the time he won his second PGA championship at Shoal Creek on the outskirts of Birmingham, Alabama, in 1984, he was among the best known and most universally popular golfers the game has known.

Supermex, as he had become dubbed, had

Ten years had passed since Lee Trevino had last won the PGA. His victory at Shoal Creek in 1984, when he scored in the 60s in every round, was all the sweeter.

by then entranced galleries the world over, not only with the excellence of a highly individual method but also with the banter that would always accompany it. He was quite likely to crack more jokes in 18 holes than he would play shots.

It was his way of keeping the pressure under control, though curiously he was not like that all the time. In the 1980 British Open at Muirfield for instance, Trevino stayed at the Greywalls Hotel overlooking the 10th hole. No one would ever have known he was there. He ate all his meals alone, in his room. He used neither the front, nor the back entrance. He came and went each day via the French windows opening onto his bedroom.

Lee Trevino goes for a distant green at Shoal Creek with a fairway wood.

Trevino was someone who could play golf when, at first glance on the course, you might think he could not hit the ball at all. His stance was open, the right shoulder would almost lunge at the ball and the flight of his shots would unfailingly follow the line of rough on the left before veering back into the middle of the fairway. It was not exactly impressive but the thing was that he did it every time.

But as time passed, so Trevino developed back problems. He underwent surgery and carried round with him a trapeze from which he would dangle by his legs every day. He seemed no longer the player he had been. He had won his 26th American tournament in 1981 but the well was apparently now dry.

From somewhere in that PGA championship of 1984, however, Trevino delved deep once again. Now 44, he became the first man to break 70 in every round (69,68,67,69) just as he had also been the first to do so in that US Open 16 years earlier. It was one possibly final glimpse of a truly great artist at work.

Yet it was not only Trevino who was the making of that particular championship, for no one chased him harder or more gallantly than Gary Player, who was then only weeks away from his 49th birthday. His challenge had crystallized on the second day when he equalled the championship record with a 63. He had gone out in 30 and had twos at all four short holes.

In one fell swoop he had caught Trevino, making up five shots on the Mexican. But Trevino was not to be intimidated. He had a 67 in the third round to Player's 69 and led by a stroke from Lanny Wadkins. The three of them played together in the last round and fate seemed to conspire against Trevino. Once, years before, he had been struck by lightning during a US Open and barely had they all set out than a thunderstorm broke. The delay lasted an hour and Trevino sheltered in the garage of a house where drinks and cookies were dispensed.

Trevino dared not sit down for fear his back would seize up but his lead was short lived. By the turn in this last round he was a stroke behind Wadkins, though by the 15th the roles had been reversed again. The short 16th was crucial, for Trevino, having hit too much club, was playing his third before Wadkins had played his second. But Trevino holed for his three and Wadkins missed for his two.

In a desperate effort to make a birdie at the 17th, Wadkins wound up with a six and dropped back to join Player, who all day had been tapping rather than knocking at the door. Trevino in any case finished with a flourishing birdie. It hardly mattered. He had won by four strokes.

Agony of Greg Norman

It could so easily for Greg Norman have been the year to end all years. In 1986 he led by a stroke going into the last round of the Masters at Augusta; he led by another stroke going into the last round of the US Open at Shinnecock Hills; he led by a stroke again going into the last round of the British Open at Turnberry; and he led by four strokes going into the last round of the PGA at Inverness in Toledo. There were grounds for calling it golf's Small Slam, but it was never the Grand Slam it might have been.

Norman, the big, dashing, flaxen-haired Australian they call the Big White Shark, did not have the jaws to finish the job. He won only one, the Open championship itself. In the Masters he was beaten by one of the all-time great finishing rounds, a 65 by Jack Nicklaus; in the US Open he beat himself, and in the PGA he fell victim to one of the most savage acts of fate the game has known.

Tied for the lead playing the last hole, Norman was beaten when Bob Tway, who already that year had won three tournaments in what was only his second season, holed a bunker shot for a birdie three. The last man to have done that when winning a major championship was Doug Ford in the 1957 Masters but he already had strokes in hand.

Tway had nothing in hand, indeed it looked more likely that he would be beaten as he squirmed his feet into the sand prior to that

Bob Tway contemplates a putt during the PGA at Inverness in 1986. But it was a bunker shot which won him the title.

Above: *Greg Norman seems happy enough. But satisfaction became disappointment as he lost a four-stroke lead to Bob Tway over the last nine holes of the PGA at Inverness in 1986.*

Right: *Hal Sutton was so good as an amateur that some thought him capable of doing a 'Bobby Jones' and winning a major championship. Instead he turned professional and took the PGA at Riviera in 1983.*

decisive shot, for Norman was only just off the green in two. Yet, cruel though the climax was for Norman, who took his disappointment as always squarely on the chin and with a brave smile, he knew too that he had only himself to blame for leaving himself in so vulnerable a position. He ought to have had the championship under lock and key long before the 18th. His last round of 76 was proof positive of that.

Yet for three rounds he had played beautifully (65,68,69) and but for the invariable quota of putts missed, which is of course the usual story, Norman would have been even further ahead than four strokes. Perhaps the story might also have been different had not heavy rain flooded the course soon after Norman had played the first hole together with Tway on the Sunday afternoon. They marked their balls and resumed under blue skies on the Monday.

With nine holes to play Norman was still coasting at four strokes to the good and was feeling, he said later, 'comfortable'. It was at the 11th that his defences first showed signs of crumbling. Unfortunate to hit his drive into an old divot mark filled with sand, he consequently had to play a semi bunker shot. He put his next into a trap well short of the green and took six. That halved his lead which was further reduced when Tway, at 6 ft 4 in (193 cm), 3 in (7.6 cm) taller than Norman, made a birdie at the long 13th. Then Norman dropped a stroke at the 14th and they were tied.

Celebrated though Tway's bunker shot was at the last, it was his chip at the 17th that had as much to do with his victory as anything. Having missed the green on the right, he could barely see his ball in tangled rough and furthermore was playing down a slope. Against all the odds, he played an exquisite shot to 3 feet (0.9 m) and saved his par.

Now came the crunch: advantage Norman with a drive safely down the middle of this drive-and-pitch par four, Tway deep in the rough. Striving might and main, Tway could only get his recovery as far as the bunker just below the green. Norman pitched on but such is the fierce back spin he gets on his ball that it dragged back into the fringe.

Up in the television commentary box, Jack Nicklaus remarked: 'If Tway was going to miss this green, that is the best place to do it.' Never was there a more prophetic remark for once Tway had holed, there was never a chance that Norman would follow him in with his little chip.

Does lightning strike only once? Not necessarily. The following spring Norman was no less poised for victory in the Masters. Again it was dashed from his grasp as, at the second extra hole, Larry Mize chipped in.

US PGA

Players from US unless otherwise stated
Prize money unchanged unless shown

1916 Siwanoy, New York
Jim Barnes beat Freddy McLeod 6 and 5
1917–18 No competition

1919 Engineers, New York
Jim Barnes beat Freddy McLeod 6 and 5

1920 Flossmore, Illinois
Jock Hutchison beat J.D. Edgar 1 up

1921 Inwood, New York
Walter Hagen beat Jim Barnes 3 and 2

1922 Oakmont, Pennsylvania
Gene Sarazen beat Emmet French 4 and 3

1923 Pelham, New York
Gene Sarazen beat Walter Hagen at 38th

1924 French Lick, Indiana
Walter Hagen beat Jim Barnes 2 up

1925 Olympia Fields, Illinois
Walter Hagen beat Bill Mehlhorn 6 and 5

1926 Salisbury, New York
Walter Hagen beat Leo Diegel 5 and 3

1927 Cedar Crest, Texas
Walter Hagen beat Joe Turnesa 1 up

1928 Baltimore, Maryland
Leo Diegel beat Al Espinosa 6 and 5

1929 Hill Crest, California
Leo Diegel beat John Farrell 6 and 4

1930 Fresh Meadow, New York
Tommy Armour beat Gene Sarazen 1 up

1931 Wannamoisett, Rhode Island
Tom Creavy beat Densmore Shute 2 and 1

1932 Keller, Minnesota
Olin Dutra beat Frank Walsh 4 and 3

1933 Blue Mound, Wisconsin
Gene Sarazen beat Willie Goggin 5 and 4

1934 Park, New York
Paul Runyan beat Craig Wood at 38th

1935 Twin Hills, Oklahoma
Johnny Revolta beat Tommy Armour 5 and 4

1936 Pinehurst, North Carolina
Densmore Shute beat Jimmy Thomson 3 and 2

1937 Pittsburgh, Pennsylvania
Densmore Shute beat Harold McSpaden at 37th

1938 Shawnee, Pennsylvania
Paul Runyan beat Sam Snead 8 and 7

1939 Pomonok, New York
Henry Picard beat Byron Nelson at 37th

1940 Hershey, Pennsylvania
Byron Nelson beat Sam Snead 1 up

1941 Cherry Hills, Colorado
Vic Ghezzi beat Byron Nelson at 38th

1942 Seaview, New Jersey
Sam Snead beat Jim Turnesa 2 and 1

1943 No competition

1944 Manito, Washington
Bob Hamilton beat Byron Nelson 1 up

1945 Morraine, Ohio
Byron Nelson beat Sam Byrd 4 and 3

1946 Portland, Oregon
Ben Hogan beat Porky Oliver 6 and 4

1947 Plum Hollow, Michigan
Jim Ferrier beat Chick Harbert 2 and 1

1948 Norwood Hills, Missouri
Ben Hogan beat Mike Turnesa 7 and 6

1949 Hermitage, Virginia
Sam Snead beat John Palmer 3 and 2

1950 Scioto, Ohio
Chandler Harper beat Henry Williams Jnr. 4 and 3

1951 Oakmont, Pennsylvania
Sam Snead beat Walter Burkemo 7 and 6

1952 Big Spring, Kentucky
Jim Turnesa beat Chick Harbert 1 up

1953 Birmingham, Michigan
Walter Burkemo beat Felice Torza 2 and 1

1954 Keller, Minnesota
Chick Harbert beat Walter Burkemo 4 and 3

1955 Meadowbrook, Michigan
Doug Ford beat Cary Middlecoff 4 and 3

1956 Blue Hill, Massachusetts
Jack Burke beat Ted Kroll 3 and 2

1957 Miami Valley, Ohio
Lionel Hebert beat Dow Finsterwald 2 and 1

(Decided by stroke-play hereafter)

1958 Llanerch, Pennsylvania
276 Dow Finsterwald 67,72,70,67
278 Billy Casper 73,67,68,70
280 Sam Snead 73,67,67,73

1959 Minneapolis, Minnesota
277 Bob Rosburg 71,72,68,66
278 Jerry Barber 69,65,71,73
Doug Sanders 72,66,68,72

1960 Firestone, Ohio
281 Jay Hebert 72,67,72,70
282 Jim Ferrier 71,74,66,71
283 Sam Snead 68,73,70,72
Doug Sanders 70,71,69,73

1961 Olympia Fields, Illinois
277 Jerry Barber 69,67,71,70
Don January 72,66,67,72
280 Doug Sanders 70,68,74,68
Barber won play-off 67, January 68

1962 Aronimink, Pennsylvania
278 Gary Player (S. Africa) 72,67,69,70
279 Bob Goalby 69,72,71,67
281 Jack Nicklaus 71,74,69,67
George Bayer 69,70,71,71

1963 Dallas Athletic, Texas
279 Jack Nicklaus 69,73,69,68
281 Dave Ragan 75,70,67,69
282 Dow Finsterwald 72,72,66,72
Bruce Crampton (Australia) 70,73, 65,74

1964 Columbus, Ohio ($100,000)
271 Bobby Nichols 64,71,69,67 ($18,000)
274 Arnold Palmer 68,68,69,69
Jack Nicklaus 67,73,70,64

1965 Laurel Valley, Pennsylvania
280 Dave Marr 70,69,70,71
282 Billy Casper 70,70,71,71
Jack Nicklaus 69,70,72,71

1966 Firestone, Ohio ($149,700)
280 Al Geiberger 68,72,68,72 ($25,000)
284 Dudley Wysong 74,72,66,72
286 Billy Casper 73,73,70,70
Gene Littler 75,71,70,70
Gary Player (S. Africa) 73,70,70,73

US PGA

1967 Columbine, Colorado ($149,100)
281 Don January 71,72,70,68 ($25,000)
Don Massengale 70,75,70,66
282 Jack Nicklaus 67,75,69,71
Dan Sikes 69,70,70,73
January won play-off 69, Massengale 71

1968 Pecan Valley, Texas ($150,000)
281 Julius Boros 71,71,70,69 ($25,000)
282 Bob Charles (NZ) 72,70,70,70
Arnold Palmer 71,69,72,70

1969 Dayton, Ohio ($175,000)
276 Ray Floyd 69,66,67,74 ($35,000)
277 Gary Player (S. Africa) 71,65,71,70
278 Bert Greene 71,68,68,71

1970 Southern Hills, Oklahoma ($200,000)
279 Dave Stockton 70,70,66,73 ($40,000)
281 Bob Murphy 71,73,71,66
Arnold Palmer 70,72,69,70

1971 PGA National, Florida
281 Jack Nicklaus 69,69,70,73
283 Billy Casper 71,73,71,68
284 Tommy Bolt 72,74,69,69

1972 Oakland Hills, Michigan ($225,000)
281 Gary Player (S. Africa) 71,71,67,72 ($45,000)
283 Tommy Aaron 71,71,70,71
Jim Jamieson 69,72,72,70

1973 Canterbury Club, Ohio
277 Jack Nicklaus 72,68,68,69
281 Bruce Crampton (Australia) 71,73, 67,70
282 Mason Rudolph 69,70,70,73
Lanny Wadkins 73,69,71,69
Jesse C. Snead 71,74,68,69

1974 Tanglewood, North Carolina
276 Lee Trevino 73,66,68,69
277 Jack Nicklaus 69,69,70,69
279 Bobby Cole (S. Africa) 69,68,71,71
Hubert Green 68,68,73,70
Dave Hill 74,69,67,69
Sam Snead 69,71,71,68

1975 Firestone, Ohio
276 Jack Nicklaus 70,68,67,71
278 Bruce Crampton (Australia) 71,63, 75,69
279 Tom Weiskopf 70,71,70,68

1976 Congressional, Maryland ($250,000)
281 Dave Stockton 70,72,69,70 ($45,000)
282 Raymond Floyd 72,68,71,71
Don January 70,69,71,72

1977 Pebble Beach, California
282 Lanny Wadkins 69,71,72,70
Gene Littler 67,69,70,76
283 Jack Nicklaus 69,71,70,73
Wadkins won play-off at 3rd extra hole

1978 Oakmont, Pennsylvania ($300,000)
276 John Mahaffey 75,67,68,66 ($50,000)
Jerry Pate 72,70,66,68
Tom Watson 67,69,67,73
Mahaffey won play-off at 2nd extra hole

1979 Oakland Hills, Michigan ($350,000)
272 David Graham (Australia) 69,68, 70,65 ($60,000)
Ben Crenshaw 69,67,69,67
274 Randy Caldwell 67,70,66,71
Graham won play-off at 3rd extra hole

1980 Oak Hill, New York ($375,000)
274 Jack Nicklaus 70,69,66,69
281 Andy Bean 72,71,68,70
283 Len Hinkle 70,69,69,75
Gil Morgan 68,70,73,72

1981 Atlanta, Georgia ($401,050)
273 Larry Nelson 70,66,66,71
277 Fuzzy Zoeller 70,68,68,71
278 Dan Pohl 69,67,73,69

1982 Tulsa, Oklahoma ($450,000)
272 Raymond Floyd 63,69,68,72 ($65,000)
275 Lanny Wadkins 71,68,69,67
276 Fred Couples 67,71,72,66
Calvin Peete 69,70,68,69

1983 Riviera, California ($600,000)
274 Hal Sutton 65,66,72,71 ($100,000)
275 Jack Nicklaus 73,65,71,66
276 Peter Jacobsen 73,70,68,65

1984 Shoal Creek, Alabama ($700,000)
273 Lee Trevino 69,68,67,69 ($125,000)
277 Lanny Wadkins 68,69,68,72
Gary Player (S. Africa) 74,63,69,71

1985 Cherry Hills, Denver
278 Hubert Green 67,69,70,72
280 Lee Trevino 66,68,75,71
281 Andy Bean 71,70,72,68
Tze-Chung Chen (Taiwan) 69,76,71, 65

1986 Inverness, Ohio ($800,000)
276 Bob Tway 72,70,64,70 ($140,000)
278 Greg Norman (Australia) 65,68,69, 76
279 Peter Jacobsen 68,70,70,71

1987 PGA National, Florida ($850,000)
287 Larry Nelson 70,72,73,72 ($150,000)
Lanny Wadkins 70,70,74,73
288 Scott Hoch 74,74,71,69
D.A. Weibring 73,72,67,76
Nelson won play-off at 1st extra hole

ACKNOWLEDGMENTS

Allsport 18, 38 top and bottom left, 46–7 bottom, 53 top, 56, 81, 114 bottom, 120 top, 124 bottom, 131 top, 143, 151, 159, 175, 182, Simon Bruty 153, David Cannon 6, 11, 16, 26, 27, 28, 36, 37, 38 bottom right, 39, 41, 42, 43, 45 bottom right, 47 top, 48, 49 top and bottom, 51 top, 54, 55 bottom, 106 top, 134, 158, 160, 183, 184, 185, 186 top, Mike Powell 186 bottom, Steve Powell 117, 133 top; Associated Press 139; Colorsport 123, 129 top and bottom, 137, 140, 141, 147; Peter Dazeley Photography 9, 12, 20–1 bottom, 24, 29, 31, 32, 34, 35 top, 51 bottom, 95, 96–7, 98 bottom, 100 top and bottom, 102, 105, 107, 111, 112, 113, 114 top, 118, 119, 150, 161, 179, 180 top and bottom, 181; Fitz-Symms 17; Hamlyn Group Picture Library 132 top, 135; The Keystone Collection 63, 64, 71, 106 bottom, 127, 138, 146, 149, 172, 174 bottom, 177, 178; The Bert Neale Collection 8, 15, 23, 25, 30, 44–5, 46 top, 75, 76, 79, 80, 97 top, 108, 110, 115, 116, 120 bottom, 122 top, 124 top, 128 top and bottom, 130, 131 bottom, 136 top and bottom, 144, 145 top, 148, 157; Pictorial Parade 125 right, 126 right; Tony Roberts 164, 165, 166, 167, 168, 169; Royal and Ancient Golf Club of St Andrews 104; Phil Sheldon 10, 20 top, 33 bottom, 35 bottom, 45 top, 50, 52–3, 55 top, 57 top and bottom, 58, 59 top, 90, 98–9, 101, 109, 121, 122 bottom, 145 bottom, 162, 163, 170, 171, 176; S & G Picture Library 73, 132–3 bottom; Bob Thomas Sports Photography 21 top, 22, 33 top, 88, 94, 142, 152, 181; Underwood & Underwood 61, 125 left; United States Golf Association 13, 14, 19, 59 bottom, 60, 61, 62, 67 top and bottom, 68, 69, 70, 72, 74, 77, 78, 82, 83, 85, 86 top and bottom, 126 left, 173, 174 top, John Kelly 53 bottom, 87, Kelly/Russell 65, 66, 84, 89.

Front covers: Allsport/David Cannon
Back cover: Phil Sheldon
Titlespread: Bob Thomas Sports Photography

INDEX

Page numbers in *italic* refer to the illustrations and captions

Aaron, Tommy, 23, 41, 175, 188
Adams, Jimmy, 121, 134, 156
Allen, James, 154
Alliss, Percy, 155
Anderson, David Jnr, 154
Anderson, Jamie, 103, 154
Anderson, Tip, 128
Anderson, Willie, 43, 58, 60, 62, 82, 86, 91, 103
Andrew, Robert, 154
Aoki, Isao, 86, 93, 152
Archer, George, 40
Armour, Tommy, 12, 71, 73, 92, 149, 155, 172, 187
AT & T pro-am tournament, 160
Auchterlonie, Laurie, 91
Auchterlonie, Willie, 154
Augusta National, 9–15, *9*, *10*, *11*, 73
Ayton, David, 154
Azinger, Paul, 102, 130, 157

Ball, Frank, 155
Ball, John, 95, 107, 137, 154
Ball, Tom, 155
Ballesteros, Severiano:
British Open, 106, 113, 127–8, 141, *142*, 145, 157
US Masters, *20*, *31*, 34–5, *34*, *35*, 37, *37*, 38, *38*, 41, 60
US Open, 93
Baltusrol, 43, 52, 56, 58–9, *58*, *59*
Barber, Jerry, 187
Barnes, Jim, 68, 71, 74, 91, 126, 155, 172, 173, 187
Barr, Dave, 93
Barrett, P.F., 91
Bayer, George, 187
Bean, Andy, 145, 157, 180, 188
Beard, Frank, 93
Beck, Chip, 93
Bell, David, 91
Bellerive, 67–8
Beman, Deane, 93
Berckmann, Baron, 10
Besselink, Al, 40
Black, John, 74, 91
Blumberg, George, 66
Bolt, Tommy, 40, 78, 79, 92, 188
Boomer, Aubrey, 147, 155
Boothby, Fitz, 154
Borek, Gene, 87
Boros, Julius, 26, 40, 43, 85, 87, 92, 93, 170–1, 178, *178*, 188
Bradshaw, Harry, 134, 156
Brady, Mike, 64, 91
Brae Burn, 64
Braid, James, 66, 95, *104*, 125, *125*, 131, 137, 138, 155
Brand, Gordon J., 157
Brewer, Gay, 26–7, 40
Brews, Sid, *134*, 155
Bridgland, Sir Aynsley, 112
British Amateur, 72–3
British Open, 9, 25, 43, 64, 73, 80, 95–157
Brown, David, 91, 103, 154
Brown, Eric, 142, 156
Brown, W., 154
Bulla, Johnny, 40, 92, 156
Bullock, Fred, 156
Burke, Billy, 40, 49, 92
Burke, Jack Snr, 91
Burke, Jack Jnr, *19*, 40, 187
Burkemo, Walter, 187
Burns, George, 69, 93
Burns, Jack, 154
Burton, Dick, 156
Byrd, Sam, 40, 187

Calcavecchia, Mark, 39, 41
Caldwell, Randy, 188
Campbell, Alex, 91
Campbell, Ben, 154
Campbell, Willie, 154
Carnoustie, 119–20, *119*, *120*
Casper, Billy, 40–1, 46, *46*, 52, 79, 80, 92, 93, 149, 177, 187, 188
Cerda, Antonio (Tony), 122, 149, 156
Chapman, Dick, 52–3
Charles, Bob, 93, 140, *141*, 142, 149, 156, 157, 178, 188
Chen, Tze-Chung, 55, 93, 188
Cherry Hills, 170–1, *170–1*
Clampett, Bobby, 93, 147
Clark, Clarence, 92
Clark, Clive, 136, 156
Coe, Charles, 40, 169
Colbert, Jim, 93
Cole, Bobby, 120, 157, 188
Coles, Neil, 98, *147*, 156, 157
Collins, Billy, 81
Compston, Archie, 64, 135, 155
Coody, Charles, 41
Cooper, Harry, 40, 71, 92, 172
Corcoran, Fred, 83
Cosgrove, Ned, 154
Cosgrove, William, 154
Cotton, Henry, 131, 132, *132*, 133–4, 146, 149, *149*, 155, 156, 177
Cotton, Toots, 133
Couples, Fred, 188
Cox, Wiffy, 92
Crampton, Bruce, 27, 41, 86, 93, 187, 188
Creavy, Tom, 187
Crenshaw, Ben, 35, *35*, 38, 41, 93, 157, 188
Crosby, Bing, 47
Crosby, Nathaniel, 47
Cruickshank, Bobby, 45, 71, 91, 92
Cupit, Jacky, 93
Curtis Cup, 106, 112

Dallemagne, Marcel, 156
Daly, Fred, 118, 122, 156
Daniels, Skip, 139
Darwin, Bernard, 97, 99–100, 114, 172
Davis, Rodger, 99, 157
Davis, Steve, 82
Demaret, Jimmy, 40, 92
Diegel, Leo, 66, 91, 92, 155, 172, 174, *174*, 187
Doleman, William, 154
Douglas, G., 91
Dow, William, 154
Dudley, Ed, 40, 149
Duncan, George, 74, 132, 138, *138*, 155
Dunhill Cup, 98–9
Dunn, Willie, 50, 91
Dutra, Olin, 40, 92, *174*, 187

Easterbrook, Sid, 155
Edgar, J.D., 187
Edwards, David, 41
Eisenhower, Dwight D., 10
Eisenhower Trophy, 44, 163
Espinosa, Al, 52, 72, 92, 174, 187
Evans, Charles Jnr, 91
Evans, Chick, 64

Faldo, Nick, *95*, 98, 100, *102*, 130–1, *131*, 157
Fallon, Johnny, 156
Farrell, Johnny, 58, *59*, 71–2, 91, 92, 155, 187
Faulkner, Max, 68, 118, 121–2, *122*, 140, 156
Fazio, George, 83, 92
Fergus, Keith, 93
Ferguson, Bob, 103, 154
Fergusson, S. Mure, 154
Fernie, Willie, 103, 154
Ferrier, Jim, 40, 187
Fezler, Forest, 93
Finsterwald, Dow, 17, 19, 40, 174, 187
Firestone, 166–7, *166–7*
Firestone, Harvey, 166
Fitzjohn, Val, 91
Five Farms, 52
Fleck, Jack, 46, *46*, 78–9, *78*, 92
Fleckman, Marty, 85, 178
Floyd, Raymond:
British Open, 157
US Masters, 26, 29–30, *29*, *30*, 35, 36, 37, 41
US Open, 43, *50*, 51, 93
US PGA championship, 165, 175, 188
Flynn, William S., 171
Ford, Doug, 17, 40, 185, 187
Ford, Gerald, *90*
Foulis, James, 91
Fownes, William C., 56
French, Emmet, 173, 187
Fresh Meadow, 52
Funseth, Rod, 41
Furgol, Ed, 58–9, 92

Gardner, Stewart, 91
Geiberger, Al, 93, 166–7, 187
George VI, King of England, 131
Ghezzi, Vic, 92, 187
Gilbert, Gibby, 34, 35, 41
Goalby, Bob, 23–4, *23*, 40, 93, 175, 177, 187
Goggin, Willie, 187
Goodman, Johnny, 43, 92, 135
Graham, David, 43, 45, 65, *65*, *66*, 69, 93, 134, 157, 188
Graham, Lou, 93, 165, 181
Green, Hubert, 22, 41, 150–1, 157, 165, 170, *182*, 188
Greene, Bert, 188
Guldahl, Ralph, 13, *13*, 14, 15, 40, 75–6, *77*, 92, 149

Hagen, Walter, 48, *48*, *63*, 82, 122
British Open, 131, 132, *133*, 139, 147, 149, 155
US Masters, 12
US Open, 63–4, *64*, 91, 92
US PGA championship, 74, 172, *172*, 173, 174, 179, 187
Halford Hewitt tournament, 109

Hamilton, Bob, 40, 187
Hancock, Roland, 71–2, 92
Hanmer, Captain Paddy, 101
Harbert, Chick, 40, 187
Hardin, Horde, *31*
Hargreaves, Jack, 156
Harman, Claude, 40, 92, 177
Harper, Chandler, 187
Harrison, Dutch, 93
Havers, Arthur, 64, 117, 147, *147*, 155
Hawkins, Fred, 17, 40
Hawtree, Fred, 115
Hayes, Mark, 123, 152
Hazeltine, 68–9
Heafner, Clayton, 54, 83, 92
Heard, Jerry, 87
Hebert, Jay, 166, 187
Hebert, Lionel, 187
Henning, Harold, 156, 157
Herbert, Lionel, 174
Herd, Alex, 154, 155
Herd, Fred, 91
Herd, Sandy, 137, 138
Hill, Dave, 68–9, 93, 188
Hilton, Harold, 95, 101, *106*, 107, 154, 155
Hinkle, Len, 93, 188
Hoch, Scott, 188
Hogan, Ben, 66, 86, 167, *168*, 171, 180
British Open, 119, *119*, 128, 148–9, *148*, 156
US Masters, 14–15, 40
US Open, 43, 45, 46, *46*, 54–5, *55*, 57, 58, 78–9, *78*, 80, 82–3, *82*, *83*, 84, 88, 92, 165
US PGA championship, 168, 174, 187
Hogan, Valerie, *82*
Hole, Frank, 123
Homans, Eugene, 45
Honourable Company of Edinburgh Golfers, 95, 101, 103
Horne, Reg, 156
Hoylake, 107–8, *107*, *108*
Huggett, Brian, 147, 156
Hunt, Bernard, 156
Hunter, Charles, 154
Hutchison, Jock, 91, 132, 155, 187

Inverness, 48–9, *48*, 65–6
Irwin, Hale, 52, 93, 141, *142*, 145, 157

Jacklin, Tony:
British Open, 98, 113, *113*, 116, 121, 130, 140–1, *140*, 144, 157
US Open, 43, 49, 65, 68–9, *68*, *69*, 93
Jacobs, Tommy, 26–7, 40, 81, 93
Jacobsen, Peter, 188
James, Mark, 157
Jamieson, Jim, 41, 175, 188
January, Don, 93, 187, 188
Jones, Bobby, 10–11, 12, 15, 24, 26, 70–1, 75, 82, 86, 107, 120, 180
British Open, 95, 113, *114*, 129, 135–6, *135*, *139*, 141–2, 155
US Open, 43, 44, 45, 49, 52, 58, *70–3*, 71–3, 74, 91, 92
Jones, R., 155
Jones, Robert Trent, 54, 58, 68, 83, 166
Jowle, Frank, 156
Jurado, Jose, 149, 155

Keeler, O.B., 142
Keiser, Herman, 40
Kerrigan, Tom, 155
Kidd, Tom, 154
King, Rufus, 169
King, Sam, 156
Kirk, Bob, 154
Kirkaldy, Andrew, 102, 103, 154, 155
Kirkaldy, Hugh, 154
Kirkaldy, James, 154
Kirkaldy, John, 154
Kite, Tom, 35, 41, *52*, 157
Knudson, George, 40
Kroll, Ted, 187

Lacey, Charles, 156
Laidlay, Johnny, 154
Lamb, Henry, 105
Langer, Bernard, *6*, 7, *28*, 36–7, *37*, 38, 41, 133, 134, 157
Lema, Tony, 26, 40, 128, *128*, 149, 156, 159
Leonard, Stan, 17
Little, Lawson, 40, 92
Littler, Gene, 41, 54, 59, 84, 92, 93, 160, 187, 188
Lloyd, Joe, 91
Locke, Bobby, 67
British Open, 117, 121, 122, 128–9, 134, 136, 144, 147, 149, 156
US Open, 92
Low, George, 91, 115
Lowery, Eddie, 60, *61*
Lu Liang Huan, 144, 157
Lucas, P.B. 'Laddie', 112
Lunn, Bob, 93
Lyle, Sandy, 36, 39, *39*, 41, *41*, *105*, 106, 130, 132, 134, *134*, 157

McCormack, Mark, 21, 175
McCulloch, Duncan, 147
McDermott, John, 43, 60–1, 62, *62*, 91
MacDonald, Robert, 91
Macfarlane, Willie, 91
Mackenzie, Alister, 10
Mackenzie, Fred, 91
McLeod, Fred, 91, 187
McNamara, Tom, 60, 62, 91
McSpaden, Harold, 187
Mahaffey, John, 32, 57, 93, 181–2, *181*, 188
Mahen, Tom, 173
Maiden, James, 91
Maiden, Stewart, 71, 120
Maltbie, Roger 38, 151
Manero, Tony, 92
Mangrum, Lloyd, 40, 83, 92
Marr, Dave, 19, 40, 177, *177*, 187
Marsh, Dr David, 100
Martin, Bob, 154
Massengale, Don, 188
Massengale, Rik, 32, 41
Massy, Arnaud, 113, 137, 155
Maxwell, Perry, 165
Mayer, Dick, 17, 79, 92
Mehlhorn, Bill, 91, 172, 187
Melnyk, Steve, 120
Merion, 44–5, *44*, *45*, 69
Mets, Dick, 92
Middlecoff, Cary, 17, 40, 79, *81*, 83, 92, 168, 187
Miller, Johnny:
British Open, 34, 141, 145, *145*, 146, *147*, 157
US Masters, 27, 32, 41
US Open, 56, 58, 87–8, *88*, 93
Mitchell, 138
Mitchell, Abe, 74
Mitchell, Bobby, 27, 41
Mize, Larry, 38, *38*, 41, 60, 186
Moody, Orville, 93
Moran, Michael, 155
Morgan, Gil, 41, 93, 188
Morris, J.O.F., 154
Morris, Old Tom, 95, 100, 154
Morris, Young Tom, 95, 103, 126, 154
Mudd, Jodie, 35
Muirfield, 101–2, *101*, *102*
Murphy, Bob, 93, 188
Musselburgh, 103

Nagle, Kel, 68, 80, 93, 118, *128*, 143, 147, 156
Nelson, Byron, 13, 14, *14*, 40, 76, 81, 92, 149, 174, 187
Nelson, Larry, 56–7, *56*, 93, 188
Neville, Jack, 160
New York Athletic Club, 53
Newport, Rhode Island, 43
Newton, Jack, 34, 35, 41, 149, 157
Nicholls, Gilbert, 91
Nichols, Bobby, 40, 85, 93, 167, 187
Nicklaus, Barbara, 27
Nicklaus, Jack, 7, 70, 78, 82, 87, 142, 146, *172*, 182, 186
British Open, 116, *124*, 127–8, *127*, *129*, 130, 131, 136, 144, 149, 150–1, *150*, *151*, 156, 157
US Masters, 20, 21, 25–9, *25–8*, 30, *30*, 31–2, 33, 38, 40, 41, 150, 185
US Open, 44, 50, *56*, 58, *59*, 66, 68, 69, 80, 84–6, *84–6*, 89–90, 92, 93, 161, 169
US PGA championship, 167, 177, 178, 179–80, *179*, *180*, 187, 188
Nickson, Tony, 114
Norman, Greg:
British Open, 98, *107*, 123, 152–3, *152*, *153*, 157
US Masters, 28, 32, 38, *38*, 41
US Open, 48, 52, 60, 93
US PGA championship, 185–6, *186*, 188
North, Andy, 54, 55, *87*, 93, 170

Oak Hill, 168–9, *168–9*
Oakland Hills, 54–5, *54*, *55*
Oakmont, 43, 56–7, *56*, 58
O'Connor, Christy Snr, 142, 156, 178
O'Connor, Christy Jnr, 157
Oliver, Porky, 40, 92, 174, 187
Olympic Club, San Francisco, 46–7, *46*, *47*
O'Meara, Mark, 157
Oosterhuis, Peter, 39, 41, 157
Ouimet, Francis, 43, 60, *60*, 61–2, *61*, 63, 91, 173
Ouimet, Wilfred, 61
Owen, Simon, 127, 157

Padgham, Alf, 149, 155, 156
Palmer, Arnold, 7, 128, 142, 146
British Open, 80, *80*, 116, 117, 118, 128, 143, *143*, 147, 156
US Masters, 13, 16–19, *16–18*, 20, 21–2, 25–6, 33, 40, 81, 175
US Open, 46, *56*, 66, 68, 69, 78, 79–80, 84–6, *85*, *86*, 87, 88, 92, 93, 170
US PGA championship, 161, 178, 187, 188
Palmer, John, 187
Park, David, 154
Park, Mungo, 103, 154
Park, Willie Jnr, 103, 154, 155
Park, Willie Snr, 103
Parks, Sam Jnr, 92
Pate, Jerry, 41, 93, 182, 188
Patton, Billy Joe, 15, 40
Paxton, George, 154
Paxton, Peter, 154
Pebble Beach, 160–1, *160*, *161*
Peete, Calvin, 188
Penna, Tony, 92
Perkins, Phil, 92
Perry, Alf, 156
Picard, Henry, 12, 40, 187
Pinehurst No. 2, 162–3, *162*, *163*
Player, Gary, 7, 150, 159
British Open, 95, 113–14, 119, *120*, 131, *131*, 136, 149, *149*, 156, 157
US Masters, 19, 20–2, *20*, *22*, 23, 26, 28, 33, *37*, 40, 41
US Open, 43, 65, 66–8, *66*, 69, 87, 92, 93
US PGA championship, 175–6, *175*, *176*, 184, 187, 188
Pohl, Dan, 41, 93, 188

Prestwick, 95, 96–7, *96*, *97*, 125–6
Price, Charles, 18–19
Price, Nick, 26, 117, 146–7, 157
Prince's 111–12, *111*, *112*
Pringle, Bob, 154
Pulford, G., 155
Purves, Dr Laidlaw, 105

Quaker Ridge, 52

Ragan, Dave, 187
Rawlins, Horace, 91
Ray, Ted, 43, 49, 56, 60, *60*, 61, 62, 65, 66, 91, *126*, 155
Rees, Dai, 143, 144, 149, 156
Revolta, Johnny, 187
Rice, Grantland, 12
Ridgewood, 52
Riegel, Skee, 14, 40
Rivero, Jose, 157
Roberts, Clifford, 10–11, 15, 18
Robertson, Allan, 95
Robertson, Peter, 91
Robson, Fred, 155
Rodgers, Phil, 93, 142, 147, 156
Rogers, Bill, 89, 93, 105, *133*, 134, 157
Rollan, David, 154
Rolland, Douglas, 154
Rosburg, Bob, 92, 93, 187
Ross, Alex, 91
Ross, Donald, 48, 54, 162, 168
Ross, Mackenzie, 123
Royal and Ancient Golf Club, 43, 95, 100, *100*, 147, 153
Royal Birkdale, 115–16, *115*, *116*
Royal Cinque Ports, Deal, 109–10, *109*, *110*, 138
Royal Liverpool, 107
Royal Lytham, 113–14, *113*, *114*
Royal Portrush, 121–2, *121*, *122*
Royal St George's 25, *64*, 95, 105–6, *105*, *106*
Royal Troon, 117–18, *117*, *118*
Rudolph, Mason, 188
Ruiz, Leopoldo, 142
Runyan, Paul, 40, 44–5, 174, 187
Ryder, Samuel, 138
Ryder Cup, 116, 138, 149, 163

St Andrews, 73, 98–100, *98–100*
St Anne's, 113
San Francisco, 52
Sanders, Doug, 93, 127, 131, 156, 157, 187
Sarazen, Gene, 10, 66, 122, 123–4, 172
  British Open, 111, *111*, 112, 117–18, 139, *139*, 147, 149, 155
  US Masters, 12, *12*, 14, *32*, 40
  US Open, 71, 74–5, *75*, 91, 92
  US PGA championship, 173, *173*, 174, 187
Sarazen, Mary, 139
Sargent, George, 64, 91
Sayers, Bernard, 137, 154
Schlee, John, 87, 88, 93
Schroeder, John, 150
Schroeder, Ted, 150
Scott, Lady Margaret, 121
Scott, Sid, 144, 156
Shankland, Bill, 156
Shinnecock Hills, 43, 50–1, *50*, *51*
Shute, Densmore, 76, 92, 149, 155, 162, 174, 187
Sikes, Dan, 188
Simpson, Archie, 154
Simpson, George, 91
Simpson, H.B., 155
Simpson, Jack, 154
Simpson, Scott, 43, *43*, 46–7, 93
Smith, Alex, 62, 91
Smith, Horton, *32*, 40, 73, *74*, 92, 135, 149
Smith, Macdonald, 73, 91, 92, 126, 155
Smith, Willie, 91
Snead, Jesse C., 41, 93, 188
Snead, Sam, 56, 83
  British Open, 129, 149, 156
  US Masters, 13, 14–15, *15*, 26, 39, 40
  US Open, 76–7, *76*, 78, 92, 178
  US PGA championship, 174, 187, 188
Sneed, Ed, 33, 41
Sommers, Ben, 84
Souchak, Mike, 26, 80, 81, 92, 137
Southern Hills, *164*, 165, *165*
Stadler, Craig, 35, 41
Stewart, Payne, 157
Stockton, Dave, 22, 41, 93, 165, 188
Stranahan, Frank, 40, 148–9, 156
Strange, Curtis, 36, 37, 41, 93, 98–9, 100
Strath, Andrew, 154
Strath, David, 154
Sutton, Hal, *186*, 188
Sutton, Norman, 122

Tait, Freddie, 155
Tatum, Sandy, 165
Taylor, J.H., 65, 66, 91, 95, *104*, 105, 115, 125–6, *125*, 131, 137, 138, 154, 155
Thomas, David, 131, 142, 156
Thomson, Jimmy, 92, 162, 187
Thomson, Peter:
  British Open, 103, 115, 116, 122, 128–9, 137, *137*, 142, 143, 144, *144*, 147, 149, 156, 157
  US Open, 93
Tillinghast, A.W., 52, 58
Tissies, Herman, 117
Tolley, Cyril, 73
Torza, Felice, 187
Travers, Jerome, 62, 91
Travis, Walter, 62, 91
Trevino, Lee:
  British Open, 27, 116, 130, *130*, 144, 151, 157
  US Open, 44, *45*, 93
  US PGA championship, 169, 170, 183–4, *183*, *184*, 188
Tufts, J.W., 162
Turnberry, *4*, 50, 95, 123–4, *123*, *124*
Turnesa, Jim, 92, 187
Turnesa, Joe, 71, 91, 172, 187
Turnesa, Mike, 174, 187
Turnesa, Willie, 120
Tway, Bob, 48, *49*, 185–6, *185*, *186*, 188

United States Golf Association (USGA), 43, 44, 50, 54, 55, 58, 61, 72, 79, 165
US Amateur Championship, 47, 52–3, 169
US Masters, 9–41, 64
US Open, 9, 43–93
US PGA championship, 9, 48, 64, 159–88

Van Donck, Flory, 137, 142, 156
Vanderbilt, William K., 50
Vardon, Harry, 12, 89, *104*, 137
  British Open, 95, *95*, 125–6, *126*, 127, 131, 138, 155
  US Open, 43, 49, 60, *60*, 61, 62, 65–6, 70, 71, 91
Venturi, Ken, 18, *19*, 40, 79, 81, *81*, 93
Vicenzo, Roberto de, 23–4, *23*, *24*, 40, 107, *137*, 136–7, 147, 148, 156, 157
Von Elm, George, 49, 92, 155
Von Nida, Norman, 121, 147, 156

Wadkins, Lanny, 93, 160, 165, 167, *180*, 184, 188
Walker, Cyril, 91
Walker Cup, 72–3, 100, 107, 124, 131, 141
Wall, Art, 17, 20, 40
Walsh, Frank, 187
Ward, Charlie, 156
Watrous, Al, 141–2, 155, 172
Watson Denis, 55, 93
Watson, Tom, *14*
  British Open, 95, *95*, 100, 116, 117, *117*, 119, 123, *124*, 127, 145, *145*, 146, 149, 150–1, *150*, *151*, 157
  US Masters, 14, *20*, 31–2, *31*, *32*, 33, 35, 41
  US Open, *43*, 47, 57, 58, 89–90, *89*, *90*, 93, 161
  US PGA championship, 181–2, 188
Way, W.H., 91
Weetman, Harry, 122
Weibring, D.A., *10*, 188
Weiskopf, Tom:
  British Open, 117, 140, 146, *147*, 157
  US Masters, 22, 27, 40, 41
  US Open, 58, 86, 88, 93
  US PGA championship, 188
Westchester Classic, 170
Wethered, Roger, 155
Whitcombe, Charles, 149, 156
Whitcombe, Ernest, 155
Whitcombe, Reg, 134, 149, 156
White, Jack, 155
White, Stanford, 51
Williams, Henry, 187
Williams, Dr John R., 168
Williams, Ted, 14
Wilson, Dick, 48, 51
Wilson, Hugh, 45
Winged Foot, 52–3, *52*, *53*
Wood, Craig, 12, 40, 53, *74*, 76, 92, 155, 187
Woosnam, Ian, 130, 153, 157
World Match-play championship, 159
World Series, 167
Worsham, Lew, 40, 77, 92
Wysong, Dudley, 187

Yancey, Bert, 34, 40, 93

Ziegler, Larry, 41
Zoeller, Fuzzy, *32*, 33, 41, 52, *53*, 93, 152, 188